NDSU LIBRARIES

**North Dakota State University
Fargo, North Dakota
58105**

GIFT OF

Catherine Cater

Professor Emeritus

English Department

North Dakota State University

2004

Publications of the American
Association for Netherlandic Studies • 5

Margriet Bruijn Lacy, Series Editor

THE LOW COUNTRIES AND BEYOND

edited by
Robert S. Kirsner
University of California, Los Angeles

UNIVERSITY
PRESS OF
AMERICA

Lanham • New York • London

Copyright © 1993 by
University Press of America,® Inc.
4720 Boston Way
Lanham, Maryland 20706

3 Henrietta Street
London WC2E 8LU England

All rights reserved
Printed in the United States of America
British Cataloging in Publication Information Available

Co-published by arrangement with
The American Association for Netherlandic Studies

Library of Congress Cataloging-in-Publication Data

The low countries and beyond / edited by Robert S. Kirsner.
   p. cm. — (Publications of the American Association for
      Netherlandic studies ; 5)
"...based on papers originally presented at the Fifth Interdisciplinary
Conference on Netherlandic Studies, held at the University of
    California, Los Angeles, in June 1990"—Pref.
    Includes bibliographical references.
  1. Netherlands—Congresses. I. Kirsner, Robert, 1941- .
          II. Series.
DJ18.L68   1993   949.2—dc20   92–33459 CIP

ISBN 0–8191–8943–X (cloth : alk. paper)

The paper used in this publication meets the minimum requirements of American National Standard for Information Sciences—Permanence of Paper for Printed Library Materials, ANSI Z39.48–1984.

Acknowledgements

Grateful acknowledgement is hereby made to the following individuals and institutions for their kind permission to reproduce or quote from works:

The Art Gallery of Ontario, Toronto, for permission to reproduce the photograph of *Van Gogh's Room* by Murray Favro, in the article by Patricia Vervoort.

Athenaeum — Polak & Van Gennep, Amsterdam, The Netherlands, for permission to reprint the poems "De afdaling," "In den beginne," "Pasen," and "Voltooiing" by Ida Gerhardt, in the article by Jacques van der Elst.

Joe Fafard for permission to reproduce photographs of *Vincent #4* and *The Painter,* in the article by Patricia Vervoort.

Uitgeversmaatschappij J. H. Kok B.V., Kampen, The Netherlands, for permission to reprint the poem "Een open hand naar de hemel" by Nel Benschop, in the article by Jacques van der Elst.

The Los Angeles County Museum of Art for permission to reproduce the photograph of *The Raising of Lazarus* by Rembrandt van Rijn, gift of H. R. Ahmanson & Co., in memory of Howard F. Ahmanson, in the article by Mary Arshagouni Papazian.

Louisiana State University Press for permission to reprint quotations from *Rituals* by Cees Nooteboom, translated by Adrienne Dixon, copyright © 1980 by Uitgeverij De

Arbeiderspers, English translation copyright © 1983 by Louisiana University Press, in the article by Christa Johnson.

Marga Minco for her kind permission to use materials from *De val,* Amsterdam, Bert Bakker, 1983, in the article by Saskia Daalder and Arie Verhagen.

The Resource Collections of the Getty Center for the History of Art and the Humanities for permission to reproduce the illustration from Caspar van Baerle's *Blijde Inkomst van Maria de Medicis,* Amsterdam, Blaeu, 1639, in the article by David Kunzle.

The Rijksmuseum-Stichting, Amsterdam, for permission to reproduce the photograph of Joachim von Sandrart's *The Company of Cornelis Bicker,* 1640, in the article by David Kunzle.

Tafelberg-Uitgewers, 28 Wale Street, Cape Town, South Africa, for permission to reprint the poem "Gebed vir Paasmôre" by Izak de Villiers, in the article by Jacques van der Elst.

Russ Yuristy for permission to reproduce the photograph of *Van Gogh Walking,* in the article by Patricia Vervoort.

Table of Contents

Acknowledgements iii

Table of Contents v

Preface ix

Art

Sandrart's **Company of Cornelis Bicker** *and the Arquebusiers Hall Civic Guard Paintings in the Afterglow of Marie de Medici's Visit to Amsterdam 1638*
David Kunzle 3

Re-Constructing Van Gogh: Paintings as Sculptures
Patricia Vervoort 15

History

The Schulenborgh Affair and Provincial Politics in Groningen
John H. Grever 37

The Passions of an Enlightened Jew: Isaac de Pinto (1717-1787) as a "Solliciteur du Bien Public"
Ida Nijenhuis 47

The Indologist P. J. Veth (1814-1895) as Empire-Builder
Paul van der Velde 55

Linguistics

The Word Order of Final Verbal Elements in Dutch: Free Variation or Meaningful Organization?
Justine A. Pardoen 71

To be or not to be in Dutch: A Cognitive Account of Some Puzzling Perfect Auxiliary Phenomena
Thomas F. Shannon 85

The Declension of Adjectives with Nominal Infinitives
Arie Verhagen 97

Dutch Modal Particles in Directive Sentences
Roel Vismans 111

Literature

Object of Desire and Undesired Knowledge in Multatuli's **Woutertje Pieterse**
Gary Lee Baker 125

Dutch Tenses and the Analysis of a Literary Text: The Case of Marga Minco's **De val**
Saskia Daalder and Arie Verhagen 139

The Pink Pages of Petit Larousse: Marnix Gijsen's "Art of Quotation"
Marcel Janssens 151

Nooteboom and Postmodernism
Christa Johnson 161

The Work of Marga Minco: A Wrangle of Time and Space
Johan P. Snapper 171

Gospel and Religion in the Poetry of Ida Gerhardt
Jacques van der Elst 181

*Politics in Frank Martinus Arion's **Nobele Wilden***
Manfred Wolf 197

Nederlandkunde

New Perspectives on the Second World War in Dutch Historiography
Bob de Graaff 207

Myth and Understanding: Recent Controversy about Dutch Historiography on the Netherlands-Indonesian Conflict
Peter Romijn 219

Afrikaans

From "Verbasterde Hollans" to "Dochtertaal van het Nederlands" to "Afrikataal": Afrikaner Linguistic Mythology in Flux
Paul T. Roberge 233

Border Literature in Afrikaans
Johan P. Smuts 247

Rethinking Afrikaans Language and Literature: Facets of a Current Debate
Hein Willemse 255

Anglo-Dutch Relations

The Lazarus Motif in Donne and Rembrandt: Some Religious and Artistic Parallels
Mary Arshagouni Papazian 269

Early Printed Books and the Low Countries: Accessing the Past through the Computer
Henry L. Snyder 281

*Politics **versus** Poetics: · The Granting of the **Privilege** of Marnix' Revised Vernacular Psalm Translation of 1591 to Vulcanius*
Richard Todd 297

Dutch-American Relations

"Dutch" Towns in the United States of America
Augustus J. Veenendaal Jr. 309

Contributors 323

Preface

This fifth volume in the series *Publications of the American Association for Netherlandic Studies* contains articles based on papers originally presented at the Fifth Interdisciplinary Conference on Netherlandic Studies, held at the University of California, Los Angeles, in June 1990. Grateful acknowledgement is hereby made of the support of this conference by the *Taalunie*[1] and of the logistic and financial aid provided by UCLA's International Studies and Overseas Programs to the local organizing body, the UCLA Netherlandic Studies Program. The program organizers — Professors Paul Sellin, David Kunzle, and I — are deeply indebted to Dean John Hawkins, Mrs. Gloria Goldberg, Ms. Lurie Johnson, and Ms. Jessica van der Valk.

Among the many participants who made the Conference a success, we would especially like to thank Prof. Dan F. McLaughlin of the UCLA Department of Film and Television for organizing a special program devoted to the work of the renowned Flemish animator Raoul Servais and his students, and for hosting the screening of the Flemish film *Het Sacrament,* based on Hugo Claus's *Omtrent Deedee.*

These Flemish film events were generously supported by the Honorable Marc Otto, Consul General of Belgium, and the Honorable Rita Omwal, representative of the Flemish Community in Washington. We would also like to thank them for their donation to UCLA of a number of art books.

We are also grateful to the Honorable John von Mühlen, the Netherlands Consul General, for hosting a reception, for making

---

[1]The binational Dutch Language Union, whose task is to co-ordinate language policy in Belgium and The Netherlands.

possible a performance by the Dutch actor Jules Croiset, and for his general support.

Finally, we wish to thank the UCLA Department of Germanic Languages, the UCLA Art Library, and the UCLA Latin American Center for hosting additional *borreluurtjes*.

Let me now turn from the Conference — a distant event — to the volume you are holding in your hands. The title — *The Low Countries and Beyond* — reflects the broad interpretation of the field of Dutch Studies vigorously encouraged by my colleague and fellow ICNS5 conference organizer, Paul R. Sellin, of the UCLA English Department. There is of course plenty of material here to delight the traditional reader; more than half of the twenty-five articles focus on topics which have always been considered *Neerlandistiek*, to wit: Dutch and Flemish literature, Dutch linguistics, Dutch history, and Dutch art history. But there is also more. A number of papers go beyond the Low Countries as such: to America, to Britain, to Canada, to Indonesia, to South Africa; to reinterpretations of Dutch art and historiography, to Anglo-Dutch and Dutch-American relations, this time even to a sister language of Modern Dutch, Afrikaans, and to its literature, and to the mythology surrounding both the language and the literature.[2]

The conference organizers believe that this broader view of Dutch Studies strengthens the field. First of all, it recognizes that the Low Countries have influenced and continue to influence more of the Modern World — and in more ways and more subtle ways — than is usually acknowledged. Yes Virginia, there is a Dutch Studies and it is not "marginal."[3] And just because the Dutch themselves (but not the

---

[2]The section of three articles on Afrikaans is perhaps prefigured by the brief remarks on Afrikaans in William H. Fletcher's "Semantic factors in Dutch gender choice" in W. H. Fletcher (ed.) *Papers from the Second Interdisciplinary Conference on Netherlandic Studies held at Georgetown University 7-9 June 1984* (Lanham, Md.: University Press of America), 50-63.

[3]For non-American readers, I should perhaps point out that the allusion here is to a famous letter written by Francis P. Church in 1897 in the *New York Sun*, in answer to eight-year-old Virginia O'Hanlon's query "Is there a Santa Claus?" The response, containing the famous phrase *Yes, Virginia, there is a Santa Claus*, used to be reprinted at Christmas by many American newspapers; cf. Reid (1991: 244). Church's response is evoked here because, just as a child needs to be reassured that the cynical adults and siblings around her are wrong

Flemish) currently make a somewhat strange fetish of the alleged small-size of their language area[4] is no reason for the rest of us — and certainly not American Neerlandici — to follow suit and to denigrate the CONTINUED cultural importance of the Low Countries. No Virginia, though the Golden Age is crucial, all did NOT end in the Seventeenth Century. We can rightly call the attention of our Anglicist and Germanist or Historian colleagues to the continued richness and relevance of Low Countries language, literature, art, and culture in their broadest sense. As Editor, I would suggest that C. P. Snow's compelling argument (in his lecture on the "two cultures") should be extended beyond the original dialogue between the Humanist and Scientist to include the Literary Scholar and the Linguist, and also the Neerlandicus and the Anglicist or Germanist. Stated forthrightly, one who has read Mann or Milton but not Multatuli, or Eliot but not Elsschot, or Goethe but not Gijsen, is not fully literate in European literature. And one who has read only Hermans but not the grammarian Den Hertog, or Van Ostaijen but not the grammarian Overdiep, is not fully literate in Dutch culture. (What, after all, is more indicative of culture and cultural attainment than intellectual effort devoted to the analysis of language itself?) With respect to literature, I would even go further and point out that in earlier editions of De Vooys and Stuiveling's *Schets van de Nederlandse Letterkunde,* a last chapter was devoted to literature in Afrikaans. It can be argued, then, that if one really wants to be grounded in Netherlandic literature in its broadest sense, one should read Breytenbach as well as

---

and that Santa Claus does exist (at least in some spiritual sense), so do Dutch scholars laboring (often in solitude) in the Diaspora need to be reassured that there really is an international discipline devoted to Dutch Studies. Furthermore, just as the cynical and doubting adults surrounding Virgina needed to be gently made aware by Francis Church of their cynicism and lack of imagination, so do the sometimes unappreciative colleagues and administrators surrounding the Dutch scholar need to be made aware of their own conceptual blinders.

[4]Consider the traditional formula *Nederland is maar een klein landje* 'Holland is only a small country', with both the adjective *klein* 'small' and the diminutive form of *land.* But of course there are more speakers of Dutch alive today than there are of Danish, Swedish, and Norwegian together. See also Kees Bastianen, "Nederlanders hebben gebrek aan zelfrespect," *De Volkskrant,* November 23, 1991, reporting on the American-born Dutch author Ethel Portnoy's address at a conference on the position of Dutch in the Europe of the future. Further brief but useful comments on this topic are to be found in Donaldson (1981:8) and Shetter (1987:138, 284).

Bordewijk, Leroux as well as Lucebert. Hopefully, the present volume — showing the tip of the tip of the iceberg — will pique the reader's curiousity about all of the areas discussed.

In closing, a few additional remarks about the volume and the editorial process are in order. The twenty-five articles presented here were gleaned from thirty-six submitted for publication, out of the more than ninety papers given at the Conference. Though each paper itself will serve as its own best introduction, the aggregate does indeed testify to the vitality, diversity, and international character of scholarship in Dutch Studies. In terms of university affiliation, 40% of the authors come from the United States, 32% from The Netherlands, 12% from South Africa, 8% from Great Britain, and 4% from both Belgium and Canada. In terms of topics and fields, the largest number of papers (28%) were devoted to literature, followed by linguistics (16%), then 12% each for history, Anglo-Dutch relations, and Afrikaans, 8% each for art and Nederlandkunde (which in the present volume is contemporary history), and finally 4% for Dutch-American relations.

The Editor would like to thank Professors Margriet Lacy, Anne Lowenthal, Arend Lijphart, Herbert Rowen, Paul Sellin, and Johan Snapper for assistance in evaluating the original manuscripts. Jane Bitar, formerly of UCLA Central Word Processing, and Mr. Michael Cohen, formerly of the UCLA Humanities Computing Facility, helped in the preparation and conversion of computer files. Mr. Drew Krum, now of the UCLA Office of Academic Planning and Budget, helped prepare the final camera-ready version of the book. The volume was produced with WordPerfect 5.1 and printed in Times Roman.

With such a variety of disciplines represented, it was not possible to achieve uniformity of style. The Editor hopes nonetheless that remaining errors will be few. He especially wishes to thank the authors who reviewed their manuscripts and proofs with care and provided essential feedback through fax machines, computer networks, and express mail. To the extent that this volume is successful, they are the reason why.

Robert S. Kirsner
Editor

References

Donaldson, B. C. *Dutch reference grammar.* 's-Gravenhage: Martinus Nijhoff, 1981.

Reid, Wallis. *Verb and noun number in English: A functional explanation.* London and New York: Longman, 1991.

Shetter, William Z. *The Netherlands in perspective: The organizations of society and environment.* Leiden: Martinus Nijhoff, 1987.

Snow, C. P. *The two cultures and the scientific revolution: The Rede lecture 1959.* New York: Cambridge University Press, 1961.

Vooys, C. G. N. de, and G. Stuiveling. *Schets van de Nederlandse letterkunde.* Groningen: J. B. Wolters, 1966.

Publications of the American
Association for Netherlandic Studies

Editorial Board

Robert S. Kirsner, Los Angeles
Arend Lijphart, San Diego
Anne Lowenstein, New York
Herbert S. Rowen, New Brunswick
Johan P. Snapper, Berkeley

Series Editor

Margriet Bruijn Lacy, Indianapolis

Volumes to date:

1. *Papers from the Third Interdisciplinary Conference on Netherlandic Studies.* Edited by Ton Broos, 1988.

2. *The Berkeley Conference on Dutch Literature 1987. New Perspectives on the Modern Period.* Edited by Johan P. Snapper and Thomas F. Shannon, 1989.

3. *The Low Countries: Multidisciplinary Studies.* Edited by Margriet Bruijn Lacy, 1990.

4. *The Berkeley Conference on Dutch Linguistics 1989. Issues and Controversies, Old and New.* Edited by Thomas F. Shannon and Johan P. Snapper, 1991.

5. *The Low Countries and Beyond.* Edited by Robert S. Kirsner, 1993.

Art

Sandrart's *Company of Cornelis Bicker* and the Arquebusiers Hall Civic Guard Paintings in the Afterglow of Marie de Medici's Visit to Amsterdam 1638

David Kunzle
University of California, Los Angeles

The idea that Marie de Medici's visit of 1638 to Amsterdam was a major, if not *the* occasion of Rembrandt's and all the other paintings of the Kloveniersdoelen (Arquebusiers Hall) was seriously mooted in the early 20th century, then dismissed by major scholars since, but has been opened up again by Gary Schwartz in his recent Rembrandt biography. Not a new idea, then, but one fraught with ramifications which have not begun to be explored.

Here I want to posit the idea that the royal entry of 1638 contributed essentially to the atmosphere in which the Arquebusiers Hall paintings were commissioned and executed, that they were done, in the words of my title, "in the *afterglow*" of that event which is extraordinary in senses both obvious and not so obvious. I've been laying siege to this topic — to use a very Dutch metaphor — by digging tunnels, "approches" as they were called then, from many sides: the political and social importance of the entry itself, and the meaning given to it by the book commemorating it; the role of the Schutters, the para-military guard protecting and embellishing the Entry, and their political interests; the participation of artists, not only the six assigned to paint the various civic guard groups, but also the designers of the theatrical displays set up for the Entry, and the engravers of those displays and of other aspects of the visit for the commemorative book; the author of that book, and his literary collaborators on the whole

Robert S. Kirsner (ed.), *The Low Countries and Beyond,* 003-013. Lanham, MD: University Press of America, 1993.

program; and finally — if I could get more documentation — I would dig a tunnel, an approach into the new building of the Arquebusiers Hall, the availability of which obviously is the primary physical factor in the commission of the paintings. And since a siege laid to one town can be furthered by laying siege to its neighbors, I would also take into account the chronologically adjacent festivals, notably that closely preceding for the Spanish Cardinal-Infant Ferdinand, whose entry into Antwerp was decorated by Rubens in 1635, and that closely following, the Entry into Amsterdam of the English Queen Henrietta Maria with her newly married children, daughter Mary and son-in-law William II, future Prince of Orange.

Obviously I can't do all of this here. I will start with the most obviously, literally visible link to Maria de Medici in the Kloveniersdoelen: the painting by Sandrart (Fig. 1) which is not immediately attractive in its present condition, lackluster in color, certainly, but deserving a color reproduction which I cannot find.

No one pretends there is any overt, visible reference to Marie de Medici in Rembrandt's Night Watch, and any of the other paintings, apart from the Sandrart. But in that work the lady certainly looms in a central and solemn — not to say forbidding — manner. She forbids us, at least, to take her lightly. She faces us in the form of an austere, Roman bust, the object of veneration of the troop gathered around it, half of whom actually direct their gaze at it, that is at her. The degree of this veneration — I'm tempted to call it a kind of adoration, akin to that normally accorded the image of a religious patron, such as might have been carried in procession by the distant ancestors of these guardsmen when their guild still had a religious function — the degree of this veneration is conjured up by the Dutch poet Laureate, Joost van den Vondel, in Dutch verses inscribed quite conspicuously (though hard to read now) on the paper below the bust:

> The standard [flag, banner, applied to the company as a whole] of Swieten [that is Cornelis Bicker, who styled himself Lord of Swieten] ventures to receive Medici; but for so great a person Dam and Market are too small, and the eyes of the citizens too weak before such rays. The sun of Christianity is not flesh nor

Figure 1

skin nor bone: so forgive [the painter] Sandrart that he paints her but as stone.

First, the obvious question: whose idea was it to include Marie de Medici, when the inclusion of an extraneous figure such as this was unheard of in the whole long history of Civic Guard group portraits? A priori one would suppose it was due to the company captain, Cornelis Bicker, whose quest for aristocratic allure may be deduced from the lordly estate and title he had recently (1632) assumed as Lord of Swieten; he was later to be burgomaster three times, 1646, the critical year 1650, and 1654, and he was brother to Andreas Bicker who set an all time record with nine burgomasterships. But the idea of including the royal visitor can equally well have come from the artist, for Joachim von Sandrart was an international comet who dazzled, briefly, in the empyreum of princely European courts before his reputation fizzled out so that he is remembered today almost entirely as an artist's biographer. Even Vasari has done better. Sandrart was born in Germany, was trained by the Dutchman Honthorst, an internationally known court painter himself, who painted Maria de Medici in the "official portrait" she chose to present, on the occasion of her visit, to the city of Amsterdam; he was the companion of Rubens in Holland, and went with Honthorst to England. In the course of his grand tour of Italy, he lived for several years with the Marchese Vincenzo Giustiniani and became, in effect, the curator of his art collections; he did portraits of the Pope, the Emperor and the Elector of Bavaria; he gained an imperial knighthood, and in emulation of Castiglione's perfect courtier and Rubens himself, displayed (in his own words) "virtuous conduct, courteous comportment, and elegant conversation" at all times.

Soon after his arrival in Amsterdam about 1636 he made friends with the leading literary figures of the city — Caspar van Baerle, who would write the book of the French Queen's Entry; Samuel Coster, who would determine the iconography of the celebrations; P.C. Hooft who would advise Coster in this, and above all Vondel who would translate van Baerle's book into Dutch, and whose numerous verses on Sandrart paintings were his first exercises in the genre. Sandrart also did portraits of the Bickers, the leading, indeed, the politically dominant family of Amsterdam at this time. Small wonder that although a newcomer and a foreigner in Amsterdam, Sandrart should be chosen to do one of the more prestigious groups in the Kloveniersdoelen; and that he should choose to elevate his subject with this thrice — or quadruply — royal personage, and high-flown verses by Vondel I have cited.

There is moreover evidence that Sandrart was first in place, in the new Kloveniersdoelen chamber. To aim for and achieve priority in this manner is typical of his character; one can imagine him pressing his patron, Cornelis Bicker, to marshal his men, and double-quick, individually in the painter's studio, and, where necessary, going to the individual guardsman's house to make the portrait sketches. My hunch is that this was organized by Sandrart with exceptional efficiency and speed given the kind of difficulties which could arise, as we know from the case of Frans Hals' Meager Company, whose members, a few years before, refused to go to Haarlem to the painter's studio, while the painter refused to come to them in Amsterdam which was, after all, very close by. Sandrart, who in his autobiography boasted of his own speed of execution, got the painting done and in place by 1640 which is the date on the painting (the date 1638 — as that of the Entry itself, appears (or appeared) inscribed after Vondel's verses). Three of the other paintings are dated or datable (including Rembrandt's) to 1642, and it is likely a big push was made in that year in order to get the whole scheme finished, perhaps in connection with another, related royal visit in April of that year by the English Queen Henrietta Maria and in order to catch up with Sandrart.

Sandrart's priority, suggested by the date on the painting itself, and actually documented in 1641, would help account for the fact that the guidebooks to Amsterdam which appeared in a cluster during the early 1660s, single out the Cornelis Bicker group and no other in the Kloveniersdoelen. The word got around, certainly by 1641 when John Evelyn visited, probably earlier if the painting was in place the previous year and even after 1642 when it was no longer alone on the walls, that the Kloveniersdoelen was worth a visit for this picture alone because it showed the famous — or infamous — Queen Mother of France, at a time when she was still an active, if embarrassing and indeed — if you were Richelieu or in his camp — dangerous figure on the European stage, at a time when the Thirty Years War still raged. Marie de

Medici, exiled from France in 1631, continued to intrigue from Brussels until 1638 when, having become an intolerable financial and political burden, she was virtually expelled. After spending some time being celebrated in Holland, she moved to England, was expelled from there also, and went in September 1641, via Holland again where she enjoyed, this time, no reception at all, to Cologne, where she died, miserable and unmourned, but conspiring to the last against Richelieu to whom she satirically left her parrot in her will. She died on July 3, 1642 — just after Rembrandt's group was put in place and just before that of Elias-Pickenoy and probably van der Helst. Her miserable death, at this moment, can only have enhanced by contrast the recent memory, kept alive by Sandrart and Captain Cornelis Bicker, and the book by Caspar van Baerle, of her moment of glory in Amsterdam, in which, I am arguing, the whole Kloveniersdoelen scheme bathes.

A prominent actress on the European stage of over forty years, the occasion of Amsterdam's first princely visit since 1618, she was not likely to be forgotten by the succeeding generation. The first reference to the Kloveniersdoelen is to be found in the diary of John Evelyn, who visited Amsterdam in August 1641, and who describes the painting — then, I assume, the only painting in place, as "paynted on a very large table [meaning canvas] Maria de Medices her statue to the breast, supported by fower royal diademes, the worke of one Vandall, who hath set his name thereon [and the date] 1. Sept. 1638." Vandall is of course the poet Vondel. Evelyn's hasty diary entry gets the name of the painter wrong, and omits that of the company captain.

The first of the guidebooks which appeared in the early 1660s in a cluster — there are least four of them, all interdependent — admires the civic guard paintings in the Kloveniersdoelen generically, then goes on to say "There is also hanging here the portrait of Maria de Medicis, who came to visit this city in the year 1638." In a new paragraph, the author, Melchior Fokkens, goes on to specify, alone among the other paintings in the room, Sandrart's of the Cornelis Bicker company, giving both names, and reproduces the verses by Vondel. Fokkens' wording was taken over by other guides, including that of Tobias Domselaer which would become standard, and which edits the text to eliminate the possibility that two separate paintings are at issue — one of Marie de Medici, and one of the Bicker company — by adding the specification that Cornelis Bicker's guardsmen are "looking at the aforementioned bust" (beeldt). Sandrart himself in his *Teutsche Academie* (1675-79) describes the Bicker company painting, the most important public work of his Amsterdam period, in these words: "In the Kloveniersduelle, the large work of a company of burghers who are engaged in receiving the Queen of France, Maria de Medici, in Amsterdam." No mention of the company commander by name, only Marie de Medici — and in a phrase suggesting that they are posed in the act of receiving her, rather than merely in commemoration of her. This wording tightens, of course, the association of painting and Entry, although it fits, in terms of composition, much better Rembrandt's Night Watch, which simulates an actual mobilization.

Schutterstukken were not normally made in commemoration of historic events, although one earlier group by Lastman and Nieulandt, was certainly intended to celebrate a moment of glorious semi-action — the moment when various Amsterdam companies were called on in 1622 to replace the garrison in Zwolle, needed for the battlefront.

Considered as a historic event, the Entry of Marie de Medici into Amsterdam (Fig. 2, on the following page) in 1638 is ambiguous and peculiar. Historians Dutch or French pay little or no attention to it in their accounts of the period or in biographies of the Queen. Yet it represents a return to the Queen's pristine glory — a totally illusory one, of course, but of such illusions are glory, and art made. Never, since Rubens painted her life in the early 1620s, had she been feted thus, as she was here, in the words and images of Amsterdam's best writers and iconographers, and in the Arquebusiers Hall.

As embodiments of princely virtue went, Marie de Medici presented a special challenge to eulogists. Rubens had tried to evade, gloss over, or repudiate serious accusations of which the worst was his subject's being implicated in the murder of her husband, which could not be proven, and the next worst was actively plotting against the authority, if not the life, of her son, King Louis XIII, which was rather too evidently the case. Since then and since her self-exile in 1631 to the court in Brussels that was soon to become the declared enemy of France, she had been plotting against the authority and the life of Richelieu, her son's chief minister, whom she blamed for all her woes.

Figure 2

Here lies the first level of paradox in Amsterdam's, and Holland's homage to the Queen: such homage was prejudicial to the French king, to whom the Dutch were now formally bound in a military as well as political, offensive alliance. In Holland, moreover, Marie had asked the Dutch to plead for her to be allowed to return to Paris; this was judged by the French to be an intolerable interference in domestic affairs. Both Richelieu and King Louis expressed their anger to the Dutch ambassador in Paris. The attempt made in Holland to get Marie permission to return failed completely, as would similar attempts made afterwards, in England. But while to the French government Marie was simply an incorrigible menace, to many Dutch she was more — and less — than a source of intrigue against their principal ally: she represented not a France allied against a common enemy, but peace with the enemy, the Spain to whom she had always been sympathetic; she represented at the very least a compromise, a road towards the end of the long war begun seventy years before.

Amsterdam, led by the Bickers, was beginning at this very moment to think more actively of peace, and work against the military and dynastic ambitions of Frederick Henry, the Prince of Orange, whose personal cause the French tried in every way to promote. Frederick Henry, too, with his wife Amalia von Solms, had welcomed the exiled Queen, who might be able to further their still secret plans to marry their son to the English king, Charles I's daughter, who was Marie de Medici's granddaughter. But the prince's military ambitions were being thwarted at this time by the covert collaboration of Amsterdam with enemy Spain, a collaboration which had already denied him possession of Antwerp. He was angry at, and even uttered dire threats against, Amsterdam. In a very real sense, the Schutters of Amsterdam stood armed against the House of Orange, too; symbolically, preventively in the late 1630s and 1640s, but soon in an active role, against Frederick Henry's son, the reckless Willem II in 1650.

The visit of a Queen who professed peace and waged a war of intrigue against the major ally of the Republic, succeeded, at the very least, in stirring up feelings, sharpening the debate over the major international and national issues facing the citizens of her host city and host country: pro and con the French alliance, pro and con dividing up the Southern Netherlands, as the French proposed, pro and con an accommodation with Spain, pro and con a monarchizing Prince of Orange, pro and con a hegemonizing Amsterdam, pro and con peace and war; soon (by 1640) pro and con an English alliance.

Prudently these issues were not addressed directly in the iconography celebrating Marie de Medici. Nor, properly studied, is this iconography even about Marie de Medici personally. Judiciously, Caspar van Baerle, Samuel Coster and — above all, I believe — P.C. Hooft, conceived as the focus of the historical-allegorical tableaux vivants traditional to such occasions, and which were placed atop triumphal arches along the route the Queen took into Amsterdam (Fig. 2), not the life and glory of Marie de Medici in the manner of Rubens in Marie's Luxembourg Palace; rather, they chose to emphasize the glory of her husband, commonly called Henry the Great, whose parallel gallery of honor in that same Luxembourg palace, promised long ago to Rubens, was still and would remain unfilled. In no fewer than five of the nine Vertooningen or displays on the triumphal arches Marie does not appear at all; these are wholly dedicated to one theme: Henri IV reuniting France, by defeating the terrors of anarchy and rebellion — those same forces which Rubens had shown defeated by Marie but which in fact sprang up afresh during and after her Regency. No flattering or falsifying "Blessings of the Regency" for the burgomasters of Amsterdam. They seized the occasion to project the great historic ally of the Dutch, Marie's husband Henry the Great, as the model of good government: tolerant of religious variety but capable of unifying factions under his firm and benevolent rule; concerned for social pacification and economic prosperity; and, of course, standing at all times armed for legitimate defense of the realm. All these issues were central to Amsterdam and the Dutch Republic. The Schutters massed below Henry the Great represented in the triumphal arch, and beside his Queen as she proceeded through Amsterdam, stood in defense of his principles which were theirs rather than hers, which had merely provoked and continued to threaten civil war in France. And when they paid homage to her they did so not as a person, but as an embodiment of monarchical glory, representing as she did four monarchies — France, of course, then Spain, England and Savoy, where her children were married. In this monarchical glory the Schutters, defenders of a merchant republic, bathed. At the Queen's Entry the shining armor of the Schutters reflected and the cannonades reverberated Marie's quadruple royal glory upon Amsterdam, the center of a republic-empire equal to any monarchy on earth.

Re-Constructing Van Gogh: Paintings as Sculptures

Patricia Vervoort
Lakehead University, Ontario, Canada

A recent phenomenon in Canadian sculpture is the translation of Vincent van Gogh's paintings into three-dimensional objects by artists having no direct ties with Dutch culture other than their mutual admiration for the painter who died one hundred years ago. The appropriation and reconstruction of van Gogh's imagery by Murray Favro (b. 1940), Russ Yuristy (b. 1936), and Joe Fafard (b. 1942) demonstrate the paradoxes involved in recycling imagery that remains recognizable, yet has been transformed. In turn, these issues invite further exploration of the concepts of originality, reproduction, and illusionism. These three Canadian artists are not alone in their attraction to van Gogh's imagery; artists of other nationalities such as Francis Bacon, Clive Barker, Ann Wilson, David Pearson, and Arnulf Rainer have also based works on those of the Dutch painter. But what distinguishes Fafard and Yuristy is the extent of their devotion to van Gogh's subjects. While Favro only utilized one van Gogh image in his *oeuvre,* the size of his *Van Gogh's Room* demonstrates that this was a major project. Fafard, Favro, and Yuristy have re-constructed van Gogh's paintings as sculptures, works which are readily recognizable as van Gogh's, but at the same time are altered and transformed to introduce a new element which is not van Gogh's. This illusionism and its accompanying issues of imitation and reproduction are the focus of this paper.

Further, these artists have alluded not only to van Gogh's style, but have also usurped his self-portraits and other highly biographical

Robert S. Kirsner (ed.), *The Low Countries and Beyond,* 015-033. Lanham, MD: University Press of America, 1993.

non-figurative works such as *The Bedroom at Arles*. Thus the very personal imagery of van Gogh has been borrowed and changed; his subjects, style, and biography have been expropriated. Usually in the past, when the composition or pose of a portrait was borrowed, the new artist substituted his own face.[1] Here Fafard and Yuristy simply adopt van Gogh's own self-portraits as images and transform them into different materials and different scales. They remain van Gogh's, but simultaneously, they are not van Gogh's.

Artists have always borrowed from other artists; it is a standard practice in the visual arts and a means of learning. In fact, as Egbert Haverkamp-Begemann has stated, artists guided by other art works "usually learned more from those examples than from reality itself."[2] In contemporary art, the issue of appropriation is central to discussions of post-modernism.[3] Art labeled post-modernist art is referential. "For example, it may 'steal' types and images in an 'appropriation' that is seen as critical — both of a culture in which images are commodities and of an aesthetic practice that holds (nostalgically) to an art of originality."[4] As Andreas Huyssen queried, "And if nostalgia it is, does it point to the exhaustion of cultural resources and creativity in our own time or does it hold the promise of a revitalization in

---

[1] For example, Rembrandt's etched *Self-Portrait Leaning on a Stone Wall* (1639) is adapted from Titian's *Portrait of a Man with A Blue Sleeve* (c1506). There are exceptions, of course, such as James Ensor's *Portrait of the Artist Surrounded by Masks* (1899) where Ensor retains the facial features of Rubens.

[2] Egbert Haverkamp-Begemann, "The Creative Copy," in *Creative Copies: Interpretive Drawings from Michelangelo to Picasso* by Egbert Haverkamp-Begemann with Carolyn Logan (New York: Sotheby's in association with The Drawing Center, 1988), 13.

[3] Bruce Cole and Adelheid Gealt, *Art of the Western World: From Ancient Greece to Post-Modernism* (Toronto: Summit, 1989), 333, "the term Post-Modernism was coined to characterize contemporary art and architecture, and while there is general agreement that Post-Modern is a new period quite distinct in form and intent from the so-called modernists, its exact tenets remain elusive." For some of the many uses of post-modernism, see Douglas Davis, "Post-Everything," *Art in America* 68 (February 1980), 11-14.

[4] Hal Foster, "Re: Post" in *Art After Modernism: Rethinking Representation*, ed. Brian Wallis (New York: The New Museum of Contemporary Art/David R. Godine, 1984), 197.

contemporary culture?"[5] In this discussion of Canadian artists, the images of van Gogh promise revitalization because they have been transformed and altered while at the same time emphasizing the breakdown of cultural boundaries. These are Canadian van Gogh's, not Dutch van Gogh's.

In the twentieth century, the availability of reproductions makes, as John Berger noted, "all paintings contemporary."[6] The fascination with van Gogh is universal partly because van Gogh's works have been so widely reproduced that van Gogh images even in recycled variations have immediate recognition value.[7] A further problem arises with what to call these recycled images, which have been identified by a variety of terms: reproduction, replication, borrowing, repetition, copying, creative copying, transformation, translation, quotation, citation, etc. None of these new works by Favro, Yuristy, or Fafard is intended to be a duplicate or copy of the van Gogh original, each is altered to reflect the new human presence. As George Kubler observed: "Every man-made replica varies from its model by minute, unplanned divergences, of which the accumulated effects are like a slow drift away from the archetype."[8] On the other hand, Anne Hollander in her discussion of re-used images called them stolen images and remarked: "The most commonly stolen goods are the arrangements that guarantee emotional responses."[9] Van Gogh's life story is so intimately bound up with his paintings in the eyes of the general public that his works, in whatever form, do guarantee an emotional response. Thus, the availability of an audience already familiar with the van Gogh legend must be a major factor in the selection of van Gogh imagery. The familiarity of van Gogh's life history and the translation of his

---

[5]Andreas Huyssen, "The Search for Tradition: Avant-Garde and Postmodernism in the 1970s," *New German Critique* 22 (1981), 25.

[6]John Berger, *Ways of Seeing* (New York: Viking, 1973), 19.

[7]John A. Walker, "The Van Gogh Industry" in *Van Gogh Studies: Five Critical Essays* (London: Jaw Publications, 1981), 41-46.

[8]George Kubler, *The Shape of Time: Remarks on the History of Things* (New Haven: Yale University Press, 1962), 71.

[9]Anne Hollander, *Moving Pictures* (New York: Knopf, 1989), 12.

letters has allowed North American artists to gain an intimate knowledge of van Gogh as a person; no other artist has made himself so accessible. All three of these artists have studied van Gogh's *Letters* and they consider van Gogh a friend.

Do images that are readily perceived as van Gogh's, despite changes in scale or material, still belong to van Gogh or do they belong to the transformers? Are they translations or originals? Literary translations usually lose some of the flavor of the original, but does the same hold true for visual translations? I think not. These Canadian works are not one-to-one correspondences with van Gogh's because the medium has changed, details added, exaggerations incorporated, and the scale either magnified or reduced. These new works were, ironically, all produced through the medium of reproductions, second-hand versions of the original paintings. Yet, as Walter Benjamin observed: the "reproduction can put the copy of the original into situations which would be out of reach for the original itself."[10] And indeed, the van Gogh imagery of these artists has placed the works in new situations; Van Gogh remains recognizable, but the transformations are also immediately perceived. As sculptures, these works by Favro, Fafard, and Yuristy cannot be ordinary copies since they use three-dimensions to re-make images that originated in two-dimensions. All three artists make additions to the original van Gogh's, additions which reiterate their roles as collaborators with the Dutch painter.

To begin with Favro's *Van Gogh's Room* (1973-74), it is a multi-media construction of wood, room-size, and by itself, virtually colourless; the work is completed only when a colour slide of the actual painting is projected on to the construction, hence Favro's label "projected reconstruction" (Fig. 1). Favro insists that he did not create this work "out of interest in history of art or a comment on art," but rather, "I wanted to see what that space would really look like."[11]

---

[10]Walter Benjamin, "The Work of Art in the Age of Mechanical Reproduction," in *Illuminations*, trans. Harry Zohn, ed. Hannah Arendt (New York: Harcourt, Brace and World, 1955), 222.

[11]"Murray Favro" in *10 Canadian Artists in the 1970s: An Exhibition for European Tour* (Toronto: Art Gallery of Ontario, 1980), 48.

Figure 1

He first worked from reproductions, and later as the work progressed, ventured to Amsterdam to see the original painting.

Favro noticed "the floor goes almost straight up and then bends back."[12] *Van Gogh's Room*, however, can't be easily occupied, because of the angles and tilt of the floor; his construction remains a sculpture to be only observed. Enclosed by three straight walls, the construction includes all the furniture and room furnishings found in the painting, even the clothing hanging on hooks is included. The construction itself has several colours: the smaller objects are painted white, the furniture is "harvest gold," and the walls are pale blue with patches of white on the walls where the paintings and window panes are located. The work is complete only when the colour slide is projected. When the *Bedroom at Arles* is projected onto Favro's construction, the window panes acquire "glass" and images appear in the "paintings," and the smooth surfaces become textured with impastoed paint. Without mechanical projection, Favro's reconstruction is only partially coloured and, in Favro's eyes, only a partial work, an ironic reversal of van Gogh's aim that in the *Bedroom*, "color is to do everything." And as the light of the projector illuminates the makeshift furniture, shadows are created which again is contrary to van Gogh's aim of "suppressing all shadows." Further, the tilted floor and the rickety furniture create an air of instability and unrest that reverses van Gogh's intention that the *Bedroom* "is to be suggestive here of rest or of sleep in general...."[13]

One addition made by Favro is the continuous black horizontal line which extends around all three walls of his construction. This line functions as a parallel to the tilt of the floor and emphasizes that the angle on the left side is more exaggerated than that on the right. It is the only obvious intrusion made by Favro that was not in the original of the *Bedroom at Arles;* the line also blatantly declares that this construction is not an exact replication.

---

[12]Marie L. Fleming, *Murray Favro: A Retrospective* (Toronto: Art Gallery of Toronto, 1983), 74.

[13]Vincent van Gogh, *The Complete Letters of Vincent van Gogh*, 2nd. ed. (Greenwich, Connecticut: New York Graphic Society, 1959), 3:86, letter 554.

Favro has disrupted the viewer's complacency. Indeed, *Van Gogh's Room* invites a variety of responses. As Marie Fleming observed, Favro's reconstruction is "thrice removed from reality," with van Gogh's painting as the first stage, the slide of it, and then the simulation of these realities by Favro.[14] Kenneth Baker summed up his reaction:

> Favro's installation seems to be an ironic statement of the difficulty of reconstructing in memory the experience of a work of art. It might also be seen as a wry reflection upon the quotient of misrepresentation in any visual reproduction of an original work....[15]

Because of van Gogh's unique vision, the painting cannot be fully recreated in actuality, and Favro's reconstruction is itself incomplete without van Gogh's own painting projected on to it. The projection required for the completion of *Van Gogh's Room* introduces slow and imperceptible changes as the slides gradually disintegrate and fade in colour the more they are used. Authenticity is maintained only by a constant replacement of the slide with new ones. Nevertheless, Favro has transformed van Gogh's *Bedroom at Arles* into an object in which the original remains recognizable, but also perceptible are the changes which signify *Van Gogh's Room*. Moreover, *Van Gogh's Room* creates the urge to compare Favro's work with van Gogh's, an activity that is impossible since these two works reside in museums an ocean apart. A comparison can only be achieved through the use of more reproductions or projections which adds an ironic reversal to Walter Benjamin's prediction that reproductions destroy the "aura" of the originals.[16] In Favro's case, the reconstruction creates the desire to see again the original.

Some of the same issues arise when the use of van Gogh's self-portraits by Yuristy and Fafard is examined. Russ Yuristy has been

---

[14]Fleming, 74.

[15]Kenneth Baker, "Report from Toronto: Ten Canadians Abroad," *Art in America*, 69 (March 1981), 53.

[16]Benjamin, 223.

exploring van Gogh's imagery in a variety of two-and three-dimensional media, all quite recent in date. For example, Yuristy's series of 25 van Gogh heads, each called *Painter* (1987-88), was inspired by van Gogh's self-portrait, the *Self-Portrait at the Easel* (1888) in Amsterdam. Yuristy made a mold and used paper pulp to create 25 similar but different works; thick paint in various colours, expressionistically applied, supplements the relief character of the paper pulp. By producing a series of the *Painter*, Yuristy displays another characteristic of the post-modern. "Seriality and repetition, appropriation, intertextuality, simulation or pastiche: these are the primary devices employed by post-modernist artists."[17] Yet, while the basic appropriated image has been repeated 25 times creating a series, the finished versions of the *Painter* result in 25 unique works.

The van Gogh *Self-Portrait on the Road to Tarascon* (1888), destroyed during the Second World War, provided the inspiration for Yuristy's large bronze relief, *Van Gogh Walking* (1987), subtitled: *Off to Paint the Sun — for Vincent* (Fig. 2). Lifesize, this is a free-standing, brightly-coloured bronze relief, a cut-out style figure supported by an irregular shape that spreads forward from the figure's feet forming a flat base that recalls the shadow cast by van Gogh in his back-lit painting. The colours are patinated on the bronze: yellows, blues, greys, and black. Van Gogh's *Self-Portrait on the Road to Tarascon* is summarized in shape and minimized in detail, the shape of the figure and the shadow dominate rather than the features of the artist's face. But Yuristy has added features to the face, the pipe, and even an image to the canvas under van Gogh's arm. All over the surface are a series of shorter, thicker raised shapes which are actually twigs pruned from Yuristy's backyard apple tree. While this may seem incongruous, it was the tree pruning in the spring of 1987 which "brought to mind those wonderful paintings of van Gogh's of orchards in bloom. I saved the twigs and branches...." Yuristy, in a written statement, went on to explain the creation of *Van Gogh Walking*:

> My inspiration came from reading Vincent's letters, in which he describes his trips to the fields to paint. I envisioned him with all his gear and folding easel on his back and his paint box in

---

[17] Abigail Solomon-Godeau, "Photography After Art Photography" in Wallis, 80.

Figure 2

hand; dressed in zinc workers denim, striding off in the early dawn, and puffing on his beloved pipe, off for another day of painting in the bright sun. This is my tribute to a passionate human being and to a great, great painter![18]

Of the three artists being examined here, Joe Fafard has had the most intense and longest involvement with van Gogh. Fafard has transformed van Gogh's self-portraits into free-standing or hanging ceramic reliefs called the *Vincent Self-Portrait Series* (1983-1987), 40 pieces which he considers to be a single work. In addition, he also created two small three-dimensional figures of van Gogh which are composites of several van Gogh paintings.

Fafard claims van Gogh's painted surfaces were already sculptural due to the build-up of pigments. The self-portraits sculptured by Fafard are a natural continuation of van Gogh's own art, "...what van Gogh would have done," says Fafard, "had he become a sculptor."[19] In the *Vincent Self-Portrait Series,* Fafard isolated the heads from their grounds, and hence much of the colour, but retained the poses, the facial expressions, and clothing of the originals. In various scales from life-size to six-feet in height, monochrome and painted, Fafard has sculpturally animated the faces of van Gogh.

For example, in *Vincent #4* from 1983 (Fig. 3), the intense sidelong glance of van Gogh's nervous eyes follows the precedent of the Oslo *Self-Portrait* (1889), one of van Gogh's last. In the painting, van Gogh smudged the paint to obliterate most of the ear, and the long sweeping brushstrokes merged the whole side of the face with the beard. Fafard has retained the nervous expression; but by modelling the ear and clarifying the beard against the face, Fafard has completed in his own way an unfinished van Gogh original. The most telling testimony of Fafard's ability to re-create rather than simply copy van Gogh's imagery is the enlargement of the eyes, a feature which makes Vincent appear alert and in control. Such minor variations constitute Kubler's notions of replication and invention:

---

[18]Written statement from Russell Yuristy, February 21, 1990.

[19]Teitelbaum, 37.

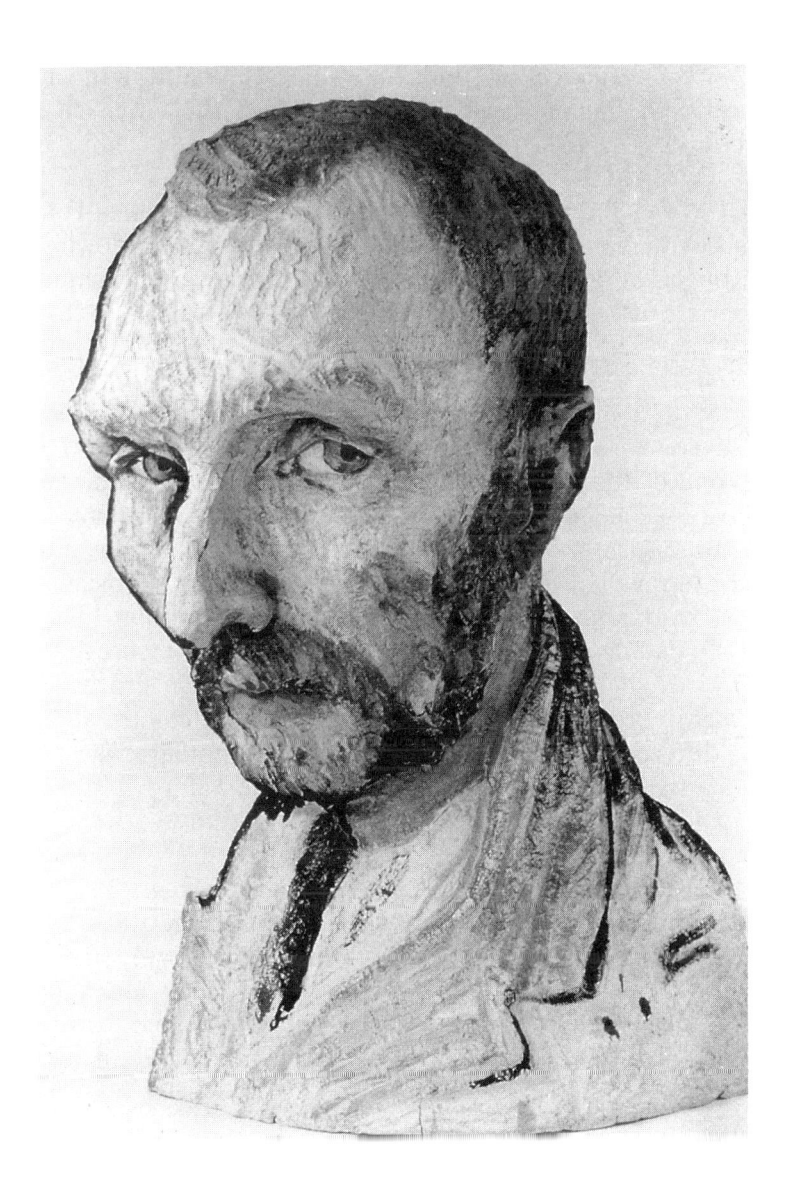

Figure 3

In every act, fidelity to the model and departure from it are inextricably mingled, in proportions that ensure recognizable repetition, together with such minor variations as the moment and circumstances allow. Indeed, when variation from the model exceeds the amount of faithful copying, then we have an invention.[20]

Vincent #4, like the others in the series, demonstrates Fafard's interactions with van Gogh, an intimacy gained from knowing his subject through not only his self-portraits, but through all his paintings. The ability to infuse life into these ceramic and bronze heads testifies that Fafard is also an inventor.

While the *Vincent Self-Portrait Series* was in progress, Fafard executed several three-dimensional portraits of van Gogh, *The Painter* of 1986 is one of these (Fig. 4). A full-length seated portrait of the artist, Fafard uses a pose which van Gogh himself never adopted. *The Painter* holds a brush in one hand and his palette in the other. On his head is the straw hat so familiar from van Gogh's Parisian *Self-Portraits*. At work, *The Painter* is studying what's before him. There is a sense of impending movement, as if he's about to lift his brush to the invisible canvas; each viewer can visualize a painting in process. *The Painter* is cast in bronze and patinated to provide the colour; all seven casts have different colouring which introduces another twist to the concepts of originality and reproduction because Fafard has created multiples of his own work.

A different full-length figure is called *Dear Vincent* (1983) and, like *The Painter*, is a composite of van Gogh's own imagery. As Fafard explained, it's "from all of van Gogh's work. I borrowed from the painting of his chair, the painting of his boots, the painting of his palette, his self-portraits, and combined them into one gesture."[21] Unlike *The Painter, Dear Vincent* is made of clay and painted in acrylics;

---

[20]Kubler, 72.

[21]Robert Enright, "Working in the Flatland: An Interview with Joe Fafard," *Border Crossings,* VII (January 1988), 18-19.

Figure 4

it is unique, there are no multiples. The intensely serious face with the large tuft of unruly hair atop the head and the blue clothing covered in swirling lines of paint derive from the Whitney *Self-Portrait* of 1889. On the candle which van Gogh holds in his hand, Fafard said: "He was really an innocent and he was lighting up things that we only begin to see a hundred years later. As he moves his hand to paint with the brush, he's also throwing some light on the subject, too."[22] Fafard's figural sculptures with their slightly enlarged heads bring van Gogh to life, recalling the painter's work and life with all its quotations from various individual works. This referential blending again refutes the notion of simple copying, expressing instead a fusion of knowledge about van Gogh the artist and van Gogh the man. The result is not a van Gogh, but rather Fafard's van Goghs.

All three of these Canadian artists have based these sculptural works on van Gogh's paintings. While it can be acknowledged that van Gogh was a painter and not a sculptor, is appropriation of his imagery by others without permission appropriate? The answer has to be an unequivocal yes because the subject matter of art cannot be legislated or censored. Further, it is not only these Canadians, but also artists of many different nationalities that have adopted van Gogh's images which only emphasizes how much van Gogh has become a commodity of mass culture. Calvin Tompkins sums up some of these issues:

> As a result of the overwhelming power of advertising, television, and the media in general, we no longer inhabit a world of real things, according to Baudrillard; reality has been replaced by the signs and images that refer to it. And art — well, art has been replaced by its simulacrum, too. The artist can no longer make art; he or she can only refer to it, and one way of doing so is by appropriating or mimicking previous art. In the process, the artist Peter Halley has written, the elements of modernism "are reduced to their pure formal state and are denuded of any last vestiges of life or meaning."[23]

---

[22]Enright, 19. Teitelbaum, 37, says "he's clutching a candle which represents his cherished colleague, Gauguin."

[23]Calvin Tompkins, *Post-to Neo-: The Art World of the 1980s* (Markham, Ontario: Penguin Books, 1988), 238.

The final question to be examined is that of meaning in the appropriated images used by these three Canadian artists. First of all, the van Gogh portraits and his *Bedroom* are not reduced to their pure formal state. All of these artists have made additions, deletions, changes in scale, materials, and especially dimensions. These are not van Gogh images simply repeated and presented as the works of other artists. Nevertheless, the arguments of the post-modern theorists emphasize that the appropriation of images is a wide-spread contemporary phenomenon in the art world. A significant oversight, however, in discussions of post-modernist appropriation is the traditional use of appropriation in the visual arts. As Leo Steinberg has stated: "all art is infested by other art." Further, he wrote:

> ...a borrower is one who takes. But the record of art reveals that giving, lending, imparting, may be equally suitable metaphors.... There are instances by the score where the artist invests the work he takes from with renewed relevance; he bestows on it a viability hitherto unsuspected; he actualizes its potentialities.... He can clear cobwebs away and impart freshness to things that were moldering in neglect or, what is worse, had grown banal through false familiarity. By altering their environment, a latter-day artist can lend moribund images a new lease on life.[24]

Steinberg's statement is particularly apt in regards to van Gogh's art, which has been reproduced so extensively as to become banal and over-familiar. These Canadian artists have altered the environment of the van Gogh's and, in the process, have imparted them with a new life. As sculptures, these van Gogh images are examples of traditional homage paid to an artist greatly admired.

To summarize, of the three artists under discussion here, Favro appears to be the most detached. He was intrigued by a particular painting and recreated it in a large-scale sculptural format in order to explore the problem of a distorted two-dimensional space in three dimensions. The quest for understanding van Gogh's *Bedroom* was

---

[24]Leo Steinberg, "The Glorious Company" in *Art About Art* by Jean Lipman and Richard Marshall (New York: Dutton in association with the Whitney Museum of American Art, 1978), 9, 25.

solved to Favro's satisfaction, his more recent productions deal with other realities and not paintings; *Van Gogh's Bedroom* was Favro's only excursion into van Gogh's imagery. On the other hand, both Fafard and Yuristy have created extensive series of works all based on van Gogh's self-portraits. Their adoption of van Gogh's own face adds an extremely personal note when they use the face of the painter they admire and don't substitute their own. However, in addition to changes in medium, there are basic differences in Fafard's and Yuristy's approaches. Fafard's van Gogh heads titled *Vincent Self-Portrait Series* is composed of forty separate pieces which to Fafard constitutes a single work. Yuristy, on the other hand, borrowed one van Gogh self-portrait and made a mold from which he formed 25 different paper pulp reliefs, works in a series.

These Canadian sculptors are dependent on van Gogh's imagery, a debt they readily acknowledge; yet this existing subject matter for them was the point of departure. Although the initial recognition of van Gogh imagery has an emotional impact, the works prompt a desire to view the original van Gogh's and, since that isn't possible, a need to examine a book of van Gogh reproductions which refers the viewer back again to the sources used by these sculptors. The use of mechanical reproductions can not be avoided in an examination of these re-constructed van Gogh's. They exemplify, as Peter Wolheim observed:

> the life of the work of art in the age of mechanical reproduction must seriously rephrase or dispense with concepts of exclusive authorship and originality, in favour of a notion of creative interdependence and received imagery.[25]

Although Wolheim believes originality is no longer a factor of importance in the visual arts, the images produced by Favro, Fafard, and Yuristy are examples of creative interdependence with van Gogh but, at the same time, could not have been produced without a degree of originality on the part of these recent sculptors. Their productions are more than received images.

---

[25]Peter Wolheim, "The Politics of Memory: Re-Reading Walter Benjamin," *Vanguard*, 15 (February/March 1986), 26.

Benjamin bemoaned the use of mechanical reproductions, prints in black-and-white, which, he said, removed the significance of a "unique existence" for the original, "its presence in time and space."[26] Yet if it were not for reproductions, these new Canadian works would not have been created in the first place, since they all depended on newer and better quality reproductions than those which concerned Benjamin. These new works, made by hand, are originals too, and each has a "unique presence" in another time and culture from that of van Gogh. They are ensuring, in some ways, the survival of van Gogh's memory, not as written history, but visually, thus fulfilling another need identified by Benjamin: that "every image of the past that is not recognized by the present as one of its own concern threatens to disappear irretrievably."[27] Accordingly, the reconstruction of van Gogh's paintings as sculptures by Favro, Yuristy, and Fafard demonstrates that these images from the past are recognized and will not disappear.

References

Arendt, Hannah, ed. *Illuminations,* trans. Harry Zohn. New York: Harcourt, Brace and World, 1955.

Baker, Kenneth. "Report from Toronto: Ten Canadians Abroad." *Art in America,* 69 (March 1981), 53-54.

Berger, John. *Ways of Seeing.* New York: Viking, 1973.

Cole, Bruce, and Adelheid Gealt. *Art of the Western World: From Ancient Greece to Post Modernism.* Toronto: Summit, 1989.

Davis, Douglas. "Post-Everything." *Art in America,* 68 (February 1980), 11-14.

Enright, Robert. "Working in the Flatland: An Interview with Joe Fafard." *Border Crossings,* VII (January 1988), 10-20.

---

[26]Benjamin, 222-223.

[27]Benjamin, "Theses of the Philosophy of History" in *Illuminations,* 255.

Fleming, Marie. *Murray Favro: A Retrospective.* Toronto: Art Gallery of Ontario, 1983.
Gogh, Vincent van. *The Complete Letters of Vincent van Gogh,* 2nd ed. Greenwich, Connecticut: New York Graphic Society, 1959.
Haverkamp-Begemann, Egbert with Carolyn Logan. *Creative Copies: Interpretive Drawings from Michelangelo to Picasso.* New York: Sotheby's and The Drawing Center, 1988.
Hollander, Anne. *Moving Pictures.* New York: Knopf, 1989.
Huyssen, Andreas. "The Search for Tradition: Avant-Garde and Postmodernism in the 1970s." *New German Critique* 22 (1981) : 23-40.
Kubler, George. *The Shape of Time: Remarks on the History of Things.* New Haven: Yale University Press, 1962.
Lipman, Jean, and Richard Marshall. *Art About Art.* New York: Dutton in association with the Whitney Museum of American Art, 1978.
Teitelbaum, Matthew, and Peter White. *Joe Fafard: Cows and Other Luminaries.* Saskatoon and Regina: Mendel Art Gallery and Dunlop Art Gallery, 1987.
Tomkins, Calvin. *Post- to Neo-: The Art World of the 1980s.* Markham, Ontario: Penguin Books, 1988.
Walker, John. *Van Gogh Studies: Five Critical Essays.* London: Jaw Publications, 1981.
Wallis, Brian, ed. *Art After Modernism: Rethinking Representation.* New York: The New Museum of Contemporary Art; Boston: David R. Godine, 1984.
Wolheim, Peter. "The Politics of Memory: Re-Reading Walter Benjamin," *Vanguard,* 15 (February/March 1986), 22-27.

Illustrations

Figure 1

Murray Favro, *Van Gogh's Room,* 1973-74. Painted wood, slides, 35 mm slide projector (multi-media construction): 269 x 365 x 365 cm. (8 1/2 x 12 x 12'). Overall size including projector space: 365 x 975 cm. (12 x 32'). Collection: Art Gallery of Ontario, Toronto.

Figure 2
Russ Yuristy, *Van Gogh Walking: Off to Paint the Sun — for Vincent,* 1987. Bronze, patinated, 168 cm. (6'). Private Collection. Photo: Courtesy of the Ufundi Gallery, Ottawa.

Figure 3
Joe Fafard, *Vincent #4,* 1983. Clay and acrylic paint, 83.9 x 56.4 x 24.9 cm. (33 x 22 1/2 x 9 3/4"). Collection: CBC, Regina. Permission of the artist.

Figure 4
Joe Fafard, *The Painter,* 1986. Bronze, patina, acrylic paint, 64.7 x 53.3 x 22.8 cm. (25 1/2 x 21 x 9"). Permission of the artist.

History

The Schulenborgh Affair and Provincial Politics in Groningen

John H. Grever
Loyola Marymount University, Los Angeles

During the early 1660s a federal dispute in The Hague escalated into a provincial crisis in distant Groningen.[1] The central figure in the conflict was the capable and ambitious Johan Schulenborgh. He was a member of the city council of Groningen, but never joined the inner circle of power brokers. Instead he became an influential deputy in the provincial delegation to the States General. After a decade of service in The Hague, the States of Groningen resolved in 1661 to revoke his commission, claiming that he had violated their instructions in approving a treaty with Portugal in which deputies had an economic stake. They had public and private funds invested in the West India Company, which had a Chamber in their capital. To recover their investments after the Portuguese reconquest of Dutch Brazil, the local Chamber had recommended a substantial indemnity.[2] The provincial assembly followed this advice, stipulating two conditions: an indemnity to be paid in cash by Portugal, with the money to be distributed among all the Chambers. But a copy of this resolution sent to Schulenborgh contained one fateful error, the result either of a negligent clerk or of

---

[1] The following abbreviations have been used: Arch., Archives; C.T., Collectie N. Tonckens; G.A., Gemeentearchief; R.A., Rijksarchief; Res., Resolution; Secr., Secret; St., States. The dates of Groningen are given in Old Style, which are ten days behind the Gregorian calendar used by the provinces of Holland and Zeeland.

[2] Extract uit het Resolutie boeck der Heeren Bewinthebbers, March 7, 1661, R.A. (Groningen), Arch. St. van Stad en Lande, 1392, 257. P. J. van Winter, *De Westindische Compagnie ter Kamer Stad en Lande* (The Hague, 1978), 155-56, 260-61.

Robert S. Kirsner (ed.), *The Low Countries and Beyond,* 037-045. Lanham, MD: University Press of America, 1993.

a trap set by his enemies. The term "conditions" had lost its plural form, so that the approval of the treaty depended only on one condition.[3]

The crucial session of the States General took place on June 23, 1661, when Schulenborgh was the "president of the week" and chaired a session which included the provincial assembly of Holland and a large number of deputies from Zeeland. In spite of strong opposition from Gelderland and Zeeland, Schulenborgh decided in favor of resuming negotiations with Portugal. In the session of August 6, over which he again presided, the States General agreed to sign the treaty.[4] Schulenborgh had notified the States of Groningen that the federal resolution of June 23 was in compliance with their instructions. He had obtained one condition, that the indemnity would be paid to the Chambers, but the second one, that it be delivered in cash, was not accepted. Since Schulenborgh believed that one condition was sufficient, he thought he had acted properly.[5]

At first, the city council and the Delegated States of Groningen, their standing executive committee, did not respond to Schulenborgh's approval of the treaty, not even when he passed through Groningen on his way to East Friesland. But Schulenborgh had political enemies. Factional rivalries involving court politics became more important than Groningen's economic interests in the West India Company. Many councilors supported Willem Frederik, the stadholder of Groningen and Friesland, because he would maintain their influence over the Ommelanden assembly, which consisted of rural deputies from the nine subquarters or country districts. The Ommelanden included a faction led by Osebrand Jan Rengers, Heer op Fraylemaborg tot Slochteren, who sought to curtail the stadholder's political power and therefore

---

[3]H. A. Poelman, "Johan Schulenborgh," *Groningse Volksalmanak* (1920), 49-53.

[4]Secr. Res. June 23, August 6, 1661, Algemeen Rijksarchief (The Hague), Arch. Staten Generaal, 3267, fols. 329, 409-10.

[5]Johan Schulenborgh, Warmold Ackama, and Johan Clant van Stedum to St. of Groningen, August 10, 1661, R.A. (Groningen), Arch. St. van Stad en Lande, 325A. Poelman, "Johan Schulenborgh," 52-53.

had gained the sympathetic support of Holland's States party.[6] The reliance upon outside assistance was caused by a perennial conflict between the two rivals in the provincial Diet: the sixteen councilors of Groningen and the huge Ommelanden assembly. This constant friction aroused mutual distrust. During the month in which the treaty with Portugal was signed, the burgomasters instructed their deputy in the States General, Warmold Ackama, to watch the moves of the Ommelanden delegates in The Hague and to gather information about their intrigues directed against "our city's rights and privileges."[7] Yet, during this period the pro-Rengers faction was still a minority in the Ommelanden assembly because most rural deputies favored Willem Frederik. The Ommelanden majority demonstrated their support when they joined the city council in granting William Frederik's young son, Hendrik Casimir, the right to succeed to the provincial office of stadholder.

In approving the signing of the treaty with Portugal, however, Schulenborgh had endorsed the policies of Johan de Witt, the Councilor Pensionary of Holland. He may also have been siding with Rengers's anti-stadholder faction in the Ommelanden. If so, this link would explain why the council of Groningen included members who opposed Schulenborgh for his connections with the anti-dynastic factions in Groningen and Holland. This connection was disclosed when on September 6, 1661, Johannes Meinardi, the secretary to the Delegated States of Groningen, entered the home of burgomaster Gerhard Swartte, and saw burgomaster Ludolf Coenders, Tobias van Iddekinge, Johan van Julsinga, Hendrick Emmelcamp, Johan Eeck, and secretary Andreas Ludolphi enjoying a glass of wine and praising the merits of stadholder Willem Frederik. Among the merry company, Coenders, Julsinga, Iddekinge, and Ludolphi were Schulenborgh's

---

[6]N. Jonckens, "Het proces-Schulenborgh (1662) in het licht van de stadhouderlijke politiek in Stad en Lande," *Groningse Volksalmanak* (1963), 65-80.

[7]Warmold Ackama to Burgomasters of Groningen, September 1, 1661, G.A. (Groningen), Oud-Archief (r.n.r.), 335r.

leading opponents.[8] It was during these days that the councilors of Groningen had repeatedly asked the Delegated States for a special meeting of the Diet to discuss the treaty with Portugal. The request was granted one day after the festive gathering of Schulenborgh's opponents.

Before the Diet session, the council of Groningen had held lengthy debates about Schulenborgh's conduct. His opponents finally emerged as the victors because, once the Diet was in session, the city joined the Ommelanden in repudiating the treaty with Portugal. The council also demanded that Schulenborgh appear in person to explain his approval of the treaty.[9] When Groningen's rejection of the treaty was revealed to the States General, the deputies of Holland protested against this repudiation of one of their colleagues. Schulenborgh had informed De Witt that the repudiation had taken place without his knowledge. The States of Holland resolved to support Schulenborgh, a defense which he had printed and sent to his friends in Groningen.[10] The council retaliated by asking a reluctant Johan Isbrants to gather information against Schulenborgh. Herman de Syghers, his fellow-deputy from the Ommelanden, was more willing to collect incriminating evidence. Willem van Raesfelt, the deputy of Gelderland, told him that Schulenborgh had called his provincial superiors "a group of drunken and reckless rogues." Coenders heard from Joost Lewe, the Ommelanden deputy in The Hague, that he described them as "tyrants and wretches."[11]

---

[8]Tonckens, "Het proces-Schulenborgh," 80-81. Gerard van Walrich to Willem Frederik, January 19, 1661, Ate Riemersma to Willem Frederik, January 20, 1661, R.A. (Groningen), C.T., 096.1122, nr. 12.

[9]Johannes Meinardi to Willem Frederik, September 6, 1661, R.A. (Groningen), C.T., 096.1122, nr. 12; Res. September 14, 1661, R.A. (Groningen), Arch. St. van Stad en Lande, Staatsresolutiën, nr. 13; Poelman, "Johan Schulenborgh," 53-54.

[10]Tonckens, "Het proces-Schulenborgh," 82.

[11]Johan Isbrants to Burgomasters of Groningen, November 15, 1661; Informatien uyt last der Ed. Mo. H. Heeren Borgemeesteren ende Raedt genomen, November 16, 1661 in G.A. (Groningen), Oud-Archief (r.n.r.), 730; R.A. (Groningen), C.T., 096.1122, nr. 12.

Schulenborgh had made enemies not only among the councilors but also among the Ommelanden deputies. He claimed that six of the nine subquarters were against him. The Rengers faction had lost influence because the syndic of the Ommelanden, Symon Wijchel, was replaced by Daniël ten Winckel, a supporter of stadholder Willem Frederik. It appeared that Willem Frederik opposed Schulenborgh because of his close contacts with De Witt and the dominant States party in Holland. George Downing, the English envoy, may have been one of the persons who persuaded Willem Frederik to ruin Schulenborgh's political career. Although Downing had a motive since he opposed the signing of the treaty with Portugal, there was a lack of clear evidence to establish this link.[12] Other opponents were the Orangist deputies from Zeeland who corresponded with Willem Frederik. They also had a motive for destroying Schulenborgh. With investments in privateering ventures against Portugal, their province passionately resisted the signing of the treaty. Whatever the exact number and identity of his enemies, they were strong enough to demand that Schulenborgh be questioned by the States of Groningen. He entered the Diet on November 22, 1661, to face his accusers. Menso Alting, the syndic of the city, charged him with a violation of his provincial instructions and with malice for having incited the States of Holland to discredit Groningen's reputation. Despite his attempt to refute the charges, the council ignored his arguments, although the Ommelanden delayed an immediate response. The next day, Schulenborgh was asked to appear in the council. Ordered to sit down on a small bench instead of his customary chair, the council decided to remove him as deputy of the States General.[13]

These actions against Schulenborgh were not supported by the whole council. Deep divisions were exposed in the meeting of November 30, when the council discussed an Ommelanden document

---

[12]Tonckens, "Het proces-Schulenborgh," 81-82.

[13]Private Notes Schulenborgh, Council Meeting, November 23, 1661, in R.A. (Groningen), C.T., 096.1122, nr. 12; Res. November 22-23, 1661, R.A. (Groningen), Arch. St. van Stad en Lande, Staatsresolutiën, nr. 13.

filled with condemnations of Schulenborgh's conduct.[14] Burgomaster Coenders had pulled this document out of his pocket and requested Iddekinge to read it aloud because he was the presiding burgomaster. All councilors were invited to present their opinions. Burgomaster Johan Tjassens initially refused, because the Ommelanden document could only be discussed in the Diet. Iddekinge insisted on hearing his opinion. Tjassens replied by condemning the actions against Schulenborgh as a plot with the Ommelanden, declaring that he never wanted to participate in such "godless procedures." But Coenders, Allard Aldringa, and Henricus Weremeus wanted to discuss the Ommelanden document. Arend van Nijeveen agreed with burgomaster Tjassens. He called the procedures a travesty of justice, and so did Eeck and Samuel Emmius. Emmelcamp and Johan Wichers again accepted the Ommelanden document, while Gerhard Horenken bluntly told the council that he knew that, the day before, several of his colleagues had met till late at night with the Ommelanden to prepare this document for the council. The next speakers, Julsinga and Rembt de Mepsche, refused to accept Tjassens's criticism. Although aware of a council majority against Schulenborgh, Tjaert Gerlacius still labeled the procedures unlawful. After burgomaster Iddekinge had given his own negative view, he announced that the majority of the council had accepted the Ommelanden document. Therefore, in the Diet meeting on the same day, the council supported the Ommelanden in withdrawing Schulenborgh's commission as deputy in the States General.

Schulenborgh's opponents remained in control of the council; on January 10, 1662, they succeeded in depriving him of his council seat and in declaring him ineligible to hold municipal offices.[15] To defend himself, Schulenborgh began to court public opinion. His three lawyers published an elaborate defense. In his father's tavern, he also sought to gain the support of well-to-do citizens and guild members who were critical of Groningen's oligarchical government and of the heavy taxes

---

[14]Private Notes Schulenborgh, Council Meeting, November 30, 1661, R.A. (Groningen), C.T., 096.1122, nr. 12; Res. November 30, 1661, R.A. (Groningen), Arch. St. van Stad en Lande, Staatsresolutiën, nr. 13.

[15]Council Secr. Res., January 10, 1662, G.A. (Groningen), Oud-Archief (r.n.r.), 317, fol. 47.

they were forced to pay.[16] More importantly, Schulenborgh still had supporters in the council, both friends and opportunists. He decided to follow the advice of one of the opportunists, Eeck, who hinted that he would regain his council seat.[17] Eeck's secret plan, however, was to leave Schulenborgh's council seat vacant, in order to make a deal which would give a federal office to his youngest son. But Eeck's plot failed because Iddekinge had a similar goal in mind for his son, and Julsinga was scheming on behalf of his brother. Therefore, Eeck turned around and rejoined the councilors who were pushing for the election of Schulenborgh. The final outcome was that a majority of ten councilors elected him as councilor and nominated him as deputy of the States General. But the six councilors who had been outvoted were determined to prevent Schulenborgh's return. These hard-core opponents were Iddekinge, Julsinga, Coenders, Geert Gruijs, Rembt de Mepsche, and Johan Drews. The same evening they approached the Ommelanden assembly in order to block Schulenborgh's election with an appeal to the provincial resolution which had declared that he was ineligible to hold office.

The next day in the Diet meeting, the Ommelanden deputies appealed to this resolution to oppose Schulenborgh's reinstatement, but the council did not accept their appeal. To avoid a deadlock, it proposed to appoint all offices, except the one of deputy in the States General. The Ommelanden agreed with this exception if it would never apply to Schulenborgh. When the council rejected this condition, a deadlock developed which lasted five days. During this stalemate the Ommelanden deputies became more and more defiant, because Schulenborgh's opponents in the council secretly encouraged them, and even used sign language in the Diet to exploit the weaknesses of their colleagues. This political strategy slowly turned the tables against Schulenborgh. The council majority began to erode, some members succumbing to the temptation to strike a bargain with the Ommelanden for their personal benefit. Eeck was one of the first turncoats. The Ommelanden promised him that the six councilors who were Schulen-

---

[16]Poelman, "Johan Schulenborgh," 56; Tonckens, "Het proces-Schulenborgh," 83.

[17]Private Notes Schulenborgh, Undated Council Meetings in February 1662, R.A. (Groningen), C.T., 096.1122, nr. 12.

borgh's enemies would help his son Johan become a member of the Admiralty College of Friesland. When several other councilors followed Eeck's example, the anti-Schulenborgh group had gained a majority. Schulenborgh was replaced by Emmius.

Schulenborgh did not accept this stunning political reversal. To regain his majority, he might have told the council about a secret plan of the Rengers faction intended to reduce the influence of the ordinary freeholders in the Ommelanden assembly by means of the creation of a separate Noble Order. The city council, however, adamantly opposed the formation of a Noble Order because it would weaken its influence over the Ommelanden. If Schulenborgh had betrayed this plan, he would have antagonized his supporters in the Ommelanden. The Rengers faction certainly turned against him during this period, although later Rengers was accused of maintaining secret contacts with Schulenborgh.[18] The most important cause of Schulenborgh's final downfall, however, was his attempt to return to the council through his contacts with the leaders of the eighteen guilds. Schulenborgh briefly succeeded in his goal. A revolt of the guilds forced the council to readmit him. But the council waited for the right moment to launch a counterattack. The political assault came during the fall of 1662 when the council suddenly imprisoned the guild leaders. Supported by the stadholder and the Ommelanden, the council began to organize a special court to put Schulenborgh on trial for his role in the popular uprising. This special court was convened on October 17, 1662. To prevent another guild revolt and to increase his influence over the province, stadholder Willem Frederik decided to send troops into the city. Although the council was not consulted, it did not protest because the soldiers intimidated the guilds. Schulenborgh understood that he would receive a death sentence from a hostile court and managed to escape, dressed as a woman, to Christoph Bernhard von Galen, the bishop of Münster.[19]

---

[18]Tonckens, "De kaart van de gebroeders Coenders en de Plannen tot Oprichting van een Ommelander Ridderschap in de 17e eeuw," *Groningse Volksalmanak* (1961), 30-34.

[19]Tonckens, "Het proces-Schulenborgh," 84-91.

The Schulenborgh Affair had started with a genuine concern to protect provincial investments in the West India Company. Personal ambitions and factional conflicts transformed this economic goal into a tactical weapon to destroy a political opponent. But the campaign against Schulenborgh developed into a provincial crisis shaped by many different forces: the interests of Willem Frederik and the States of Holland, the grievances of the guilds, the fiscal policy of an oligarchical government, and finally the long standing rivalries between the capital and the Ommelanden. What made the outcome of the struggle unpredictable was the impact of ambition and self-interest. Council members changed sides for personal gain the way modern investors move their accounts within a family of mutual funds.

The Passions of an Enlightened Jew:
Isaac de Pinto (1717-1787) as a "Solliciteur du Bien Public"

Ida J. A. Nijenhuis
University of Groningen

The age of Enlightenment encouraged, amongst other things, the pursuit of "le bien public." The phrase "solliciteur du bien public" was used by both Isaac de Pinto (1717-1787) and his admirers to define his activities as a champion of the sephardic community's interests but also to account for his publications as a "philosophe." In this paper these two aspects of De Pinto's life, namely enlightened philosophy and protection of sephardic interests, will be presented in combination.* Attention will be concentrated on an issue which takes the reader from the salons of Amsterdam and Paris to that continent which bewildered the enlightened eighteenth-century public: America.

Isaac de Pinto was an experienced financier — cum — economist from Amsterdam who wanted to become a respected resident in the Republic of Letters. His publications on eighteenth-century topics such as public credit and debt, luxury, and the jealousy of trade in his days, earned him an international reputation as a minor "philosophe." In retrospect his originality clearly lies in these fields of political and financial economy.[1] Yet De Pinto was — and still is — most widely

---

*Preparation of this paper has been supported in part by a grant from the Fonds Doctor Catharina van Tussenbroek.

[1] For this contention see Richard H. Popkin, "Isaac de Pinto's criticism of Mandeville and Hume on luxury," *Studies on Voltaire and the Eighteenth Century*, 154 (1976) 1705-1714, and the chapters on De Pinto's political and financial economy in my dissertation (forthcoming).

Robert S. Kirsner (ed.), *The Low Countries and Beyond,* 047-054. Lanham, MD: University Press of America, 1993.

known for his *Apologie pour la nation juive* (1762)[2] in which he tried to rebut Voltaire's injurious remarks on the Jews. By publishing this essay De Pinto tried to kill two birds with one stone: on the one hand it gave him the opportunity to elaborate his views on the singularity of the Sephardim, earlier expressed in a legal dispute between the Portuguese community of Bordeaux and the French authorities; on the other hand his first publication in French was meant to result in a striking debut in the Parisian enlightenment circles.

Until now historiography has dealt only with the debate ensuing from De Pinto's rather partial defense of his co-religionists.[3] What I would like to do is add another, so far neglected aspect: the origin of the *Apologie*'s argumentation. In brief, one can say that the argument of the *Apologie* ran along socio-historical lines. According to De Pinto Voltaire's accusations against the Jews lacked evidence and did not discriminate between Ashkenazim and Sephardim. The gap between these two communities resulted from specific historical conditions and manifested itself clearly in social behaviour:

> The manners of the Portuguese Jews differ completely from those of other Jews. The former don't grow beards, nor do they assume any peculiarity in their dress, the well-to-do among them push on refinement, elegance and splendour in this respect as far as the other Nations of Europe, from which they do not differ but for their worship.[4]

---

[2]*Apologie pour la nation juive, ou Réflexions critiques sur le premier chapitre du VIIe tome des oeuvres de M. de Voltaire* [Amsterdam and Paris, 1762]. Citations will be made from the reprint of the apologie in [Ant. Guénée] *Lettres de quelques juifs Portugais et Allemands à M. de Voltaire* (Lisbonne=Paris, 1769) 7-42.

[3]Cf. J. S. Wijler, *Isaac de Pinto, sa vie et ses oeuvres* (Apeldoorn, 1923) 34-61; Peter Gay, *Voltaire's Politics. The Poet as Realist* (Yale UP, 1982, orig. publ. 1959) 351-354; the same, *The Party of Humanity. Essays in the French Enlightenment* (New York, 1971) 97-108 ("Voltaire's Anti-Semitism"); Arthur Hertzberg, *The French Enlightenment and the Jews. The Origins of Modern Anti-Semitism* (Columbia UP, New York and London, 1990, orig. publ. 1968) 179-187 and passim; Richard H. Popkin, "The Philosophical Basis of Eighteenth-Century Racism," *Studies in Eighteenth-Century Culture* 3 (1973) 250.

[4]*Lettres de quelques juifs,* 15. Hertzberg, *French Enlightenment,* 181 also quotes this passage but incorrectly translates "recherche" (in this case meaning "refinement") into "learning."

According to De Pinto, Voltaire, being prejudiced against the Jews in general, could not accept the fact that the Portuguese Jews had assimilated succesfully with Christian society. Consequently, the charges Voltaire brought against the Jews were irrelevant to the case of the Sephardim and had to be qualified with respect to the Ashkenazim:

> ...one should not attribute to [their] ancient, divine and sacred Religion the baseness of sentiment of certain German and Polish Jews. It is necessity, it is persecution, it is misadventure that made them like those who, while professing a different Religion, live under the same circumstances.[5]

Indeed, all human activity was dominated by identical passions whose various conjunctions depended on recurring "circonstances." These conditions set the pace of the everlasting battle between vice and virtue in every human being. Referring to Abbé Du Bos and Montesquieu, De Pinto acknowledged only one determinant factor causing dissimilarity among mankind:

> Only the difference in climates can cause any physical alteration perceptible in the universal arrangement of a people taken together, and can influence morals.[6]

However, moral principles, of which De Pinto reckoned education to be the most effective, could restrain the physical agent's decisive influence. Education could exert a positive influence upon "circonstances" and improve a people's disposition. This "eternal truth" should not be tampered with "in order to ridicule the Jews and make them hateful."[7] As both Sephardim and Ashkenazim were living in societies where climate's preponderance had been succesfully curbed, De Pinto's message was clear: the Jews did not differ in

---

[5] Ibidem, 23-24.

[6] Ibidem, 34-35. For the origin and development of the climatic theory with respect to America, see A. Gerbi, *La disputa del Nuevo Mundo. Historia de una polémica 1750-1900* (México, 1982, orig. publ. 1955) 49-65.

[7] *Lettres de quelques juifs*, 35.

character from their fellow human beings and were subject to the same passions. Some of them were depraved, but then so were some of the Christians.

The climatic line of reasoning must have sounded quite familiar to De Pinto's readers. However, they would have been inclined to connect its substance with several writings on America and its inhabitants. They must have been surprised by De Pinto's use of this argument in connection with the Jews. Of course the real polemic on the future of the American continent did not start until 1768, when Abbé Corneille de Pauw published his disparaging *Recherches philosophiques sur les Américains*.[8] In fact, De Pinto borrowed the argument from the first batch of eighteenth-century publications on the New World and transferred it to his refutation of Voltaire. A hitherto unpublished correspondence[9] between young De Pinto and the French traveler and academician Charles Marie de la Condamine (1701-1774) shows how the philosophe-to-be practised the line of defense summarized above in a dispute on (South-) American Indians. Apart from this issue, the letters show an eager De Pinto, hankering after "nouvelles" from the Republic of Letters in general and from La Condamine's friend Voltaire in particular. Also, the correspondence constitutes a curious comment on the current political situation, in which France and the Dutch Republic featured as enemies in the War of the Austrian Succession.

De Pinto probably wrote his first letter to La Condamine in the late summer of 1746. At that time he participated, like his brothers Aron and Jacob, in the family's banking and trading business. But unlike them, so it seems, he had already developed a taste for learning and letters, a felicitous inclination in a period witnessing the advance of the Enlightenment as a way of life.[10] At his wedding, in 1734, young Isaac was hailed by the sephardic poet Saldaña as a future

---

[8]See Gerbi, *La disputa del Nuevo Mundo*, 66 ff. and H. S. Commager and E. Giordanetti, *Was America a Mistake? An 18th-century Controversy.* New York, 1967.

[9]British Library London (BL), Bentinck Papers, Correspondence vol. I (1730-1748) f181-f200 (pagination is not conform chronology).

[10]Cf. Norman Hampson, *The Enlightenment* (Harmondsworth, 1968) 128 ff.

Alexander the Great.[11] A seventeen-year-old boy already versed in natural and moral philosophy, history, poetry, rhetoric, politics and theology: who would not be impressed? A few years later, in his native town, he acted as the secretary of a small academy which also constituted the audience to his lectures, one dealing with the intricate relationship between truth and error, another condemning the abuse of learning.[12]

The members of this sephardic learned society had been presented with some copies of La Condamine's *Relation abrégée d'un voyage fait dans l'intérieur de l'amérique méridionale* (Paris, 1745). Later on, De Pauw used this travel story to substantiate his unfavourable statements on the native population of America.[13] Though La Condamine went not as far as De Pauw to dismiss the New World as a total creative mistake, he certainly did not attribute many virtues to the Indians. The primitive populace he had encountered in South America showed "how little Man, left to plain nature, deprived of education and society, differed from Animal."[14]

De Pinto wrote La Condamine that he had not been able to stop reading his copy: he started 9:00 a.m. and finished at 2:00 p.m. (which amounts to digesting about 20 pages per hour). He had a lot of questions to ask: What about the number of America's authentic inhabitants relative to that of Europe? Had it occurred to La Condamine that the Americans lacked the restraints on population

---

[11]"Panegirico Proso-Poetico" Ets Haim Library Amsterdam (EH), ms 48E10. On Saldaña see R. G. Fuks Mansfeld, *De Sefardim in Amsterdam tot 1795* (Hilversum, 1989) 139.

[12]"Discours académique sur l'abus qu'on fait de l'étude et de sciences," EH, ms 48A19 (XI); "Paradoxe soutenu de plusieurs exemples pour prouver que la verité nous conduit souvant à l'erreur et l'erreur à la verité," EH, ms 48A19 (XII).

[13]Though not corroborated by evidence, perhaps the fact that La Condamine's travel story was read by the members of De Pinto's academy reflects the long-standing sephardic interest in the origin of the American Indians, see Richard H. Popkin, "The Rise and Fall of the Jewish Indian Theory" in: Yosef Kaplan, H. Méchoulan and Richard H. Popkin, eds, *Menasseh ben Israel and his World* (Leiden, 1989) 63-82. For De Pauw's use of La Condamine see Gerbi, *La disputa del Nuevo Mundo*, 132-134.

[14]As cited in ibidem, 133.

growth common to Europeans, like warfare, seafaring and monastic life? Evidently De Pinto denied the supposed negative influence of the New World's climate on propagation. In case the spirit of perfection, which had rendered Europe its highest degree of development, would pervade the expanding American populace "the Europeans had everything to fear and once again the World's complexion would be altered." It would even be conceivable that

> one day, the European Colonies would break away from obedience to their far-distanced masters. Would this kind of Revolution not cause a turnabout in Politics and Commerce?[15]

Of course, in 1746 this alarming perspective did not seem to be an actual problem to the young philosophe, but something to occur in centuries to come. However, when this revolution actually took place in 1776, De Pinto had great difficulty in coming to terms with his fulfilled prophesy: "I believe England, at this very moment, will triumph over its Colonies" he wrote in his defence of the British government against its rebellious subjects in North America.[16]

La Condamine replied graciously in a letter dated September 17, 1746.[17] He had not dilated upon the matter of the native population in his *Voyage en Amérique* because his readership consisted of "académiciens" as well as *Robinson Crusoe* fans. He was not as optimistic as De Pinto, though, when assessing the chances of improvement with respect to the American "sauvages." Where the latter was thinking in terms of centuries, the Frenchman did not expect changes to take place before millennia had elapsed. But then, everything was possible, even the fact that France in due time would turn into a barbarian country!

---

[15] De Pinto to La Condamine, s.d., s.l., BL, Bentinck Papers, Correspondence vol. I (1730-1748) 181-182.

[16] *Seconde Lettre de M. de Pinto, à l'occasion des troubles des Colonies, contenant des Réflexions politiques sur les suites de ces troubles, et sur l'Etat actuel de l'Angleterre* (La Haye, 1776) 17.

[17] La Condamine to De Pinto, Etouilly, September 17, 1746, BL, Bentinck Papers, Correspondence vol. I (1730-1748) 186-187.

Secretary and members of the Amsterdam "société amicale" were not satisfied with La Condamine's airily reply. Some of their questions, De Pinto wrote in his next letter, remained unanswered: could he explain to them why the indigenous inhabitants of the New World acted like "automates?" If climate caused their indolent behaviour would not the European colonists have become infected as well? In any case, De Pinto was convinced of the Indians' capability to learn, especially when they associated with Europeans. This contact would result in a mixture of characters and in the end would generate a polite nation. He also referred to Charlevoix' *Histoire et description generale de la Nouvelle-France* (1744) which was rather mild in its judgement of the Iroquoian Indians.[18]

La Condamine did not have De Pinto's confidence in the outcome of a melting pot of characters, as is demonstrated by his later remarks regarding the mestizos: they constituted "a kind of people possessing nothing but the vices of the nations whose blend they are."[19] Personal experience, he told De Pinto, had taught him the plain truths he had communicated in his book. Bartolomé de las Casas in his day had rightly pleaded the case of the Indians with respect to their exploitation by the Spaniards, but even he "does not think highly of their mind... I have seen," La Condamine continued,

> as a rule, pride amongst the Negroes, and hatred or affection with respect to their masters... I have encountered among them moral vices and virtues, but nothing of the kind amid the Indians.[20]

Their future was a dim one, as they were rapidly decreasing in number due to smallpox, infertility, exploitation, and interbreeding. It

---

[18]De Pinto to La Condamine, s.d., s.l., ibidem, 184-185.

[19]Cited in Gerbi, *La disputa del Nuevo Mundo*, 133 from La Condamine's *Journal du voyage fait par ordre du Roi, à l'Équateur* (Paris, 1751-1752).

[20]La Condamine to De Pinto, Etouilly, October 12, 1747, BL, Bentinck Papers, Correspondence vol. I (1730-1748) 195-198. La Condamine misrepresented Las Casas who did believe in the mental capabilities of Indians; they just had to be instructed by the right kind of Spaniards, cf. Popkin, "Philosophical Basis of Racism," 247-248.

seemed as if they had already degraded to the point where they had nothing more in common with humanity.

This, then, seemed to be the end of the discussion. The older philosophe took refuge behind his years of travels and encounters to impress his young correspondent. But De Pinto did not acknowledge defeat: both he and La Condamine knew perfectly well that an entire nation could not be judged upon the basis of a limited number of random encounters, he wrote to his learned friend.[21] Some fifteen years later De Pinto still relied on this undeniable truth when castigating the famous "philosophe de Ferney." And yes, even Voltaire had to concede the point. In a reaction to De Pinto's *Apologie* he wrote: "I was wrong to attribute to a whole nation the vices of some individuals."[22] De Pinto was deeply satisfied with this answer, even publishing it some years later.[23] His public appearance in the dispute with Voltaire gained the sephardic philosophe the explicit citizenship of the Republic of Letters, a status already privately practiced and coveted in his letters to La Condamine. As shown above, this correspondence reveals that De Pinto's criticism of Voltaire originated from the earlier debate on American Indians. The *Apologie*, one might say, was an elaborated version of De Pinto's defense of the Indians. As he has been criticized for his partiality with respect to the Sephardim, it is perhaps good to know De Pinto did not restrict his protective abilities to the Jewish minority. He was, indeed, a true "solliciteur du bien public." In comparison, the fact that neither Voltaire nor La Condamine ever restated their offending remarks on Jews and Indians respectively, was small beer.

---

[21]De Pinto to La Condamine, s.d., s.l., ibidem, 191-192.

[22]Gay, *Voltaire's Politics*, 352.

[23][Isaac de Pinto], *Réponse à deux critiques qui ont été faites de l'Apologie de la nation Juive etc., ... avec la lettre de l'auteur à M. le Mrl de Richelieu qu'à M. de Voltaire et leurs réponses* (La Haye, 1766). The correspondence between Voltaire and De Pinto with respect to the latter's *Apologie* was reprinted in the *Mercure de France* (May, 1769) 85-86.

The Indologist P. J. Veth (1814-1895) as Empire-Builder

Paul van der Velde
Leiden University

Introduction. In an article on P. Baldaeus, a seventeenth-century scholar of Indonesia, P. J. Veth stressed on the one hand the absence in the Netherlands of biographies of important figures while noting on the other the abundance of biographical dictionaries "...which labor under the burden of trifling details about insignificant people who owe the undeserved immortalizing of their names... to some trashy composition or a bundle of insipid doggerel."[1] Little has changed in this respect since 1857, when Veth committed these words to paper. Biography as a historical or literary genre has never been popular in the country, although recently literary biography has come to enjoy increased popularity.[2] In order not to fall victim to Veth's own words just quoted, I had to decide whether Veth belonged to the category of insignificant or important people. I discovered very quickly that, apart for the obligatory life history in the necrologies of the Royal Dutch Academy of Arts and Sciences, nothing has been written about Veth.[3] Fortunately, according to Veth himself, this means very little: "One seeks in vain for light on many a person who one may suspect accomplished great things and led a remarkable, and often even

---

[1] P. J. Veth, "Philipus Baldaeus," *De Gids,* 31-3 (1867: 193-214).

[2] *Aspecten van de Literaire Biografie* (Kampen, 1990).

[3] P. A. van der Lith, "Pieter Johannes Veth," *Jaarboek van de Koninklijke Academie van Wetenschappen* (1896), 1-42.

Robert S. Kirsner (ed.), *The Low Countries and Beyond,* 055-067. Lanham, MD: University Press of America, 1993.

adventurous, life."[4] Veth's life was not a series of mighty deeds, and he could not claim an adventurous existence, but his life, which spanned the century, is noteworthy because of his intense interaction with the movements and currents of the nineteenth century.

Veth was involved in or influenced by romanticism, positivism, modern theology, liberalism, Spinozism, social Darwinism, the Geographical Movement, and imperialism, which are essential parts of the image of the nineteenth century.

At the same time, he was a member of a great many organizations which served as breeders of Dutch imperialism. The Veth collection of the Leiden University Library, which contains 2,500 letters, reveals that he was in correspondence with a great number of prominent nineteenth-century personalities, such as Wallace, Roland Bonaparte, Thorbecke, Fransen van de Putte, Van Hoevell, Potgieter, Geel, Busken Huet, Bakhuizen van den Brink, Van Vloten, Roorda, De Jonge, Muller, and Fruin.[5] This interaction between Veth and the national and international community seems to me to justify the writing of his biography.[6]

In an article in the *Times Literary Supplement* of 14 April 1989, the French historian J. Le Goff fiercely attacks the *Annales* school and puts forward an argument for a biographical approach to history. What appeals to me most of all is its temporal aspect, the span of a human life, that he cites as the advantage of biography.[7] Seen in this way, Veth becomes the mortar for holding together aspects of nineteenth-century events which until now have been studied only in their isolation and therefore appear unrelated. In my biography of Veth, I will emphasize the quest for the roots of Dutch imperialism, liberalism in

---

[4]Veth, "Baldaeus," 193.

[5]*Collectie Westerse Handschriften BPL 1756* (Leiden University Library).

[6]W. Dilthey, *Der Aufbau der Geschichtlichen Welt in der Geisteswissenschaften* (Stuttgart, 1928), 5: 247-249.

[7]J. Le Goff, "After *Annales*, The Life as History," *Times Literary Supplement* (14 April 1989).

the colonial context, the link between cultural nationalism and imperialism, the influence of science on colonial policy, and the working of the scientific lobby in practice.

Education and Cultural Background. Veth, who was born in 1814, sprang from a Patriot, bourgeois, Protestant element of the Dordrecht middle class. At the French school, which followed the principles of the Enlightenment, such practical subjects as mathematics, geography, and English were taught. English as the subject matter of a regular course was then quite exceptional in The Netherlands. It soon became apparent that Pieter was a prodigy who could make the transition to the "Latijnse school" (grammar school) with ease. After completing Grammar School, where mainly Greek and Latin were taught, Veth went to Leiden University, where training in theology prepared him for the pulpit. With the exception of the church and trade, career opportunities were extremely limited for someone from the middle class. It was only after the '50s of the last century that, under the influence of increasing specialization, the universities would open new career possibilities to sons of the middle class.

When Veth enrolled at Leiden University in 1852, the Netherlands was plunged into a national identity crisis as a result of its defeat in the war with Belgium. In Leiden, however, which in the third decade of the nineteenth century was described as a city of light, a lively cultural atmosphere prevailed. During the first two years of his study, in which he had to obtain a Bachelor of Arts degree as a prerequisite for theological study, Veth was exposed to the broadly oriented European romanticism embodied in such writers as Scott, Byron and Hugo. This interest in Romantic literature was stimulated by membership in many literary societies, to which people like Beets and Kneppelhout also belonged. Ten years later Kneppelhout was to describe it as "that Romantic time."[8]

In the aftermath of the Belgian Revolt and under the influence of the literary scholar, Professor J. Geel, broadbased Romanticism was

---

[8] J. Kneppelhout, "Mijn Zwarte Tijd," *De Gids,* 8-2 (1844): 162.

narrowed to national romanticism.[9] The influence of Geel's evocative and ironic literary style had a great effect on Veth's style, along with its influence upon his attitude to life. In *Gesprek op den Drachenfels,* Geel wrote that one's personality should be expressed in one's own literary style, in which clear and preferably controversial opinions regarding social problems should be expressed.[10] Veth carried this maxim in his mind throughout his life.

During his study for a degree in theology, Veth's interest in the Orient, which had developed during the first years of his study, received a practical boost from his study of Hebrew and Arabic: From a theological point of view he did not escape the influence of supranaturalism, a movement within Protestant theology inspired by positivism which questioned the supernatural character of revelation and considered Christianity primarily as a rational religion. In 1837 the lecture, "Das Leben Jesu," by the modern theologian D. F. Straus brought Veth's vocation, which had already become a faint echo under the influence of positivism and Romanticism, to an end. The doubts about the Protestant faith which disclosed themselves in Veth were a foreshadowing of the grave doubts manifested among many clergymen in the '50s under the influence of Spinozism. In 1838 when Veth received the prestigious offer of a position as tutor in English and Malay at the Royal Military Academy in Breda, an officers training school, he did not hesitate for a moment.

In the three years that he spent at Breda, Veth learned Malay. His teaching duties at the Military Academy were not onerous. Having successfully defended his dissertation in 1840, Veth was proposed as successor to Juynboll, the professor of Hebrew and Arabic at the Atheneum (university college) in Franeker. Three months later, shortly before giving his inaugural lecture, Veth received the doctorate honoris causa. He never completed his thesis, however. While at Franeker he was greatly influenced by contacts with the first modern theologian in the Netherlands, J. M. Scholten. Building on Straus's ideas, Scholten

---

[9]G. P. M. Knuvelder, *Beknopt Handboek tot de Geschiedenis der Nederlandse Letterkunde,* 34th ed. (Den Bosch, 1974), 99.

[10]J. Geel, *Gesprek op den Drachenfels,* 3rd ed. (Amsterdam, 1977), 72-75.

no longer considered Christianity as a revealed religion but emphasized the ethical values which it represented. This ethical approach to Christianity was to become one of the most prominent pillars of modern Dutch imperialism. Immediately before the Franeker Atheneum was closed in 1843, Veth was appointed to the Amsterdam Atheneum as professor of Oriental languages and Hebrew, succeeding T. Roorda. It was there that Veth resumed his studies of the Netherlands Indies, which he had begun in Breda but had been forced to halt temporarily in Franeker because of a lack of materials.

Orientation toward the Netherlands Indies. Veth's social life in Amsterdam, which depended on his interest in the Netherlands Indies, became more active. He became a committee member of the Dutch Bible Society, in which capacity he stimulated the translation of the Bible into the languages of the archipelago. In addition he became a member of the board of governors of the Society for General Welfare *(Maatschappij tot 't Nut van het Algemeen)*; in this capacity he took up the cudgels for the improvement of education in the Netherlands and the Netherlands Indies. In the same year, 1843, he became editor of the cultural monthly *De Gids*. Through his long service as editorship in *De Blauwe Beul* (The Blue Executioner), he belonged to the Romantic, liberal avant-garde in the Netherlands. Until the split within the editorial board of *De Gids* in 1855, when Veth aligned himself with the positivists, he enjoyed a close friendship with its founder, E. J. Potgieter. Following in the footsteps of Geel, Potgieter had made Dutch Romanticism national and oriented toward the seventeenth century. In his book *Jan, Jannetje and hun Jongste Kind* (Jan, Jannetje and Their Youngest Child), published in 1841, Potgieter criticized the defeatist attitude prevailing in the Netherlands, which he immortalized in the character of *Jan Salie*. This orientation toward the Golden Age was later to become an integral component of nationalist and imperialist terminology.

Up to 1848, in contrast to Potgieter, Veth belonged to the defeatists, who saw no future for the Netherlands as an independent nation. "Are we not blood of Germany's blood, bone of her bone?" he wrote in an often-quoted article in *De Gids* about a Lower Rhine-

Dutch song festival in Arnhem.[11] In another, much less cited article which he wrote on the occasion of the bicentenary of the Peace of Munster, he qualified his position by emphasizing the sound common sense and home life of the Dutch, which distinguished them from the Germans.[12]

After the liberal revolution of 1848 (which was as unexpected then as the recent changes in Eastern Europe were in 1991), Veth, like many others, sought to justify the Netherlands' right to independent existence by appealing to its role in the Netherlands Indies. Some twenty years later this would result in the ideology of "the small great nation" — small in Europe, great in the world. From 1846 onwards, in the wake of unrelenting criticism of his achievements in Arabic by the Arabist R. P. A. Dozy, Veth devoted himself more and more to the Netherlands Indies. For this reason, from 1846 on he maintained an intensive correspondence with Van Hoevell, who was banned from the Indies after 1848, and he became a member of the Amstel Club in 1846. This group of moderate Liberals was closely watched by the police because of a suspect anti-monarchist attitude. In articles which circulated within the club, Veth pioneered the liberalization of the relationship between the mother country and the colony.

Veth's view of science manifested itself in written rebuttals of Dozy in which he stressed the extension of knowledge through the compilation of summaries of true scientific value.[13]

The first such product in the extension of knowledge saw the light of day in 1854. This was *Borneo's Westerafdeling* (The Western Division of Borneo), in which Veth brought together everything then known about that part of the island.[14] The book was widely acclaimed

---

[11]P. J. Veth, "Het Derde Nederrijnsch Nederlandsch Zangersfeest te Arnhem," *De Gids* 11-2 (1847), 399.

[12]P. J. Veth, "De Duitschers en de Nederlanden voor den Munsterschen Vrede," ibid., 817-34.

[13]*BPL 1756*, Veth to Dozy, 1844.

[14]P. J. Veth, *Borneo's Wester-Afdeling. Geografische, Statistische, Historisch.* 2 vols. (Zaltbommel, 184-56).

and had an exemplary effect on other authors who, like Veth, devoted themselves to the dissemination of knowledge about the Netherlands Indies. One example of such a collective project is the *Aardrijkskundig en Statistisch Woordenboek van Nederlandsch-Indie* (Geographical and Statistical Dictionary of the Netherlands Indies).[15] Works like these in part enabled the Dutch parliament in 1865 to take control of affairs in Indonesia, which until then had always been the province of the colonial ministry. It was only then that a policy of openness in colonial affairs, which had been introduced in 1848, could be consummated.

On the basis of his two controversial articles in *De Gids* in 1848, "De openbaarheid in koloniale aangelegenheden" (Openness in Colonial Matters) and "De politieke demonstratie in Batavia" (Political demonstrations in Batavia), Veth became the extraparliamentary voice of the Liberals in colonial affairs. (In the years 1850 to 1852, Veth and D. C. Steyn Parve edited *De Indiër,* a weekly which, because of its radical ideas about the Netherlands Indies, was viewed with suspicion by the Colonial Ministry): He showed himself as an advocate of freedom of the press, openness in colonial affairs, the abolition of slavery, and the abolition of the so-called "Cultivation System" of enforced agricultural ion. As a founder-member of the Royal Institute for Linguistics and Anthropology (1851) and as a co-founder of the Indies Society *(Indisch Genootschap)* (1854), he devoted himself to these ideas. Veth's favorable review of Multatuli's *Max Havelaar* in 1860 made a very large contribution to forcing open the discussion of the relationship between the mother country and the Netherlands Indies.[16]

The liberalization of this relationship had never got off the ground after the fall of the first Thorbecke cabinet in 1853, and was only brought up for discussion again during the second Thorbecke cabinet (1862-66). In 1863, Veth was appointed to the commission set up to consider reforming the training of Indies civil servants. The activities of this commission resulted in the foundation of the

---

[15]*Aardrijkskundig en Statistische Woordenboek van Nederlands-Indie.* 2 vols. Amsterdam, 1859-69.

[16]P. J. Veth, "Multatuli versus Droogstoppel," *De Gids,* 24-1, 1860.

Government Institute for Indies Civil Servants *(Rijksinstelling voor Indische Ambtenaren)* in 1865. In view of this prevailing liberal climate, it is not surprising that Veth, who had acquired a reputation as an expert on Indies matters, was appointed a professor at the institute.

The Road to the Netherlands Indies. In his inaugural lecture Veth summarized what in his view the nature and aims of education in the linguistics and ethnology of the Netherlands Indies should be. For him linguistics and ethnology were synonymous with (anthropo)geography, which was supposed to be an encyclopedia of all that was known on this subject. He also foresaw that this encyclopedia would quickly become outdated under the pressure of scientific specialization. However, a new encyclopedia could be compiled upon the basis of the new specialist knowledge, and so on and on.[17]

The aim of training was to produce competent and humane civil servants, whose duty it was, because of their knowledge of the native languages and cultures and their own superior Western culture, to lead the natives toward a better future inspired by the West. Veth trained many civil servants who, at the end of the nineteenth century, were being appointed to administrative positions from which they could implement the "ethical" policy.[18]

Although Veth had been in constant contact with politicians since 1848, the proximity of The Hague made this contact much more direct than before. Since politics in the '60s was strongly affected by the redefinition of the relationship with the Netherlands Indies, Veth was often consulted on colonial problems by politicians. In *De Gids* he lashed out at the defeat of the Cultivation law *(Cultuurwet)* proposed by his friend I. D. Fransen van de Putte, the colonial minister.[19] The main tenor of the article, which had a strongly positivist slant, was that whatever was valid for Europe also held good for the Netherlands Indies. "One has only to avoid the Communist [read: Conservative!]

---

[17] P. J. Veth, *Over de aard en het doel van het onderwijs in de land- en volkenkunde van Nederlandsch-Indie voor toekomende ambtenaren* (Leiden, 1864).

[18] Ibid.

[19] P. J. Veth, *De Cultuurwet* (Leiden, 1861).

concepts that we avoid here like the plague, but which we hail in Java as the highest wisdom."[20]

The *Tijdschrift voor Nederlandsch-Indie,* of which Veth was editor-in-chief from 1867 to 1871, concentrated its attacks upon the Cultivation System. When, by 1870, the Cultivation System had been largely dismantled and the agrarian law of De Waal made possible the private ownership of land in the Netherlands Indies, Veth saw his long struggle rewarded. However, this liberalization was largely confined to Java. Another formidable obstacle obstructing liberalization — one often overlooked — was the abstention policy or *Onthoudingspolitiek*; a policy opposing the expansion of direct colonial rule to the Outer Territories. Only after Dutch authority had been established over the outer provinces would economic exploitation of these areas become possible. For this reason Veth argued that Dutch control should be extended, especially in those regions (Borneo, Sumatra, and New Guinea) where he saw the Dutch position threatened by other colonial powers. He thought that the Netherlands was powerful enough to maintain itself in the competitive Darwinian world. He realized that Darwinism could not be countered and recognized in it precisely the instrument that he needed to strengthen his arguments for the extension of Western civilization by every means available.[21] In this attitude Veth revealed himself as a rational follower of Spinoza who coupled rationalist-based thought with the world view of modern physics.

The Empire Builder. While the dissolution of the Cultivation System resulted in increasing economic relations between the Netherlands and the Netherlands Indies, the outbreak of the Achin War in 1873 led to intensified political relations between the mother country and the colony. The failure of the First Achin expedition was seized upon by Veth as an opportunity to argue for the extension of colonial authority to the Outer Territories and for strengthened economic exploitation of these areas.[22] In his opinion the defeat had been the result of a lack

---

[20]Ibid., 231.

[21]P. J. Veth, *Het land van de Paradijsvogel en den Orang Otan* (Leiden, 1870-71). (Translation of A. R. Wallace, *The Malay Archipelago*).

[22]P. J. Veth, *Achins Betrekkingen tot Nederland* (Leiden, 1873).

of knowledge of the area, a deficiency that could be eliminated by scientific expeditions: He called upon all his acquaintances in the worlds of politics, science, and business to support him in his aims. In order to put his ideas into practice, he founded, in collaboration with others, a Geographical Society *(Aardrijkskundig Genootschap)* in 1873, which he presided over for a decade and in which he remained a driving force.[23] The founding of the society gave him entry into a broad European geographical movement.[24]

Through publication of the *Tijdschrift van het Aardrijkskundig Genootschap* (Journal of the Geographical Society) and by organizing meetings throughout the country, Veth endeavored to organize the anti-abstention forces. Within three years the Society had developed into a colonial lobby of eight hundred well-placed members girded for the fray. From its inception this lobby displayed national and even Great Netherlands aspects and agitated vigorously against the "Jan Salie" spirit which, even after thirty years, hung like a miasma over the Netherlands.[25] Within the context of Europe, the Netherlands was indeed a small country, but its colonial possessions made it a major power within its own civilizing mission. The ideology of "the great small nation" had already gained ground. The great powers had to be made to realize that the Netherlands was prepared to defend its colonial heritage. As long as the Dutch government continued to refuse to consider any territorial expansion, the equipping of scientific expeditions would, in Veth's view, heighten the prestige of the Netherlands abroad.

The Netherlands Indies was the main field of interest for the Geographical Society, but other regions also enjoyed its attention: the North Pole (seven polar expeditions were mounted by the Society), the kindred Boers of South Africa, and the adjacent Congo Basin, where

---

[23]P. G. E. I. J. van der Velde, "Van Koloniale Lobby naar Koloniale Hobby. Het Koninklijk Nederlands Aardrijkskundig Genootschap en Nederlands-Indië, 1873-1914," *KNAG Geografisch Tijdschrift*, 22-3 (1988): 211-21.

[24]P. G. E. I. J. van der Velde, "Van Sabang tot Merauke. Het Nederlandse imperialisme in het licht van een oplaaiende discussie," *Theoretische Geschiedenis*, 15-2 (1988), 250-54.

[25]Van der Velde, "Van Koloniale Lobby naar Koloniale Hobby," 220.

the Rotterdam African Trading Company had built up an informal empire with its numerous trading posts.

As chairman of the executive committee, however, Veth devoted most attention to the organization and conduct of the Sumatra expedition of 1877-79.[26] In 1876 he retired from the editorial staff of *De Gids* because he had begun to find it too solemn and mild-mannered. Moreover, his writings filled the bulk of the Society's journal and he was very occupied with his *magnum opus* on Java. The Sumatra expedition enjoyed considerable support from private individuals in the Netherlands. It had a dual purpose. There was the scientific and economic goal, the discovery of a transportation route from the Ombilin coalfields, which was closely tied up with the political aim, the extension of authority into an area of Sumatra through which the Society hoped to find a way to transport the coal. The supporters of abstention still managed to keep the upper hand, however, so that, to Veth's great disappointment, the aims of the expedition were not achieved.[27] Fresh proposals by Veth for the mounting of expeditions to Borneo, Timor and New Guinea did not find adequate support. Furthermore, in 1880 the focus of interest shifted to South Africa, where the Boer Republics had been annexed by perfidious Albion in 1879.

One of the main figures in the international protest movement against the English annexation, which led finally to a temporary dissolution, was Veth,[28] who in the meantime had evolved into an international figure with a reputation as an authority in the field of the Netherlands Indies. Amongst other reasons, this was the appearance of his standard work on Java, which appeared in 1882.[29] Finally, in

---

[26]P. G. E. I. J. van der Velde, "Een vergeten koloniale lobby. Het Koninklijke Aardrijkskundig Genootschap en de Sumatra, 1874-1879," Den Haag, 1986. Leiden University M.A. thesis.

[27]*Midden-Sumatra. Reizen en onderzoekingen der Sumatra expeditie, uitgerust door het KNAG.* (Leiden, 1881-92), I: 14.

[28]P. J. Veth, *Onze Transvaalsche Broeders* (Leiden, 1880).

[29]P. J. Veth, *Java.* 3 vols. (Leiden, 1875-82).

1883, he played a prominent role in the realization of the international colonial exhibition in Amsterdam, which stressed the importance of the Netherlands as a colonial power. Veth, who was never to set eyes on the Indies, was able, thanks to the eruption of Krakatoa that same year, to catch a glimpse of his love because for weeks it colored the night sky red.

In 1884, Veth's weakened health compelled him to move to Arnhem. In the same year he retired as President of the Geographical Society, and his honorable retirement as professor of the geography and ethnology of the Indian Archipelago at the State University of Leiden, a position he had held since 1877, followed in 1885.

Closing Remarks. In 1894, on the occasion of his eightieth birthday, Veth was presented with a *Festschrift*.[30] The contributions to this volume mainly reflect the broad scientific activity of Veth. The dedication to the book reads, "To the Nestor of colonial geography." In this case, geography should be taken in its wider nineteenth-century sense, including, among other fields, natural history, anthropology, and ethnography. The collection does not disclose what has become apparent from this article, that Veth, in addition to his scientific endeavors for the extension of knowledge of the Archipelago, was also a practical man who for a long time, as one of the main figures of the colonial lobby, helped to establish the Netherlands as a colonial empire. When Veth died in 1895 the expansionist policy of pacification, which he had supported, was vigorously continued and in 1914 would lead to the Pax Neerlandica for the whole of the Netherlands Indies.

Veth was soon forgotten, amongst other reasons because the encyclopedic scientific practices which he advocated were already obsolete by the time of his death. His hope that the various specialties would raise the standard of the encyclopedia were only partly fulfilled, even though his *Java* was reprinted twice. Now, a century afterwards, his life is again attracting attention because of his deep involvement in nineteenth-century society, movements, and events which — until the present — have been viewed in isolation, and which can now be brought into a comparative relationship, offering a new outlook upon the

---

[30]*Feestbundel ter Gelegenheid van zijn 80ste geboortedag aan Dr. P. J. Veth* (Leiden, 1894).

nineteenth century and the relationship between mother country and colony. Veth will emerge from this development as an overlooked empire-builder.

Linguistics

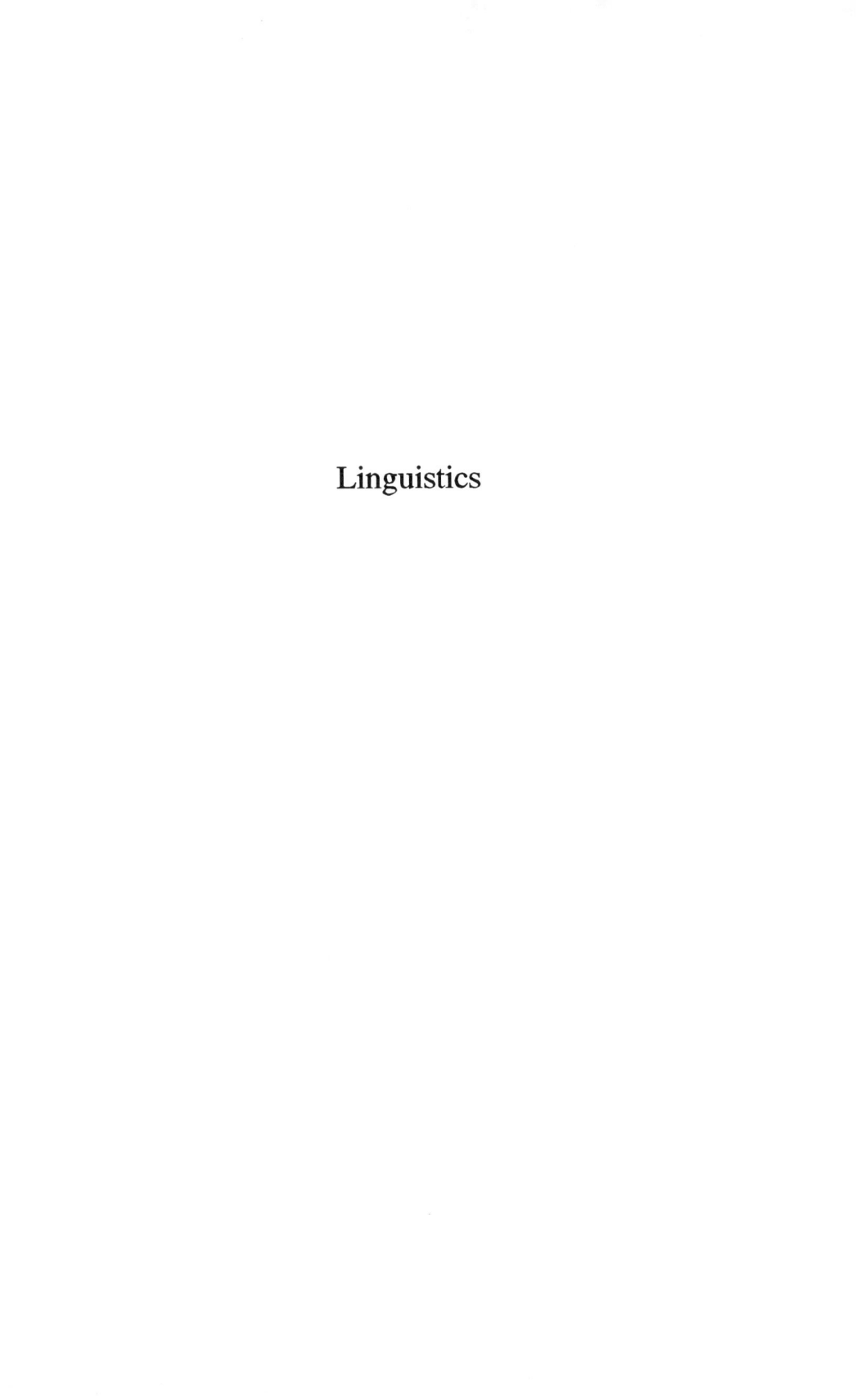

The Word Order of Final Verbal Elements in Dutch: Free Variation or Meaningful Organization?

Justine A. Pardoen
Free University, Amsterdam

1. Introduction.* In Dutch verbal groups in clause final position, the position of the finite verb in relation to other verbal elements is not fixed. In this respect Dutch differs from German, for in German the finite verb always follows the other verbal elements. In Dutch the finite verb may either precede the non-finite verb, as is illustrated in 1a and 2a, or follow the non-finite verb, as in 1b and 2b. The order of the verbal elements in the a-sentences is often referred to as the RED ORDER, and the one in the b-sentences as the GREEN ORDER. I will do so as well.

(1) a. omdat het zwembad gisteren *is gesloten* (red order)
    [because the swimming pool yesterday is closed]
    "because the swimming pool was closed yesterday"
 b. omdat het zwembad gisteren *gesloten is* (green order)

(2) a. omdat we gisteren *hebben gewerkt* (red order)
    [because we yesterday have worked]
    "because we worked yesterday"
 b. omdat we gisteren *gewerkt hebben* (green order)

---

*I have greatly benefited from discussions with Arie Verhagen. This research was supported by the Foundation for Linguistic Research, which is funded by NWO, the Netherlands Organization for Research. It was carried out within the research project "Functional study of language: Grammar and Pragmatics," Vrije Universiteit Amsterdam LETT/88-10.

Robert S. Kirsner (ed.), *The Low Countries and Beyond,* 071-083. Lanham, MD: University Press of America, 1993.

The green and the red order seem to be in free variation. In principle, the difference in word order does not seem to be systematically associated with a difference in interpretation. In some cases, however, one may intuitively feel some preference for one order over the other. In the following examples, for instance, several people would prefer the green order.

(3) a. ? omdat het zwembad al jaren is gesloten
 b. omdat het zwembad al jaren gesloten is
    [because the pool for years now closed is]
    "because the pool has been closed for years now"

(4) a. ? omdat de meningen nogal zijn verdeeld
 b. omdat de meningen nogal verdeeld zijn
    [because the opinions rather divided are]
    "because (the) opinions are rather divided/rather differ"

In the linguistic literature on this subject, the difference between the a-sentences and the b-sentences in 3 and 4 is accounted for by two different analyses for these sentences.[1] It is said that, with the red order, the combination of the finite verb and the participle in 3a and 4a always constitutes a perfect tense. The b-sentences, however, may be interpreted as having a nominal predicate with the present tense. As in Dutch the red order is never used in nominal predicates with a "real" adjective, it is argued that the red order is less acceptable when the participle functions as a "real" deverbative adjective.

Not surprisingly, all examples given in the literature to illustrate this difference contain a form of the auxiliary *zijn* 'to be'. However, even when the verbal group contains a Vf of *hebben* 'to have' we may feel a preference for one order over the other, as is the case in the following example (cf. Janssen 1986:77). Several people would prefer the green order here.

(5) a. ? omdat de legers elkaar vrijwel hebben afgeslacht
 b. omdat de legers elkaar vrijwel afgeslacht hebben

---

[1]Cf. Michels 1959, Sassen 1963, and De Rooij 1987.

[because the armies each other practically slaughtered have]
"because the armies (have) practically killed each other off"

It is not satisfactory to relate the difference with *hebben* 'to have' in 5a and 5b to the difference between a verbal predicate and a nominal predicate. Even if it were, such a statement would only express the difference in interpretation and would not explain why it takes the form it does. We still have to answer the question of HOW a given interpretation is related to word order.

Accordingly, I will here suggest an analysis that relates the two different word orders in the final verbal group more explicitly to the interpretation of the whole sentence in which they occur. Until now, word order in Dutch final groups has been treated exclusively as an isolated phenomenon.[2]

I will show that these differences in word order can best be described as differences in the way verbal elements are grouped together in a given interpretation, both with respect to each other and with respect to the other sentence elements. With the proposed analysis we will be able to account for the fact that in some cases a different word order yields a different interpretation, whereas in others it does not. From this it follows that a preference for one order over the other can be explained.

First, I will propose that we assign an interpretation structure to a sentence, as a method for describing a given interpretation. We will then consider more closely the interpretative effects of the green order compared with the red order, and relate them to the general function of word order. Finally, I will discuss some relevant discourse data in

---

[2] In the Dutch grammar *ANS* (Geerts et al. (eds.) 1984), it is suggested that the difference between the red and the green order might be a difference between written and spoken language. But de Hoop en Smabers 1987 show that this suggestion can not be justified. In their conclusion they also suggest that an approach is needed in which the syntactic environment is taken into account.

order to show that they support my analysis. I will confine myself to verbal groups that consist of a finite verb (Vf) and a participle (P).

2. Interpretation structure and the function of word order: a description of the way an interpretation is constructed. To describe the interpretation given to a sentence, I will propose a graphically represented interpretation structure. Such an assigned interpretation structure depends on the given interpretation: it is a description in retrospect.[3] Reading an interpretation structure from left to right represents the way in which, going from left to right, the successive elements have been added to the foregoing, according to the interpretation given to the sentence.

I will formulate the function of word order as follows. In general, an element that precedes another element can be INDEPENDENTLY ADDED TO THE FOREGOING. The construed interpretation of the preceding element will in that case not be influenced by any elements following it. In other words, an element coming first is CONCEPTUALIZED INDEPENDENTLY of any following elements.

Sometimes, however, our interpretation will be best explained by pointing out that some elements have not been conceptualized independently. A restrictive relative clause, for instance, characteristically influences the conceptualization of the preceding nominal constituent it modifies. In this case we would say that this nominal constituent is not conceptualized independently from the relative clause following it. The same holds true for articles and a following noun.

I will now turn to the interpretation structures of sentences with the red order compared with sentences with the green order. In explaining the difference, I will make use of the notion of independent conceptualization.

---

[3]The explicit view that a description of the grammatical structure of a sentence depends on a given interpretation is also found in Uhlenbeck 1962, and more recently in Keijsper 1985, Daalder (1987; 1989), Onrust 1988, Verhagen (1986; 1990) and publications of Langacker, e.g. (1986; 1987a; 1987b). Some of my assumptions and terminology bear a resemblance to the work of these linguists. Compared with each other, their approaches diverge. This issue will be pursued in a larger study in which I am engaged.

As we saw in the introduction, combinations of Vf + P with the red order are always construed as a verbal predicate. To account for this, I propose that with the red order, the Vf is always first linked up with the following elements. Consider the interpretation structure given in 6a for the sentence in 1a above. What we see here is that P following Vf cannot be independently added to the foregoing. This is another way of describing the observation that the unity of Vf and the elements following it always receives a verbal interpretation. We will return to this interpretive aspect in greater detail in the next section. Accented elements have been marked with ^.

(6) a.   omdat het zwembad gîsteren is geslôten

Accordingly, the interpretation structure for 3a will be as given in 7a.

(7) a. ? omdat het zwembad al jâren is geslôten

The interpretation structure in 7a shows why the red order may be judged as less acceptable here, for the group *is gesloten* is added to *al jaren*. This yields an interpretation in which the event of the closing of the swimming pool is said to have been taking place for years now. To avoid this interpretation, we may prefer the green order as in 7b.

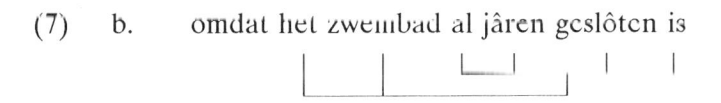

(7) b.   omdat het zwembad al jâren geslôten is

As is shown in 7b, a participle preceding Vf may be conceptualized independently. This means that the idea evoked by P is added to the foregoing independently from the following Vf. This is also shown in the following examples with *vrijwel* 'practically'.

(8) a. dat hij het vrîjwel beslôten heeft

[that he it practically decided has]
"that he has practically made the decision"

In 8a, P can be added independently to the foregoing. In other words, there is no need to assign an interpretation structure as given in 8b below. The interpretation according to 8b would imply that *vrijwel* says something about the group *besloten heeft* as a whole. Instead, *vrijwel* in Dutch says something about a state *(besloten)* as a result of some process, and not about the process itself as taking place in the course of time (cf. Vandeweghe 1988).

(8) b. dat hij het vrîjwel beslôten heeft

Now we can understand why, in this case, the red order would render the sentence less acceptable. Note that the same holds true for the red order in 4a above.

What I will claim now is the following. With the green order, P is in principle conceptualized independently from Vf, as in 7b and 8a. In some cases, however, it is obvious that an independent conceptualization of P is not possible. In those cases we assign an interpretation structure in which P and Vf are taken together as a group with respect to the foregoing. This is shown in 6b for the sentence in 1b above.

(6) b. omdat het zwembad gîsteren geslôten is.

Independent conceptualization of P in this sentence would suggest that Vf could be taken to refer to a particular moment yesterday, which is not a suitable interpretation here. However, whenever it makes sense to add P independently from Vf to the foregoing, we will do so.

In order to explain the generalizations above, I will now discuss the meaning of a past participle, as well as the meaning of accent, in relation to the different interpretations of the green and the red order.

3.   The interpretative effect of the green and red order with a past participle. I propose that a past participle denotes an ATEMPORAL STATE, to be understood as DUE TO SOME EVENT DENOTED BY THE VERB IN THE STEM OF P. In denoting this state no reference to (the course of) time is being made, neither with respect to the moment at which the state arises, nor with respect to the time interval in which the event took place. Thus, it needs to be stressed that neither the state nor the event is in the center of the attention and that neither refer to time. A participle is atemporal just like a "real" adjective. At the same time, it denotes an event. This may be seen as constituting the verbal aspect of a participle. Both aspects are equally present in the meaning of P (See also Langacker 1987a and Van der Wal 1986).

In Keijsper 1985, a study of the relation between accentuation and word order, it is proposed that an accent on a linguistic element X evokes the idea of "not X," but immediately replaces this idea with the idea evoked by X itself (an accent on X explicitly denies the thought of the absence of "X").[4] When we relate this to the red order, we find the following. Vf is always combined with P first. Therefore, an accent on P will involve the idea evoked by "Vf + P" as a whole (in Keijsper's terms: Vf is in the scope of the accent on P). As the idea of "Vf + P" as a whole is interpreted as something taking place in time, the replacement of "not (Vf + P)" by "Vf + P" is interpreted as A CHANGE TAKING PLACE IN THE COURSE OF TIME, the process denoted by P being taken as responsible for this change. This is why the red order is always given a verbal interpretation: it evokes a DYNAMIC interpretation.

---

[4]In referring to Keijsper 1985 I want to emphasize that her work on word order and accentuation has inspired me very much. I can only represent her ideas very briefly here.

With the green order, however, an accent on P will always replace the idea of "not P" into "P" before the Vf has been added. As a result, we interpret the change from "not P" into "P" NOT as taking place in the course of time, but only as a change of our thoughts, taking place in our heads. The effect will be that we revise our idea about the world. First we pictured the world at a certain moment as containing "not P," but we revise our picture. This is why a STATIC interpretation is evoked: the process itself is not pictured as a change taking place in the course of time. This is what might be called the adjectival function of the green order.

As we saw above, however, the green order also allows us to first add Vf to P, in which case P is not conceptualized independently, so that an accent on P in fact involves a change from "not (P + Vf)" to "P + Vf." The corresponding interpretation may also be called verbal, just as with the red order: with P not independently added to the foregoing, no 'state reading' will be elicited, and the 'event reading' is foregrounded. This explains why the interpretation of the red order and the green order do not differ much in their actual effect in those cases when P with the green order is not conceptualized independently. Only when P with the green order is conceptualized independently from Vf does there emerge a difference in interpretation between the green order and the red order. In such cases we sense that the alternative provided by the red order would yield a different interpretation. That is, the dynamic interpretation of the red order could make the sentence sound more active, which may lead us to prefer the green order.

4.   Clauses with red and green order and their function in discourse. In the preceding section, I claimed that a sense of dynamism is characteristic of the interpretation of sentences with the red order, whereas it may be absent with the green order. From this, it is to be expected that with the red order, the entities referred to in the clause will be seen as participants in the denoted process; participants which are assigned a certain process role within a hierarchy of process roles (to be compared to the notion of 'action chain' in Langacker 1987b). The highest process role is assigned to the most powerful participant with respect to the process (compare the notion of 'higher participant' in Kirsner 1976). I refer to it as the process-external participant. A participant affected or effected by the process is lower in the hierarchy and will be assigned a process-internal role (cf. Pauw 1984). With the red order, the process roles and their postion in the hierarchy is focussed upon.

With the green order, however, this sense of dynamism is generally absent: the clause does not present a change taking place in the course of time. It is therefore to be expected that, with the green order, the process role of the entities referred to is not focused upon.

Consider the following "real world" examples from the Eindhoven Corpus (also "Corpus Uit den Boogaart" 1975) with the green order.

(10) Daarom waste ze ook nooit d'r haar, omdat daar de hand van Miss Beryll op *gerust had.* (rno:24463)
"That is why she never washed her hair, because the hand of Miss Beryll had rested on it."

(11) Dat hij voor die verloren mensen zijn zoon *gegeven heeft,* die ons verlost van alle zonden. (rno:28455)
"That for those lost people, he gave his son, who frees us from all sin."

(12) Dit werd anders, toen zijn lichamelijke toestand zoveel *verbeterd was,* dat hij... (rno:26674)
"This changed when his physical condition had so much improved, that he..."

The static character of these sentences may be described in different ways. In 10 we might call *de hand* 'the hand' an external participant. We would not, however, call it an agent here, because the hand is not understood to be doing something itself. Similarly, although in 11 *hij* 'he' may be seen as an external participant, and *zijn zoon* 'his son' as an internal participant, the sentence does not convey information about an agent doing something to someone else. That is, the clause says something about his son, by predicating a relation with *hij*. The process role of *zijn zoon* is not important here. More important is its function as a relevant entity in the current discourse: it is made the topic in the following clause. The same static interpretation will be given to 12, where "his condition" is characterized, whereas the change from which it results is itself not pictured in the course of time, and no external participant is presumed to be involved.

Compared with the green order, clauses with the red order always favor a dynamic interpretation. They convey information about a process that took place in the course of time, and in which participants are involved. Consequently, part of this information is that the external participant is an agent and that the internal participant is an affected or effected participant. Moreover, clauses with the red order always evoke the thought of an agentive participant, even when it has not been mentioned. Consider the following examples from the Eindhoven Corpus with the red order.

(13)   Door dat eens geziene, nooit verjaagde visioen dat hem sindsdien met begeerte *had gekweld.* (rno:25905d)
"[...] by this vision, which had been seen once but never dispelled, which had tortured him with desire ever since."

(14)   Nadat ik mijn auto *had gewassen en opgepoetst,* mijn tuin *had aangeharkt,* uitgebloeide bloemen *had verwijderd,* vazen *had gevuld* met pioenrozen (...), het alfabet *had opgezegd* van achteren naar voren, een douche *had genomen,* enz... (rno:25771)
"After I had washed and polished my car, had raked the garden, had removed overblown flowers, had filled vases with peonies (...), had recited the alphabet from the end to the beginning, had taken a shower, etc..."

(15)   Toen de ketter 's morgens vroeg door de straten *was geleid,* hadden de begeleidende soldaten alle (...) vensters onder schot gehouden (...). (rno:26693)
"When the heretic had been led through the streets in the morning, the accompanying soldiers had kept all the windows covered."

The dynamic interpretation of these sentences can be recognized in different ways. In 13 we interpret the external participant "the vision" as an agent doing something to "him." This dynamic effect of the red order is coherent with the presence of *met begeerte* 'with desire', which says something about the way in which this vision tortured him. The sentence in 14 reports all the actions conducted by the agent. The sole function of the internal participants referred to is to specify the kind of action. That is, their relevance is limited to their process role, which is typical for the use of clauses with the red order. Finally, the sentence in 15 conveys that an event took place, experienced by the heretic. At the same time, it is presumed that there is a participant that did something to the heretic. This agentive participant is referred to by *de begeleidende soldaten* 'the accompanying soldiers' in the next clause. As a result, we interpret *toen* 'when' as referring to a moment during the process itself, which is consistent with the dynamic interpretation.

5. **Conclusion.** I have proposed an analysis for Dutch sentences containing a combination of a finite verb with a past participle. Utilizing the notion of 'independent conceptualization,' this analysis relates word order directly to interpretation. A crucial component of the analysis is the use of interpretation structures.

In contrast to the traditional analysis, which deals only with the combination of a past participle with a Vf of *zijn*, the one presented here covers combinations with a Vf of *hebben* as well. It explains why sentences with the red order (Vf + P) evoke a sense of dynamism, whereas this is absent with the green order (P + Vf). Finally, I have briefly indicated how these different orders function in discourse.

To conclude, I believe that much is to be gained by studying word order phenomena in terms of the distinction between independent and dependent conceptualization. As I will show elsewhere, the analysis presented here can be extended not only to sentences with verbal elements other than past participles, but also to entirely different kinds of word-order phenomena which hitherto have not been treated in relation to those considered here.

References

Geerts, G., W. Haeseryn, J. de Rooij, M. C. van den Toorn (eds.). 1984. *Algemene Nederlandse spraakkunst.* Groningen: Wolters-Noordhoff.
Daalder, S. 1987. "Grammar as a product of text interpretation." *Voortgang: Jaarboek voor de Neerlandistiek* 8:163-176.
_____. 1989. "Continuative relative clauses." In Norbert Reiter (ed.), *Sprechen und Hören. Akten des 23. Linguistischen Kolloquiums,* 195-207. Tübingen: Niemeyer.
Hoop, H. de en P. Smabers. 1987. "Rood of groen?" *NTg* 80:287-302.
Janssen, Th. A. J. M. 1986. "Het voltooid deelwoord." *GLOT* 9:57-78.
Keijsper, C. E. 1985. *Information structure — With examples from Russian, English and Dutch.* Amsterdam: Rodopi.
Kirsner, R. S. 1976. "On the subjectless 'pseudo-passive' in Standard Dutch and the semantics of background agents." In Charles N. Li (ed), *Subject and topic,* 385-416. New York: Academic Press.
Langacker, Ronald W. 1986. "An introduction to cognitive grammar." *Cognitive Science* 10:1-40.
_____. 1987a. "Nouns and verbs." *Language* 63:53-94.
_____. 1987b. "Grammatical ramifications of the setting/participant distinction." In Jon Aske a.o. (eds.), *Proceedings of the thirteenth annual meeting of the Berkeley Linguistics Society,* 383-394.
Michels, L. C. 1959. "Op de grens van copula en hulpwerkwoord." *Taal en Tongval* 11:206-212.
Onrust, M. 1988. *Eindverslag ZWO-project 300-163-017.* Manuscript.
Pauw, Annelies. 1984. "Transitiviteit, intransitiviteit en constructies met *zich.*" *Spektator* 13:417-439.
Rooij, J. de 1987. "Waarom het naamwoordelijk gezegde groen blijft." *Onze Taal* 55 (nr.11):142-144.
Sassen, A. 1963. "Endogeen en exogeen taalgebruik." *NTg* 56:10-21.
Uhlenbeck, E. M. 1962. "De beginselen van het syntactisch onderzoek." *Taalonderzoek in onze tijd,* 18-37. Den Haag: Servire.

Uit den Boogaart, P. C. (ed.). 1975. *Woordfrequenties in geschreven en gesproken Nederlands.* Utrecht: Oosthoek, Scheltema and Holkema.
Vandeweghe, W. 1988. "Omgevingen van vrijwel." *TABU* 18:93-108.
Verhagen, A. 1986. *Linguistic theory and the function of word order in Dutch. A study on interpretive aspects of the order of adverbials and noun phrases.* Dordrecht: Foris.
_____. 1990. "De interpretatiestructuur van passieve zinnen." *Forum der Letteren* 31:81-92.
Wal, M. J. van der. 1986. *Passiefproblemen in oudere taalfasen.* Leiden University doctoral dissertation.

To be or not *to be* in Dutch:
A Cognitive Account of Some Puzzling Perfect Auxiliary Phenomena

Thomas F. Shannon
University of California, Berkeley

1. Introduction. The question of the factors governing the selection of the perfect auxiliary in Dutch is an old, but still controversial one. As opposed to recent proposals in formal grammar (cf. Hoekstra 1984), I regard perfect auxiliary choice not as governed by formal syntactic factors but rather by certain semantic parameters. In considering the semantics of the clause crucial to the issue, this approach returns to a more traditional view, but also pursues new insights from recent research in cognitive grammar and the theory of transitivity. Elsewhere (Shannon 1989, 1990, to appear) I have demonstrated that this approach is able to describe and explain the diachronic development of the perfect auxiliaries in Germanic and Romance, as well as the variation to be observed across and within these languages. This paper considers further variation in Dutch described in recent studies by de Rooij and Hofmans which were not previously available to me.

2. A Cognitive Account of Perfect Auxiliary Selection in Dutch. My approach views perfect auxiliary selection in terms of prototype theory: prototypical transitive events (1) are encoded in the perfect with HAVE, whereas BE is used with prototypical mutative events (2).

(1)   **Prototypical transitive events:**
      Transpire in physical space; involve two entities that are differentiated from each other, from their setting, and from the

observer; involve two entities that participate in an interaction and are asymmetrically related; describe interactions in which the first participant moves toward and makes contact with the second participant; describe interactions in which the second participant is affected and reacts externally by changing state or moving.

(2) **Prototypical mutative events:**
Transpire in physical space; involve only a single entity, differentiated from the setting and from the observer; describe an event in which the single participant is affected and changes externally by changing state or moving.

In particular, perfect auxiliary selection is related to transitivity, in the sense of Hopper and Thompson 1980. They define transitivity as a complex, semantically determined global property of clauses, consisting of the ten parameters listed in (3), to which I add the corresponding mutative properties.

(3) **The Transitivity/Mutativity Parameters**

	High Transitivity	Low Transitivity	High Mutativity
PARTICIPANTS	2 or more (A & O)	1 participant	1 participant
KINESIS	action	nonaction	action (event)
ASPECT	telic	atelic	telic
PUNCTUALITY	punctual	nonpunctual	punctual
VOLITIONALITY	volitional	nonvolitional	nonvolitional
AFFIRMATION	affirmative	negative	affirmative
MODE	realis	irrealis	realis
AGENCY OF A	high in potency	low in potency	low in potency
AFFECTEDNESS OF O	totally affected	not affected	(=A) totally affected
INDIVIDUATION OF O	highly individuated	nonindividuated	highly individuated

In certain ways the two prototypes are similar, and yet in others they are quite different. Both concern the effectuation of a change, but differ in how this change is brought about and to whom it occurs: with prototypical transitives an agent causes a change in a patient, while in prototypical mutatives a patient subject undergoes the change without outside intervention. Regarding transitivity parameters, the prototypes differ in number of participants (two vs. one), volitionality (volitional vs. nonvolitional), potency of A (potent vs. nonpotent), and affectedness (O affected vs. A affected). Similarities between the prototypes deal with aspectual and modal dimensions: both agree in kinesis (action), aspect (telic), affirmation (affirmative), and mode (realis). These parameters of agreement relate to the effectiveness of the change, the attainment of the resultant state in the patient.

I maintain that perfect auxiliary choice is based on the prototypes, which are clearly related to these parameters: while prototypical HAVE-aux clauses have the properties listed for high transitivity, prototypical mutative clauses evince the high mutativity features. Generally, the prototypes are followed; however, when there is variation, it can be accounted for it terms of these parameters. Though we cannot normally predict when a language will be sensitive to a given parameter, when it is, we can predict what effect it will have — i.e which auxiliary it will condition. When one of the factors on which the two prototypes are opposed is relevant, the perfect auxiliary matches the corresponding prototype. But when one of the parameters held in common is involved, a switch is only found with mutatives, and then always from BE to HAVE. Previously I demonstrated that all these parameters can effect perfect auxiliary choice; in this paper I will discuss further cases in Dutch and show how they follow from our account.

3. **Perfect Auxiliary Variation in Modern Dutch.** De Rooij 1988 presents an in-depth study of perfect auxiliary variation with four Dutch verbs: *zijn* 'to be', *gaan* 'to go', *vergeten* 'to forget', and *verliezen* 'to lose'. Since I have dealt with these verbs previously (Shannon 1989), we will not consider them here individually. Instead let us consider the effects of our transitivity parameters on perfect auxiliary choice. De Rooij observes a number of factors affecting the choice of perfect auxiliary. Two of them — durativity and telicity — relate to aspect. Since prototypical mutatives are non-durative and telic, the presence of either (or both) of these features in a clause may motivate the use of HAVE, which is the general default aux for duratives (states and activities), instead of BE, which is much more restricted aspectually. De Rooij observes e.g. that in older stages of Dutch and to a certain extent in existing dialects, the presence of durative adverbs promotes the use

of HAVE with *zijn* (cf. 4a), which nowadays otherwise almost always takes BE, as well as with *gaan* (cf. 5a).[1]

In non-durative, telic uses much more closely approximating the mutative prototype, however, we find BE (cf. 4b, 5b). This switch to HAVE is clearly related to the transitivity parameters, specifically aspect: as we would expect, non-telic, durative uses of otherwise mutative verbs foster the selection of the default auxiliary HAVE.

(4) a. Jan **heeft/is** jaren in Amerika *geweest.*
"Jan has been/was in America for years."

b. De kinderen **zijn/hebben** naar het bos *geweest.*
"The children have been off to the woods."

(5) a. Hoe lang **heeft/is** hij nou wel met dat meisje *gegaan?*
"How long did he go with that girl?"

b. De jongens **zijn/hebben** vroeg naar huis *gegaan.*
"The boys went home early."

Another factor in perfect auxiliary choice which de Rooij points out in varying guises is volitionality. For example, speakers feel the subject of *vergeten* (104ff.) and *verliezen* (125f.) with HAVE to be more "active," "in control," "responsible" or "involved" (*betrokken*), while with BE it is more "passive," less "betrokken." With *vergeten* this entails that the two meanings distinguished in traditional grammars also tend to match different auxiliaries: in the sense 'to neglect to do something' the subject is clearly more responsible and the regular auxiliary is HAVE, whereas with the meaning 'to lose mental contents' the subject is not responsible and thus the regular aux is BE (cf. 6a vs. 6b and de Rooij's maps 15/17), although there is certainly a bit of variation here. With *verliezen,* on the other hand, the greater involvement in the event can be as a possessor (e.g. inalienable vs. alienable possession) as in (7a), where for some HAVE refers to his own

---

[1]In our examples, which are taken from the literature cited, the perfect auxiliary is in **bold**, the main verb in *italics,* and the modal in ***bold italics***.

leg but BE refers to another's leg; or as an 'agent' (cf. 7b, where the subject is responsible for his loss).

(6) a. Nou **heb**(/**ben**) ik m'n regenjas *vergeten*!
"Well I forgot my umbrella!"

b. De datum **ben**(/**heb**) ik *vergeten*.
"I have forgotten the date."

(7) a. Hij **heeft**/**is** een been *verloren*.
"He lost a leg."

b. Hij **heeft** zijn huis *verloren* (bij 't gokken).
"He lost his house (by gambling)."

This is exactly as we would expect, given our prototype approach: when there is a split like this, HAVE expresses features characteristic of high transitivity (volition/potency of the subject), whereas BE expresses features characteristic of high mutativity (non-volition and lack of potency).

Other factors which I had previously ascertained (Shannon to appear) and explained in terms of our parameters were also noted by de Rooij in modern Dutch. Thus, for some speakers the fact that the resultant state no longer obtains can be signalled by the use of HAVE instead of BE, e.g. with *vergeten* and *verliezen* (97f., 104; 131); HAVE seems to reverse BE's implicature of the present relevance of the result (cf. the next section). Moreover, the presence of a strong negator such as *nooit* 'never' can bring about HAVE-switch, e.g. with *vergeten* (97). Finally, iterativity, which is apparently what Honselaar 1987 means by "SAMENVATTEND," may possibly also cause a shift to HAVE (100). For further explanation of cases such as these, see Shannon (to appear).

4. HAVE-Switch with Irrealis. Several scholars (Kern 1912:280ff.; Honselaar 1987; and de Rooij 1988.24ff. et passim, who terms it "marginal" in modern Dutch) have noted a curious effect of irrealis on mutatives: although otherwise BE is used, there is a certain tendency towards HAVE in irrealis contexts.

(8) a. Ik **had** nog maar wat *gebleven,* als ik jou was (geweest).
"I would have stayed a while longer, if I were [had been] you."

b. **Had** hij gisteren *gekomen,* dan was alles in orde geweest.
"Had he come yesterday, then everything would have been okay."

c. **Was/Had** ik er maar bij *geweest.*
"If I only had been there."

d. **Hadden** jullie maar niet zo eigenwijs *geweest,* dan **had** het niet *gebeurd.*
"If you only hadn't been so pig-headed, it wouldn't have happened."

The same effect of irrealis, as well as a number of other factors, can be found throughout the history of The Germanic languages. In Shannon (to appear) I account for this in terms of the mutativity-reducing effect of these environments. With irrealis the change is specifically claimed not to have taken place and HAVE seems to cancel the implicature of the present relevance of the result which BE otherwise can have. Moreover, the notion of control and/or volitionality, which is clearly related to the transitive prototype and therefore HAVE, may also be relevant in this context. De Rooij (1988:26) quotes Paardekoper, who claims that HAVE is used in irrealis only when it's a matter of volition ("een zekere opzet"); cf. (9a vs. b). Furthermore, if I understand Honselaar (1987:65) correctly, he also appeals to the notion of control and/or volitionality in this regard. Once again, a transitivity/mutativity factor plays the role expected of it given our prototype approach.

(9) a. **Had** ie nou wat vriendelijker *geweest,* dan **had** het niet hoeven te *gebeuren.*
"Had he been somewhat more friendly, then it wouldn't have had to happen."

b. ***Had** ie nou majoor *geweest,* dan **had** het niet hoeven te *gebeuren.*
"Had he been a major, then it wouldn't have had to happen."

5. **AUX-Switch with Modals.** Finally, modal auxiliaries also show auxiliary variation in the perfect. In the double infinitive construction the modal normally determines the perfect auxiliary (= HAVE); however, with modals there is a tendency for BE to occur with mutative 'main verbs' (although HAVE is usually also possible, at times even preferred). Cf. Kern (1912:282), Hofmans (1980 et passim), Honselaar (1987:65), Geerts (1984:520f.), and Hoekstra (1984:270ff.), who notes parallels in Italian. With passive infinitives the use of BE appears to be quite widespread, perhaps even the only acceptable possibility (cf. Kern 1912:282; Hoekstra 1984:274).

(10) a. Hij **heeft/is** niet *durven/kunnen komen.*
"He has not dared/been able to come."

b. We **hebben/zijn** *moeten verhuizen.*
"We have had to move."

c. Hij **heeft/is** niet *willen gaan.*
"He did not want to go."

d. Het huis **heeft/is** *verkocht moeten* worden.
"The house had to be sold."

e. De arrestant **heeft/is** *proberen/trachten* te *ontsnappen.*
"The suspect tried to escape."

What seems to be going on here has become known in the generative literature as 'clause union' or 'restructuring.' Basically, it is the syntactic and semantic (even phonological?) amalgamation of two more independent clauses into a single clause, such that the 'modal' and the 'main verb' form a single complex predicate. This leads to a potential reanalysis of the construction in which the main verb forms the head and the modal is reduced to a kind of defocussed modal operator on it, leading to the use of BE.

Until recently, it has not been very clear what the facts are in this area of variation of modern Dutch. Fortunately, in a very important series of articles — which have apparently hitherto gone completely unnoticed in the literature on this subject — Hofmans (1980, 1982a, 1982b) has uncovered several regularities here through detailed empirical work. Table 1, on the following page, summarizes his findings. His factors which favor HAVE or BE include: type of modal auxiliary (*kunnen* and *moeten* are 'pro-BE', but *mogen* and *willen* 'pro-HAVE') or semi-modal (*durven* vs. *wensen te*) and the main verb (*gaan* vs. *groeien*). Space does not permit the necessary full discussion of these matters, but let us consider each of these points at least briefly with respect to our account of perfect auxiliary selection.

First of all, why are *kunnen* and *moeten* much more pro-BE, and *mogen* and *willen* pro-HAVE? Hoekstra (1984:174) claims that the difference between root and epistemic meaning is relevant and that only the epistemic meaning is found, but this appears to be incorrect. Rather, this too relates to transitivity factors: the pro-BE modals do not impute any volition and/or control over the situation to their subject (*kunnen, moeten*), whereas the pro-HAVE modals do impute such control (*willen, mogen*). In this context, Hoekstra (174) specifically claims that with modals HAVE imputes volitional control, but BE does not. Since volitional control is a high transitivity feature, it stands to reason that its presence favors HAVE, and its absence favors BE.

The other factors are presently much less clear to me. The cline of semi-modals appears to be due to at least the following factors: (1) lesser/greater clausal integration (signalled inter alia by [lack of] extraposition and presence/absence of *te*); (2) presence vs. absence of volitional control (e.g. *proberen* vs. *wensen*); (3) frequency (e.g. *proberen* vs. *trachten*), which is probably also related to (1). The semi-modals *laten, horen, zien, voelen* of course are pro-HAVE: since they include another participant, they are clearly much more transitive anyway. But why do the main verbs show their different pro-HAVE or pro-BE behavior? I must admit I'm still at a loss to account for this. While it is not surprising that more prototypical mutatives like *gaan, vertrekken,* and *vallen* are more pro-BE than less prototypical BE-verbs like *verschijnen* or *blijven*, I cannot see why *stijgen* is so low on the list, unless it has to do with frequency. Though the list is too small to invite

Table 1

MAIN CLAUSE

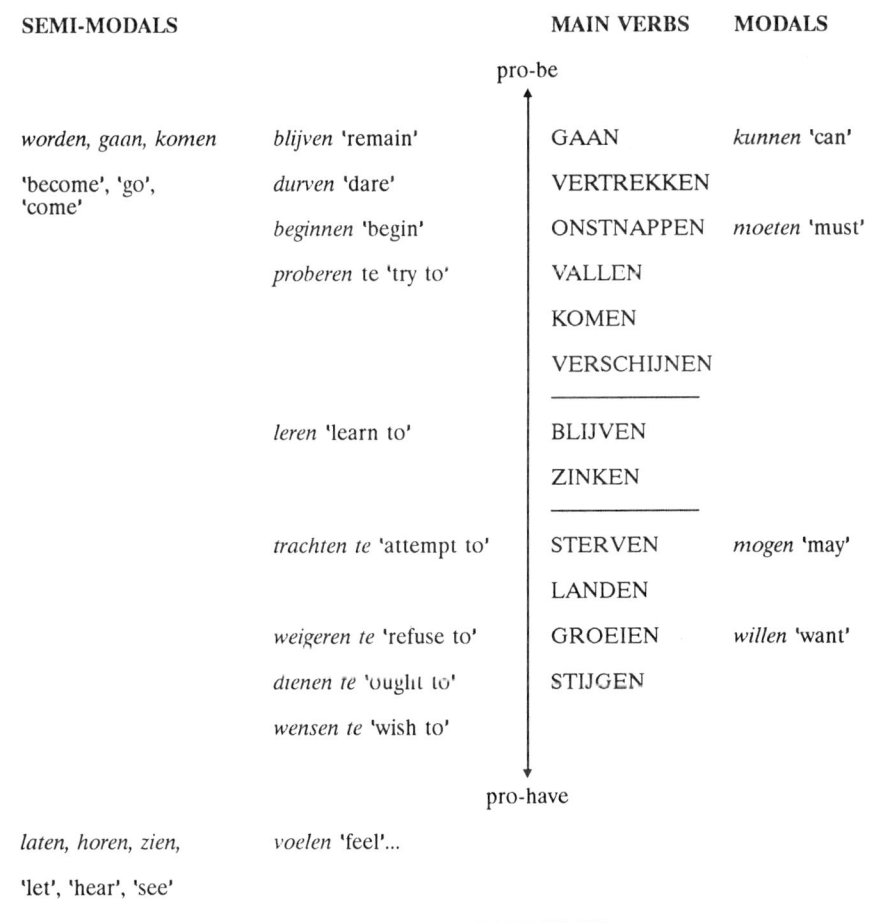

SEMI-MODALS		MAIN VERBS	MODALS
		pro-be ↑	
worden, gaan, komen 'become', 'go', 'come'	*blijven* 'remain'	GAAN	*kunnen* 'can'
	durven 'dare'	VERTREKKEN	
	beginnen 'begin'	ONSTNAPPEN	*moeten* 'must'
	proberen te 'try to'	VALLEN	
		KOMEN	
		VERSCHIJNEN	
	leren 'learn to'	BLIJVEN	
		ZINKEN	
	trachten te 'attempt to'	STERVEN	*mogen* 'may'
		LANDEN	
	weigeren te 'refuse to'	GROEIEN	*willen* 'want'
	dienen te 'ought to'	STIJGEN	
	wensen te 'wish to'		
		↓ pro-have	
laten, horen, zien, 'let', 'hear', 'see'	*voelen* 'feel'...		

SUBORDINATE CLAUSE

sweeping generalizations, it appears that true motion verbs like *gaan* or *vertrekken* are generally more pro-BE than statal inchoatives like *sterven, groeien*, which of course do not impute volitional control to their subject. Clearly the topic requires further scrutiny.

Finally, our old friend irrealis effects aux-switch here too: when perfect forms with dependent mutative infinitives occur in irrealis contexts (cf. 10), BE cannot be used and only HAVE is acceptable (11), a fact which Hoekstra (1984:274) found "puzzling." Given our approach, this is not at all puzzling: once again, since irrealis lessens the mutativity of the clause, it stands to reason that precisely this context should not allow the use of the perfect auxiliary which normally is associated with mutative clauses (BE) and requires a switch back to the non-mutative auxiliary (HAVE).

(11) a. Hij **had/*was** niet *durven/kunnen komen.*
"He would not have dared/been able to come."

   b. We **hadden/*waren** *moeten verhuizen.*
"We would have had to move."

   c. Hij **had/*was** niet *willen gaan.*
"He would not have wanted to go."

   d. Het huis **had/*was** *verkocht moeten worden.*
"The house would have had to be sold."

6. Conclusion. This paper has applied a theory of perfect auxiliary selection based on transitive (HAVE) versus mutative (BE) prototypes and transitivity parameters to a number of cases of variation in Dutch unearthed recently by de Rooij and Hofmans. In each instance it was seen that the facts fall out nicely from our account, which shows clearly the underlying semantic motivation of the correlations found. These arguments therefore provide further reason for preferring such a semantically based account over other, formal approaches, which to my knowledge are not able to explain such facts in a similarly insightful and unitary manner.

References

Geerts, G., et al. (eds.). 1984. *Algemene Nederlandse spraakkunst.* Groningen: Wolters-Noordhoff.

Hoekstra, Teun. 1984. *Transitivity. Grammatical relations in government-binding theory.* Dordrecht: Foris.

Hofmans, Mark. 1980. "*Hebben* of *zijn*: een enquête naar het gebruik van 'hebben' en 'zijn' in de konstruktie Thww + Mnww + HWW in Nederland en Vlaanderen." *Rapport d'Activités de l'Institut de Phonétique* 14 (August 1980): 83-129. Also appeared in *Tijdschrift van de Vrije Universiteit Brussel* 1981, Nr. 1: 62-114.

_____. 1982a. "*Hebben of zijn* en de deverbalisering van de modale werkwoorden in het Nederlands." In M. Dominicy (ed.), *Linguistics in Belgium 5,* 81-109. Brussels: Didier/Hatier.

_____. 1982b. "Aspects of deverbalisation: The semi-modals." In Saskia Daalder and Marinel Gerritsen (eds.), *Linguistics in the Netherlands 1982,* 83-94. Amsterdam: North-Holland.

Honselaar, Wim. 1987. "*Zijn* vs. *hebben* in het samengesteld perfectum." *De nieuwe taalgids* 80: 55-68.

Hopper, Paul and Sandra Thompson. 1980. "Transitivity in grammar and discourse." *Language* 56: 251-299.

Kern, J. H. 1912. *De met het participium praeteriti omschreven werkwoordsvormen in 't Nederlands.* Amsterdam: Johannes Mueller.

Rooij, Jaap de. 1988. *Van hebben naar zijn.* Amsterdam: P. J. Meertens Instituut.

Shannon, Thomas F. 1989. "Perfect auxiliary variation as a function of transitivity and *Aktionsart.*" In Joseph Emonds et al. (eds.), *Proceedings from the Western Conference on Linguistics. WECOL 88.* Vol. 1, 254-266. Department of Linguistics: California State University, Fresno.

_____. 1990. "The unaccusative hypothesis and the history of the perfect auxiliary in Germanic and Romance." In Henning Andersen and Konrad Koerner (eds.), *Historical Linguistics 1987. Papers from the 8th International Conference on Historical Linguistics (8.ICHL)* (Lille, August 31 - September 4, 1987), 461-188. Amsterdam: Benjamins.

_____. To appear. "Explaining perfect auxiliary variation: Some modal and aspectual effects in the history of Germanic." To appear in Shaun Hughes and Joe Salmons (eds.), *Proceedings of the Third Symposium on Germanic Linguistics.* Amsterdam: Benjamins.

The Inflection of Adjectives with Nominal Infinitives

Arie Verhagen
Free University, Amsterdam
and
The University of California, Santa Barbara

1. **Introduction.**[*] The aim of this paper is primarily to present an analysis of certain infinitival constructions in Dutch; on the basis of this analysis, I will also draw a conclusion about the general analytical framework. The topic of the discussion can be exemplified by the italicized parts in the following sentences:[1]

(1) In de raming is rekening gehouden met *het volledig functioneren van de bestaande opleidingen* (amb:52301).
"In the estimate, *the complete functioning of the existing training programs* has been taken into account."

---

[*] I wish to thank Justine Pardoen for her important contribution to my thinking about the problems discussed in this paper. Thanks are also due to the students who participated in a seminar on word order phenomena at the Free University and to the discussants at the Fifth Interdisciplinary Conference on Netherlandic Studies. This research was carried out within the Free University research program "Functional Language Research: Grammar and Pragmatics" (LETT/88-10). Part of the work was done while I was a visiting scholar at the University of California, Santa Barbara, on a fellowship awarded by the Netherlands Organization for Scientific Research (NWO), grant S 30-317.

[1] These and most of the other examples used in this paper come from the so-called Eindhoven Corpus, in the version available at the Free University in Amsterdam; this version includes a subcorpus containing language written by government officials (cf. Renkema 1981). Examples from this corpus are presented with a reference to a subcorpus and a number.

Robert S. Kirsner (ed.), *The Low Countries and Beyond*, 097-109. Lanham, MD: University Press of America, 1993.

(2)   Wat *het toekomstige functioneren van de FMO* betreft vragen deze leden zich af of niet de kans bestaat dat zich de volgende ontwikkeling zal voordoen (amb:52882a).
"As far as *the future functioning of the FMO* is concerned, these members [of Parliament] wonder if the chance does not exist that the following development will occur."

Both sentences contain a nominally used infinitive in a construction introduced with the neuter article/pronoun *het* 'it/the' and containing a complement introduced with the preposition *van* 'of'. Also, the infinitives are preceded by adjectives in both 1 and 2, but in 1 the adjective is not inflected, while in 2 it is: it has the suffix *-e*. This latter difference constitutes the particular topic of this paper.

This variation sometimes also occurs with certain common nouns.[2] An analysis of the variation with nominal infinitives will thus ultimately have to be embedded in a more comprehensive one, but I will confine myself here completely to the infinitives, although I believe the analysis to be in fact more widely applicable.

2.   Elementary observations.   Let us first consider a few more examples.

(3)   Wel zal het punt komen, dat, terwille van *het goed functioneren van de democratie,* de overheid nauw wordt betrokken bij het in stand houden van de dagbladen van verschillende richting (dbl:9140).
"What definitely WILL happen is that the point will be reached where, for the sake of *the proper functioning of democracy,* the government will become closely involved in preserving the daily newspapers of opposing persuasion[s]."

(4)   Automatisch roept *het plotseling opdagen van een inspecteur* spanningen op (pwe:36445).

---

[2]Cf. Honselaar 1980 and De Rooij 1980, and the references cited there, for overviews and data.

"Automatically *the sudden appearance of an inspector* raises tensions."

(5) Juist *het plotselinge optreden van een lekke band* brengt menig bestuurder in een soort paniekroes (obl:12442).
"Precisely *the sudden occurrence of a flat tire* puts many a driver into a panic attack."

(6) Demeter is pas de laatste die van *het angstwekkende verdwijnen van haar dochter* hoort (pwe:35192).
"Demeter is the very last person to hear about *the frightening disappearance of her daughter.*"

When we consider the semantic relations between an adjective and an infinitive and between these elements and the remainder of the clause, it appears that good paraphrases are rather different for the inflected and the non-inflected cases. In the non-inflected cases, the adjectival information is in some sense related directly to the rest of the sentence, as is illustrated by the following paraphrases:

(1)' ...the completeness of the functioning of the existing training-programs.../...the functioning of the existing training-programs being complete...

(3)' ...democracy functioning well.../...the quality of democracy...

(4)' ...the suddenness of an inspector appearing...

The three inflected cases, on the other hand, are better paraphrased as follows:

(2)' ...the way the FMO will function in the future...

(5)' ...the occurrence of a flat tire, which is (always) sudden...

(6)' ...her daughter's disappearance, which is/was frightening...

The point is that the content of examples 2, 5, and 6 is not rendered adequately by paraphrases of the sort given in 1', 3', and 4'; for example, 6 is not about the fearfulness of the daughter's disappearance, while 4 IS (also) about the suddenness of an inspector's appearing.

Note also that the meaning of the verb "functioning" differs with the inflection of the adjective: in the two non-inflected cases 1 and 3, it is in fact rather vague, coming close to simply "being," while in the inflected case 2 it is more specific, coming more closely to "operating," "working."

Cases 4 and 5 both contain the adjective *plotseling* 'sudden', but in one case without, and, in the other, with the suffix. Examination of the context reveals that this difference can be made sense of. In 4 this can already been seen in the sentence itself: it is about tensions being raised, and this is naturally related to the suddenness of the inspector's appearance. In the case of 5, only the WIDER context can provide justification for the use of *-e*: Without the inflection of the adjective, the sentence would effectively produce an unmotivated CHANGE in the topic of the discourse. The adverbial "precisely" would also apply specifically to the suddenness, while this makes no sense in the context (there being nothing to contrast it with). The inflection thus allows for the addition of this piece of information of suddenness, but without it being made so important that it becomes the discourse topic at this point.

3. **Grammatical and linear modification.** The final considerations of the preceding section provide us with the elements necessary for a more generalized account of these phenomena as well as others, as I will now demonstrate.

I propose that the suffix *-e* be taken as a grammatical indication of modification; i.e., as indicating that the base with which it is associated is to be interpreted as A DISTINGUISHING ASPECT of something else, as being IN A MODIFYING RELATION to something else (irrespective of its position).

One thing that this proposal immediately captures is why no inflection occurs with nominally used copular verbs, or rather: why an inflected adjective is not interpreted as predicative, and why *worden* 'to become' and *zijn* 'to be' cannot be taken as copular verbs when accompanied by such an adjective. Consider, for example:

(7) ...haar hele zijn van vlees en bloed en gevoel (rno:25080)
"... her entire being of flesh and blood and feeling"

The element *zijn* cannot be taken as a copula with the adjective in the function of predicate nominal (significantly, in the Eindhoven corpus it was not even given the code of a verb, but rather that of a noun).

The distinguishing, modifying nature of inflected adjectives is also nicely demonstrated by the English translations of cases of so-called substantival use of inflected adjectives:

(8) Het mooie moet nog komen
"The beautiful [part] is still to come"

(9) Dit is nu juist het aardige
"This is precisely the nice [thing about it]"

But when there IS a nominal element following, this is naturally taken as the element modified by the inflected adjective. Thus, a sequence like *het moderne denken* 'modern thinking' (pwe:35377) can be interpreted in the following way:[3]

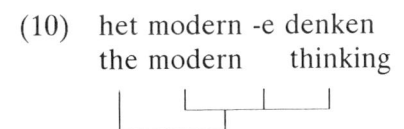

(10) het modern -e denken
the modern thinking

The interpretation of *moderne* is established as the combination of the meaning of the elements *modern* and *-e*; to this complex, which is a modifier of something else, given the meaning of *-e*, the meaning of *denken* is then added. This phrase, meaning thinking specified as modern, is added to the meaning of the article/pronoun *het*; the entire

---

[3]Here I follow a line of thinking expounded in work by Daalder (e.g. 1989) and others (cf. Pardoen, this volume).

complex then can be taken to mean: something identifiable, which is specified as the thinking of modern times. (The graph is to be read from bottom to top, and, at each level, from left to right.)

I will call a representation like 10 an INTERPRETATION STRUCTURE of a phrase; cf. Pardoen (this volume) for another application of this approach to sentence meaning.

Since the suffix marks the adjective as modifying the element following it (*denken* in 10), that element is interpreted as the modified one; in terms of structuralist notions: it is the "head" of the phrase. However, no such consequence follows when the adjective is NOT inflected. In such cases, we build an interpretation in which there is no grammatically indicated modification, but ONLY LINEAR MODIFICATION (cf. Bolinger 1965),[4] so that the meaning of the infinitive following the adjective is taken as modifying the meaning of the adjective; the latter then effectively functions as the "head" of a phrase. Thus, a phrase like *[het] ondubbelzinnig kennen* 'knowing unambiguously/unequivocal knowledge' (pwe:35857) means something like: "absence of ambiguity in knowing/knowledge" (this fits the context, which is concerned with the consequences of allowing subjective elements in rational knowledge). This means that in the interpretation structure 11,

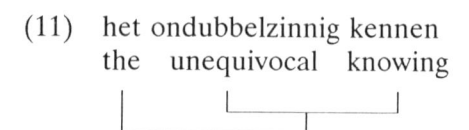

(11) het ondubbelzinnig kennen
      the unequivocal   knowing

kennen 'knowing' modifies the idea "unequivocal," while the latter does not modify the former; hence the paraphrase "absence of ambiguity in knowledge." The general pattern should now be clear: also in the paraphrases of the non-inflected cases 1', 3', 4', we see that the idea denoted by the infinitive functions as a modification of the idea denoted by the adjective. In all instances the infinitival idea denotes the specific respect in which the idea denoted by the adjective

---

[4]Perhaps one could also assume linear modification in the case of an inflected adjective; i.e., besides grammatical modification. I have not considered that possibility here, as it is not strictly germane to the present discussion.

is to be interpreted: 1 is about the completeness *of the training-programs functioning,* 3 is about the "goodness" *of democracy,* and 4 about the suddenness *of an inspector's appearance.*[5]

4. Internal and external complements. In the non-inflected cases, the element used as a specification for another is, as an infinitive, a rather abstract one. Hence it is not at all strange that a phrase such as in 11 may evoke a reaction of puzzlement: "unequivocal knowledge OF WHAT?" There is a sense of incompleteness. In the case of 11, the phrase does fit the context (that of a philosophical discussion), but this use of a non-inflected form is not very common.

The unusualness of 11 is highlighted by the figures in Table 1 (on the following page), which sums up the distribution, in the corpus used (cf. note 1), of prepositional complements in definite nominal infinitives with a preceding adjective (the absolute numbers are given between parentheses).[6]

There is clearly a high preference for infinitives with non-inflected adjectives to take a prepositional complement. We may see this as a consequence of the fact that the bare infinitive as such is semantically abstract and therefore usually does not suffice to specify the adjectival concept. Hence the large majority of cases in which the infinitive is accompanied by a prepositional phrase adding extra specification.

That the main role of the complement is to render the abstract infinitival concept more specific derives further support from another

---

[5]This accords with Honselaar's (1980:201) observation that "[t]he relation between the meaning of the adjective and the meaning of the noun is indeed unspecific for the Adjective-∅ Noun pattern as a whole, but almost always very specific for given instances." In my analysis (when extended to Honselaar's data), this would be due to the fact that the following element specifies the respect in which the general meaning of the adjective is to be taken; thus, *een goed violist* 'a good violinist' means: someone who is good as a violinist, while *een goede violist* indicates a violinist of whom "good" is a distinguishing aspect, not necessarily as a violinist.

[6]Thanks are due Yoshi Ono at UCSB for showing me how to calculate the tables.

Table 1
Distribution of Prepositional Complements

	Inflected	%	Non-inflected	%
- with prepositional complement:	(17)	38	(63)	70
- without prepositional complement:	(28)	62	(27)	30
Total:	(45)	100	(90)	100

χ^2 (1, N=135) = 12.91, $p<0.05$

consideration of the same data: one focusing on differences between the two groups in the relations of prepositional complements to the infinitive. The majority of such complements have the preposition *van* 'of'; these may sometimes be paraphrased as the SUBJECT of the infinitive, sometimes as an OBJECT. Now consider Table 2:

Table 2
Distribution of 'SUBJECT' and 'OBJECT' *van*-Phrases

	Inflected	%	Non-Inflected	%
- 'SUBJECT':	(13)	93	(23)	40
- 'OBJECT':	(1)	7	(27)	60
Total:	(14)	100	(57)	100

χ^2 (1, N=71) = 12.39, $p<0.05$)

I interpret this distribution as follows. With an inflected adjective, we have A CERTAIN TYPE of infinitival idea, i.e. specified with a distinguishing aspect. But with a non-inflected adjective, the subsequent prepositional phrase is used as a specification of the (abstract) infinitive. Now objects, as INTERNAL participants of a process, can provide such a specification, i.e. distinguish one subtype of a process from another (building a house is a different kind of process than building an argument); but especially agentive subjects, as EXTERNAL participants, do not provide such a specification (building by John is not, as a process, distinguishable from building by Bill).

We can sharpen this idea by means of the notion of interpretation structure. We may say that the combination of an infinitive and an inflected adjective is in general sufficiently specific to be CONCEPTUALIZED INDEPENDENTLY,[7] i.e. to be added to the meaning of the foregoing (witness the LOW frequency of complementation). A following prepositional phrase will then be added to the foregoing by itself. Thus, the interpretation structure of cases like these will be as follows:

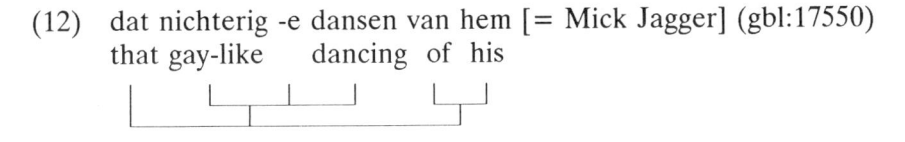

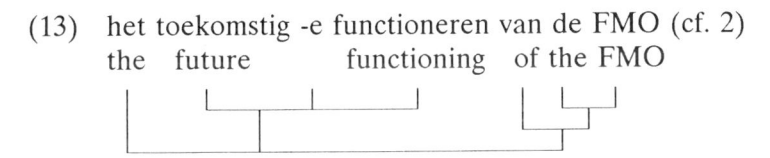

(12) dat nichterig -e dansen van hem [= Mick Jagger] (gbl:17550)
 that gay-like dancing of his

(13) het toekomstig -e functioneren van de FMO (cf. 2)
 the future functioning of the FMO

But with an non-inflected adjective, the infinitive is not readily conceptualized independently (witness the HIGH frequency of complementation), so that a following prepositional phrase will generally FIRST be added to the interpretation of the infinitive. This group is then added to the adjective and finally the entire complex is added to the article. This corresponds to interpretation structures like the following:

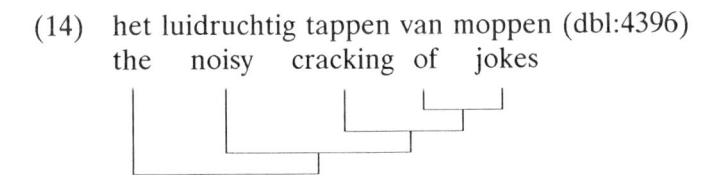

(14) het luidruchtig tappen van moppen (dbl:4396)
 the noisy cracking of jokes

---

[7]This notion replaces the concept of 'independent perceivability' in Verhagen 1986; cf. Pardoen, this volume.

(15) het ongemotiveerd afbreken van de zwangerschap (amb:52561)
    the unmotivated breaking-off of the pregnancy

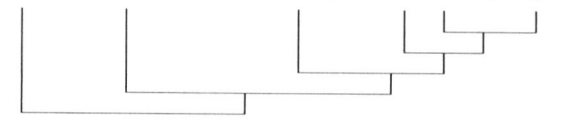

(16) het goedkoop inkopen van agrarische grondstoffen (dbl:8617)
    the cheap buying of agricultural raw-materials

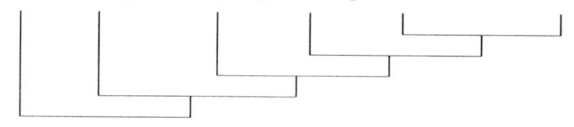

The examples just given all involve nouns functioning as objects, clearly internal participants. If this approach is correct, we expect those cases where the paraphrase with a subject is appropriate to involve non-agentive subjects, i.e. subjects that do not have an external, but an internal participant role, in intransitive situations. This is in fact precisely what seems to be the case. For example, many of the infinitives in this class are verbs of appearance and disappearance, with internal participants as subjects. Also, some other infinitives typically have a vague meaning, approaching "to be" (recall the difference in the interpretation of "functioning" between 1 and 3 on the one hand, and 2 on the other). In such cases, too, the role of the complement is to specify the infinitival idea; the infinitive is not conceptualized independently from the complement:[8]

(17) het plotseling opdagen van een inspecteur (cf. 4)
    the sudden appearance of an inspector

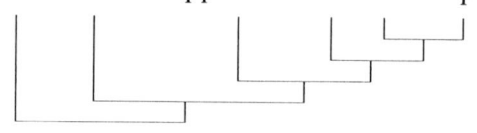

---

[8]Thus we seem to have a kind of 'ergative patterning' here: WITH inflection we have AGENTIVE SUBJECTS, WITHOUT it we have OBJECTS AND NON-AGENTIVE SUBJECTS. But note that the marking does not involve the nouns, and that the pattern is not absolutely general; cf. the discussion in the text.

A special case is the one that involves "predicatively" used adjectives. Here we would rather take the adjective and the infinitive as a complex predicate before adding the *van*-phrase as a further specification:

(18) het doorzichtig maken van allerlei samenhangen
      the transparent making of all-kinds-of connections

Note that this is still an INTERNAL participant; the participant modifies the infinitive before the entire group is added to the article (cf. the interpretation structures in 12 and 13).

Finally, note that the relation between interpretation structure and the differentiation of internal and external participant roles is not indicated grammatically, but only motivated pragmatically. What is grammatical is the inflection of the adjective: when it is there, the adjective is a modifier; when not, it may function like a head of a phrase. Thus we sometimes do encounter cases like 19:

(19) Waarom geen mogelijkheden gezocht in het stimuleren van *het coöperatief werken van aanwezige landbouwers*? (amb:52553)
      "Why not look for possibilities in (the) stimulating (of) *the cooperative working of farmers* present?"

Given the meaning of *werken* 'to work', there is no alternative to taking the farmers as external participants, more or less agentive. It must be noted, however, that 19 as it stands is not a very good sentence. Examination of the context reveals that the topic of the discourse is the question whether the farmers should go on working individually (with the risk of loosing their farms), or not. The absence of inflection here allows the adjectival idea to contribute directly to the development of the discourse theme, but as a consequence the meaning of "to work" is "downgraded," so to speak, to that of a modification of the concept of cooperation, which makes the sentence somewhat awkward.

Similarly, an infinitive with an inflected adjective occasionally has an 'object'-complement. Consider the following example:

(20) Zij hoefden zich niet met *het verachtelijke bewerken van de grond* bezig te houden.
"They did not have to occupy themselves with *the despicable working of the land.*"

The adjective provides as background information the motivation for the actual topic ("They," i.e. medieval noblemen) for not wanting to work the land: it is disgusting, they despise it. In fact, cases like 19 and 20 corroborate the analysis, since they are not excluded in principle, although they do require somewhat specific contexts, or might fit the context better if they were formulated differently.[9]

5. By way of conclusion: a methodological comment. In this paper, I have tried to recognize both the specific role of a grammatical morpheme, the suffix -*e*, and the way elements are, in ad hoc interpretations of sentences, grouped together (conceptualized independently or not). As a result, we have been able to give an integrated analysis of several phenomena, on the levels of phrases, sentences, and discourse. Thus, there are no separate theories (strictly ordered components of morphology, syntax, or pragmatics) for these levels; rather, they are just that many points on the continuum of "text," to the interpretation of which grammatical elements contribute, and which is structured, at least partially, in the process of interpretation itself.

---

[9] For instance, the only example like 20 in the Eindhoven Corpus (gbl:14363) might involve a mistake. It reads: *Zij daagde uit maar was tegelijkertijd schrikachtig-afwerend bij het ruige benaderen der mannelijke belustheid* 'She was provocative, but at the same time jumpy-repelling in the [her?] rough approach of male eagerness'.

References

Bolinger, D. L. 1965. "Linear modification." In D. L. Bolinger, *Forms of English. Accent, morpheme, order,* 279-307. Cambridge, Mass.: Harvard University Press.

Daalder, S. 1989. "Continuative relative clauses." In Norbert Reiter (ed.), *Sprechen und Hören. Akten des 23. Linguistischen Kolloquiums,* 195-207. Tübingen: Niemeyer.

Honselaar, W. 1980. "On the semantics of adjective-noun combinations." In A. A. Barendsen, B. M. Groen, R. Sprenger (eds.), *Studies in Slavic and general linguistics,* Volume I, 187-206. Amsterdam: Rodopi.

Pardoen, J. A. 1992. "The word order of final verbal elements in Dutch: free variation or meaningful organization?" This volume.

Renkema, J. 1981. *De taal van "Den Haag". Een kwantitatief-stilistisch onderzoek naar aanleiding van oordelen over taalgebruik.* 's-Gravenhage: Staatsuitgeverij.

Rooij, J. de. 1980. "Ons bruin(e) paard I/II." *Taal en Tongval: Tijdschrift voor Dialectologie* 32:3-25/109-129.

Verhagen, A. 1986. *Linguistic theory and the function of word order in Dutch. A study on interpretive aspects of the order of adverbials and noun phrases.* Dordrecht: Foris.

Dutch Modal Particles in Directive Sentences

Roel Vismans
University of Hull

1. Introduction. Particles have received more attention from linguists in the past few years than ever before. This may have something to do with the fact that particles are mainly pragmatic operators, and pragmatics as a sub-discipline of linguistics has become more prominent in the past ten years or so. This paper is about Dutch modal particles in directives; i.e., particles whose focus is an order, request, or command, and whose function is to modify that order, request, or command. It reports on an experimental study with the objective to determine the presence or absence of a rank order in a particular set of modal particles in Dutch. This set consists of the nine particles *dan, eens, even, maar, misschien, nou, ook, soms,* and *toch*. These nine particles have in common that they can be used in directives. However, before reporting on the experiment and discussing its results, the paper first briefly describes the syntactic paradigms within which these nine particles can occur, followed by a section on modality, and one on directives and politeness.

2. Syntactic paradigms. A precise definition of the word *directive* will be given in section 4. Suffice it to say here that *directive* is a pragmatic term for a category of sentences which are used by a speaker to get something done by the hearer. In Dutch, several syntactic paradigms offer themselves for this. First, straight imperatives can be used, e.g.:

Robert S. Kirsner (ed.), *The Low Countries and Beyond,* 111-121. Lanham, MD: University Press of America, 1993.

1. Ga (mp) zitten.
   "Sit down."

2. Kom (mp) binnen.
   "Come inside."

where (mp) indicates the position of the modal particle (or indeed particles, although clusters of particles are not discussed here). Questions can be used too, usually with a modal verb like *kunnen, mogen,* or *willen,* e.g.:

3. Kun je het raam (mp) dichtdoen?
   "Can you close the window?"

4. Wil je het zout (mp) aangeven?
   "Will you pass the salt?"

5. Mag ik de peper (mp) hebben?
   "May I have the pepper?"

When the question is used to elicit permission, the modal verbs *kunnen* or *mogen* are used:

6. Kan ik het raam (mp) dichtdoen?
   "Can I close the window?"

7. Mag ik je (mp) storen?
   "May I disturb you?"

Finally, statements with a modal verb expressing obligation (i.e. *moeten*) can also be used:

8. Je moet (mp) uitkijken.
   "You must watch out."

9. Je moet je (mp) vasthouden.
   "You must hold on tightly."

In each of these paradigms, a different sub-set of modal particles can be inserted in the slot indicated by (mp). In imperatives this sub-set consists of *dan, eens, even, maar, nou,* and *toch*. The sub-set for questions comprises *eens, even, misschien, nou, ook,* and *soms,* and that for statements *eens, even, maar,* and *ook*. As we can see, only *eens* and *even* can occur in all three paradigms. It should be noted here that a possible rank order (such as the present investigation tries to establish) would apply only to the separate sub-sets of modal particles that can occur in these syntactic paradigms and not across the board to the set of 'directive' modal particles taken as a whole. Furthermore, the option NOT to use a modal particle is always open to a speaker too, so each paradigm includes a zero-option (0). The various syntactic possibilities have been summarized in Table 1.

Table 1

Syntactic paradigms for directives in Dutch

Syntactic Paradigm	Possible Modal Particles
1. Imperative *Ga zitten.* *Kom binnen.*	*dan* *eens* *even* *maar* *nou* *toch*
2. Question *Kun je het raam dicht doen?* *Wil je het zout aangeven?* *Mag ik de peper hebben?* *Kan ik het raam dicht doen?* *Mag ik je storen?*	*eens* *even* *misschien* *nou* *ook* *soms*
3. Statement *Je moet uitkijken.* *Je moet je vasthouden.*	*eens* *even* *maar* *ook*

3.   **Modality.** Modality has been studied by philosophers, and more precisely logicians, since Aristotle. Linguists' interest in modality is, however, rather more recent. One of the main problems is of course that to adapt a logical system to something as inherently illogical as human language is very difficult, if not downright impossible. Nevertheless, the insights of modal logicians (such as Hintikka and Von Wright) have contributed significantly to the understanding of linguistic modality in recent decades.

In Volume 2 of his *Semantics,* Lyons distinguishes three basic kinds of modality: alethic, epistemic, and deontic. This is not necessarily an exhaustive list of possible kinds of modality, but it is sufficient for our present purposes. Of these, two are concerned with propositions. Alethic modality deals with their "necessary or contingent truth" (Lyons 1977, 791), and epistemic modality with their verifiability and falsifiability. Deontic modality, on the other hand, is not (or to be more precise, not directly) predicated of propositions in the way alethic and epistemic modality are. It is expressed in directives (orders, commands, requests) and it predicates the proposition which is also contained in the directive in such a way that the proposition "describes the state-of-affairs that will obtain if the act in question is performed" (ibid., 823). Within each kind of modality, there seems to be a basic polarity between necessity and possibility (e.g. verifiability/falsifiability in epistemic modality), which in the case of deontic modality can be rephrased as a polarity between obligation and permission (and, as Lyons points out, their "negative" counterparts: prohibition and exemption).

This polarity is recognised by other linguists, but instead of a rigid model with just the two poles, data for English, German, and Dutch seem to suggest more of a sliding scale of deontic modality ranging from obligation to permission (or vice versa). Lyons himself does not mention this possibility in the context of deontic modality, although he suggests a related scale for objective epistemic modality. Bearing in mind the vast complexity of deontically modalised expressions, which can include a range of modal verbs as well as modal particles, in a wide variety of languages, it seems that we can postulate such a sliding scale for deontic modality, operating between the deontically necessary and the deontically possible.

4. Directives and Politeness. The term directive was launched into the linguistic debate by Searle 1976, who saw directives as one of five categories of speech acts. The literature on speech acts has of course been quite prolific in the past twenty years, and it would be inappropriate to enter into a detailed discussion of speech act theory here. However, an interesting angle is provided by Leech 1983, who mentions speech acts in the context of a wide-ranging discussion of pragmatics. In this he draws on Grice's Co-operative Principle (1975), extending it to include several other Principles (of his own making), thus formulating his own "Interpersonal Rhetoric." For present purposes, Leech's most important addition to Grice's theory is the postulation of a Politeness Principle as a significant complement to the Co-operative Principle. A very brief explanation of what is meant by these Principles is perhaps required. Put simply, Grice's Co-operative Principle tries to capture the unwritten laws of normal human conversation, which tell people to speak truthfully, economically, with relevance and with clarity. Leech's Politeness Principle seems to add to that the unwritten laws of civilised verbal behaviour, which tell people to be tactful, generous, approbatory, modest, accordant, and sympathetic.

According to Searle's (1976:11) definition, directives "are attempts... by the speaker to get the hearer to do something." Leech accepts Searle's basic classification of speech acts (although he renames some of them; thus, directives become 'impositives'), and links directives to one of his own four types of 'illocutionary functions.' This is the competitive function where "the illocutionary goal competes with the social goal," the latter being defined as "establishing and maintaining comity" (Leech 1983:104), in other words: being polite. If the illocutionary goal of a directive is to force one's interlocutor into performing an action, usually for the benefit of the speaker, there is an obvious conflict with politeness.

Leech, through pragmatics and his own brand of speech act theory, provides a theoretical framework within which politeness can be studied. Brown and Levinson 1978 describe a wide variety of the actual politeness strategies which people apply, and which appear to be universally available. This has become a classic study of politeness phenomena with a wealth of examples from English, Tamil (spoken in

India and Sri Lanka), and Tzeltal (a Mexican Indian language). According to Brown and Levinson, every person has what is called 'face': "the public self-image that every member (of a society) wants to claim for himself" (Brown & Levinson 1978:66). Face has a positive and a negative aspect, where negative face may be paraphrased as the desire for privacy ("the want of every 'competent adult member' (of society) that his actions be unimpeded by others" (ibid., 67)), and positive face as the desire for recognition, affection, or love ("the want of every member that his wants be desirable to at least some others" (ibid.)). A person's face can be threatened by the actions of others, but since it is in everybody's interest that other people's face is maintained, we will want to minimize that threat. Therefore, a rather complicated process of choice is open to us. We can opt either to carry out the face-threatening act (FTA) or not to. If we choose to carry out the FTA, we can do it 'off record' or 'on record.' One of Brown and Levinson's examples of an off-the-record FTA is to say: "Damn, I'm out of cash, I forgot to go to the bank today." This may be explained as a request for a loan, but it can also be conveniently ignored. By performing a FTA on the record, the speaker commits himself or herself to it, but it can be done with or without 'redressive action.' If it is done without redressive action, it is done baldly; e.g., by means of a straight imperative, following Grice's Co-operative Principle (e.g.: "Lend me a fiver"). Redressive action, on the other hand, is a way of acknowledging the threat in the FTA and attempting to counteract it (and in the process breaking Grices's CP). This can be done by means of positive politeness or negative politeness (attempts to satisfy the hearer's positive or negative face respectively). An example of positive politeness would be to use a term of endearment and/or offer reassurance (e.g.: "Can I borrow five pounds from you dear? I'll pay you back tomorrow."). An example of negative politeness would be to question indirectly (e.g.: "Do you think you can lend me five pounds?").

Brown and Levinson chart forty politeness strategies: fifteen for positive politeness, ten for negative politeness, and fifteen for performing FTA's of the record. An explanation of the use of modal particles in directives in Dutch will have to be sought among the negative politeness strategies. A directive can be seen as a threat to the hearer's negative face, because it is an attempt on the part of the speaker to interfere with the hearer's freedom of action, an attempt to get the hearer to do something. Brown and Levinson's strategy 2 of negative politeness is formulated (in true speech-act-theory fashion in the shape of imperatives) as: question, hedge. And in Brown and Levinson's definition, a hedge is: "a particle, word, or phrase that modifies the degree of membership of a predicate or noun phrase in a set; it says of that membership that it is partial, or true only in certain respects, or that it is more true and complete than perhaps might be expected" (ibid., 150). Brown and Levinson continue to describe hedges expressed in particles in a number of languages (notably Tamil and Tzeltal) in great detail. And they acknowledge that a particular group of particles may have an internal rank order of politeness, corresponding to varying degrees of threat to the hearer's face.

5. **Dutch Modal Particles in Directives: A Quantitative Investigation.** If a case can be made for a sliding scale of deontic modality, as argued in section 3, and there is also a possible sliding scale of politeness in hedges, especially in connection with directives which are manifestations of deontic modality, then there might well be a correlation between the two scales. In that case there might equally well be a rank order of modal particles when used in connection with directives in the same syntactic paradigm, with one at the top of the scale expressing deontic necessity and being perceived as least polite, and another at the opposite end expressing deontic possibility and being perceived as most polite, with the remaining particles plotted at intervals between the two extremes.

This hypothesis was tested in a study carried out at the Erasmus University in Rotterdam in March 1990, in which a large group of law students were asked to take part. Eventually, the reactions of 111 subjects who took part and fulfilled certain criteria (native speakers of Dutch having lived in the Netherlands all their lives) were analysed. These students were asked to indicate for 52 pairs of sentences which of the two was the more forceful (the actual question was: *Geef voor ieder van de zinsparen aan uit welke van de twee zinnen volgens u de meeste dwang spreekt).* Each sentence was a mutation of the directive *de deur dichtdoen* 'close the door'. The 52 pairs were put together using 19 original sentences, seven imperatives *(doe de deur* (mp) *dicht),* seven questions *(kun je de deur* (mp) *dicht-doen?)*, and five statements *(je moet de deur* (mp) *dichtdoen)*. In each of these three categories, the only variable was the modal particle used (including 0), and sentences were only compared within each category. This led to 10 pairs of statements, and 21 pairs each of imperatives and questions.

The pairs were presented to the subjects in a random order, visually on slides and at the same time aurally on audio tape (with unmarked intonation). Each sentence pair was shown for ten seconds, with a spoken presentation at the beginning and at the end of the ten seconds, and each new pair was introduced by a short bleep. The subjects were given a sheet of paper with 52 pairs of boxes marked A and B, and were instructed to record their choice for each pair as A or B by putting a cross in the appropriate box. They were also asked to provide information relating to their age, sex, and their geographic history. In all, the test took no longer than 20 minutes and was conducted just once in a large lecture theatre.

This particular presentation was arrived at after a pilot study, comparing this method with a seemingly more straightforward method of testing, which involved subjects grading each sentence for forcefulness on a scale from one to seven. In this pilot study (reported in Vismans 1991), the data from the binary choice test (as used in the Rotterdam experiment) proved more reliable.

The data from the test carried out in Rotterdam were analysed using the frequencies function of the statistical computer package SPSS-X. This computed the scores for each sentence in a pair, thus indicating which of the two sentences was seen by general consensus of the subjects to be more forceful (and by implication less polite). If the subjects were consistently applying an underlying rank order in their choices, this would lead to the emergence of this ranking. For if sentence x in pair $A(x,y)$ is more polite than sentence y, and sentence x in pair $B(x,z)$ is more polite than sentence z, and sentence z in pair $C(y,z)$ is more polite than sentence y, then we can establish a ranking in which x is most polite and y is least polite.

This can be demonstrated using the category statements in the study. The outcome of the frequency count for statements is given in

Table 2

Frequencies of votes for each modal particle in: *Je moet de deur* (mp) *dichtdoen* 'You must (mp) close the door' in answer to the question "Which of the two sentences is the more forceful?"

mp	count in %	x>y	60.4% consistent
maar	7.2		1.5
ook	92.8	*ook*	98.5
even	83.8		92.5
maar	16.2	*even*	7.5
0	59.5		53.7
eens	40.5	*0*	46.3
eens	58.6		62.7
ook	41.4	*eens*	37.3
0	62.2		67.2
ook	37.8	*0*	32.8
even	29.7		25.4
ook	70.3	*ook*	74.6
eens	76.6		80.6
even	24.4	*eens*	19.4
0	86.5		89.6
even	12.6[*]	*0*	10.4
eens	88.3		94.0
maar	11.7	*eens*	6.0
0	96.4		97.0
maar	3.6	*0*	3.0

[*] 0.9% gave a nil return

Table 2, on the preceding page. Column 1 of Table 2 gives the particular pair of modal particles, column 2 the "votes" for each modal particle in percentages, and column 3 indicates which of the modal particles has been "voted" the more forceful, and by implication less polite. What we can see from Table 2 is the clear emergence of a ranking with the sentence with *maar* as the most polite and the one with 0 as the least polite. It is important to stress here that this table does not indicate the degree to which one sentence is more polite than another (and indeed the whole experiment is not geared to finding out the "distance" between the modal particles concerned). The politeness ratings are, therefore, relative.

Reference was made earlier to the assumed consistency of the subjects' application of their internal rank order. An ideal, homogeneous speech community would of course be in complete agreement about the rank order of modal particles. However, speech communities are rarely, if ever, homogeneous. Hence, it cannot be assumed that each subject would apply exactly the same rank order. But what can be assumed is that subjects would apply their individual rank orders consistently. It has been possible to work out which subjects were in fact consistently applying their rank order, and which were not, with 60.4% of the subjects being consistent. The frequency count of just those consistent cases is given in column 4 of Table 2 and it shows that except in one case, the votes have become more polarised, more clear-cut.

What does this tell us? It seems to lead to the conclusion that in Dutch statement directives, there is a rank order of politeness in the sub-set of possible modal particles that can be used, which (going from least polite to most polite) looks as follows:

0, eens, ook, even, maar.

And in conjunction with a possible scale of deontic modality, this rank order seems to suggest that it does indeed exist. Remember that in section 2 we rephrased the necessity-possibility polarity in deontic modality as a polarity between obligation and permission. *Je moet de deur maar dichtdoen* seems to lie closer to the possibility end of that polarity (permission) and *Je moet de deur eens dichtdoen* lies closer to the necessity end of the polarity (obligation), with the sentence with the 0-option (*Je moet de deur dichtdoen* 'You must close the door') reaching the top of the scale.

A detailed analysis of the imperative sentences and questions has not yet been completed, and space does not permit presentation of the data here. However, initial indications seem to suggest that in these categories, too, the modal particles have a definite rank order.

References

Brown, P. & S. Levinson. 1978. "Universals in language usage: Politeness phenomena." In E. N. Goody (ed.) *Questions and politeness: Strategies in social interaction,* 56-289, Cambridge: Cambridge University Press.

Grice, H. P. 1975. "Logic and conversation." In P. Cole, P. & J. L. Morgan (eds.) *Syntax and Semantics,* vol. 3: *Speech Acts,* 41-58. New York: Academic Press.

Leech, G. N. 1983. *Principles of pragmatics.* London: Longman.

Lyons, J. 1977. *Semantics.* Cambridge: Cambridge University Press.

Searle, J. 1976. "A classification of illocutionary acts." *Language in Society* 5:1-23.

Vismans, R. 1991. "Dutch modal particles in directive sentences and modalized directives in English": *Multilingua* 10:111-122.

Literature

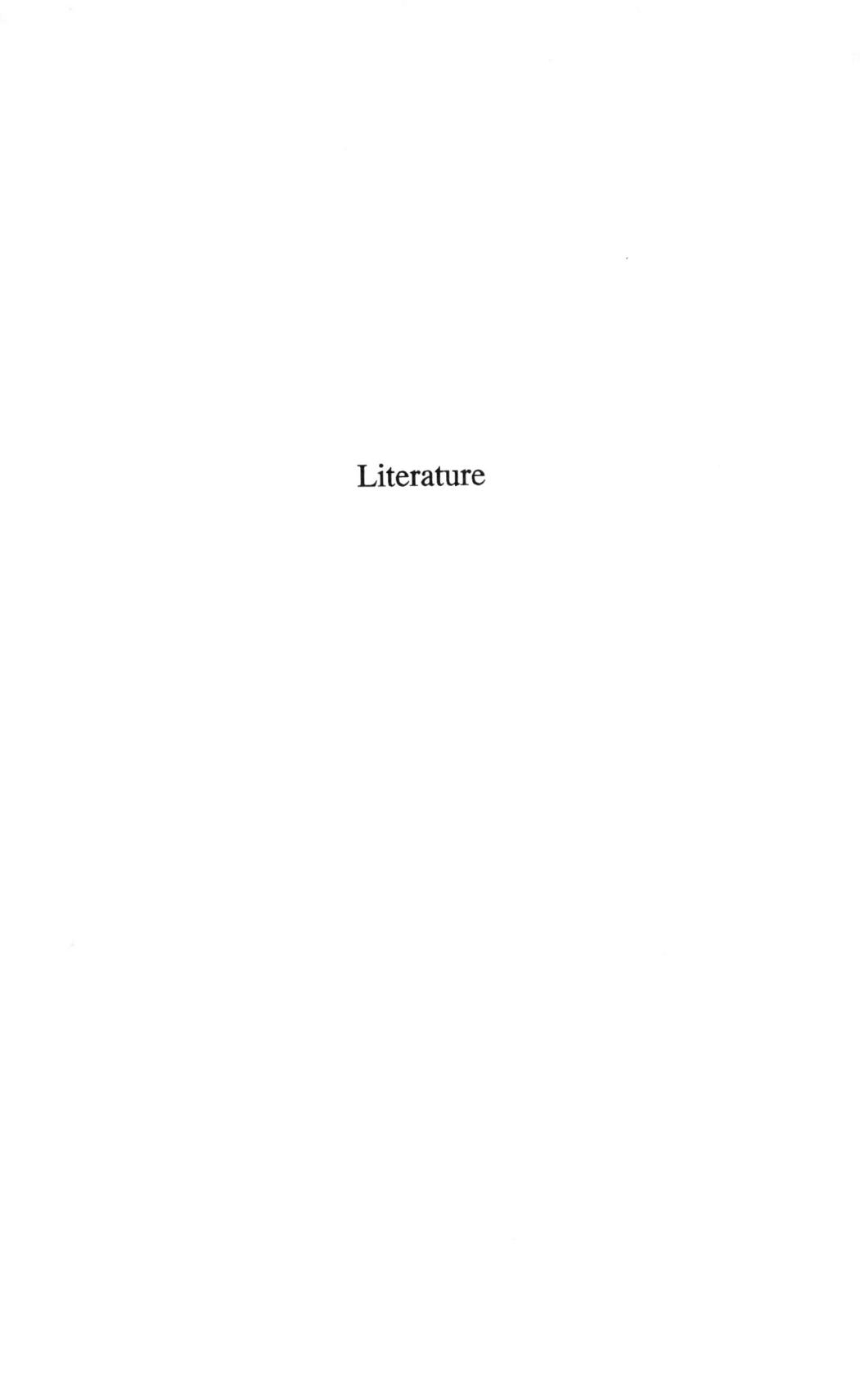

Object of Desire and Undesired Knowledge in Multatuli's *Woutertje Pieterse*

Gary Lee Baker
Denison University, Granville, Ohio

Although Multatuli's *Woutertje Pieterse* is not a story in the traditional sense, i.e., one that incorporates a sense of closure or reconciliation, it is a narrative woven together by recurring themes and, of course, by its protagonist Wouter Pieterse. Peter King writes: "This is not a novel, he tells us, and if it were, it would not be written like this. It *is* a narration (*een geschiedenis*) but it is also poetry, the author's lyrical utterance."[1] The Woutertje-narrative lacks any kind of formal structure and defies traditional conceptions of genre. Nonetheless, as all narration, it contains, or is the result of, the desire to communicate something. As Peter Brooks states, "Desire is always there at the start of a narrative, often in a state of initial arousal, often having reached a state of intensity such that movement must be created, action undertaken, change begun."[2] Our narrator, who apparently works from archives, notes, and memory,[3] is courageous

---

[1] Peter King, *Multatuli*, Twayne World Authors Series 219 (New York: Twayne Publishers, Inc., 1972): 112.

[2] Peter Brooks, *Reading for the Plot* (New York: Vintage Books, 1985): 38.

[3] In talking about the type of collar Wouter wears to work, the narrator explains that s/he cannot say with certainty what the fashion was at the time, "Because of a regretful gap in my archive — unfortunately more traces of this will turn up" "Door 'n verdrietige gaping in m'n archief — daarvan zullen zich méér sporen vertonen, helaas! — ..." Multatuli, *Woutertje Pieterse*, ed. Garmt Stuiveling (Amsterdam; G. A. van Oorschot, 1950): 338. The narrator's memory is part of that archive. S/he cannot remember specific places sometimes, "Also

Robert S. Kirsner (ed.), *The Low Countries and Beyond*, 125-137. Lanham, MD: University Press of America, 1993.

enough to commence with the story despite considering it a difficult task, "Er is moed nodig om 'n verhaal te doen aanvangen in een plaats die op 'dam' uitgaat."[4] (7) Of course the city is Amsterdam. A setting that ends in "dam" is already an indication that the story will not finish, because a "dam" is a blocking device, in this case blocking the flow of narrative. The fact that no reconciliation takes place in Woutertje's story indicates clearly that the narrator does not have control or mastery of his/her material.[5] This becomes most evident in Wouter as he shifts his focus from one object of desire to another.

One who intends to write something about *Woutertje Pieterse* is inclined to grasp for materials that deal with how books are structured, their openings, endings and middles. Edward Said states in his book *Beginnings,* "...for the writer, the historian, or the philosopher the beginning will emerge reflectively and, perhaps, unhappily, already engaging him in an awareness of its difficulty."[6] The story does not begin with Woutertje's birth but with the moment he is exposed to the

---

without referring to my complete lack of memory for locales — there is not a town, place, or village where I know the way — ..." "Ook zonder me nu te beroepen op m'n volslagen gebrek aan lokaal-memorie — er is geen stad, vlek of dorp in de wereld, waar ik de weg weet — ..." (304). When describing boys who sing a nasty song to a drunken preacher, the narrator admits, "I was not able to retain that poetic work. Which is a shame. And to *make up* something and pass it off as the exact text contradicts my principles." "Ik heb dat dichtstuk niet kunnen machtig worden. Wat jammer is. En iets te *maken* en dat uit te geven als de juiste tekst, strijdt tegen mijn principes" (57).
    It should be noted here that all further references to the text of *Woutertje Pieterse* in the present article are to the edition by Stuiveling cited above. All translations from Dutch into English are my own. To my knowledge, no decent translation of *Woutertje Pieterse* exists in English as yet.

[4]"Courage is necessary in order to go ahead with a story in a place that ends in 'dam'"

[5]I will continue to refer to the narrator as his/her because I am not yet sure who it is. Though Multatuli, whoever that is, appears to be the author, the narrator cannot be determined because s/he seems to have no body in the text. None of the persons in the novel reacts to the narrator although s/he is continuously present. And since the repetition of experience is often the motivation for narrative, the narrator could only be one of two figures. It is either "Fancy" retelling the unpleasant loss of Wouter as hope for imagination in society, or Wouter lamenting his loss of "Fancy" due to his quest for the middle-class lifestyle. Only these two could have been present in all instances in the text.

[6]Edward Said, *Beginnings: Intention and Method* (New York: Basic Books, Inc., Publishers, 1975): 35.

influences of Fancy, meaning the initial point at which his desires in life scrape against the rough, solid, and petrified surface of Dutch middle-class values. The story-worthy conflict commences with the main character on his way to sell his New Testament for the works of a romance writer named Glorioso. The reader is offered a story with little sense of a beginning and even less of a feeling of conclusiveness. Frank Kermode explains in *The Sense of an Ending,* "We cannot, of course, be denied an end; it is one of the great charms of books that they have to end."[7] In *Woutertje* the reader is denied just that; there is a last word in the narrative, "introduceren" (501), which incidentally sounds more like the start of something than an ending. The ending we receive is obviously interrupted and not of the type intimated by Herrnstein Smith in *Poetic Closure,* "Perhaps all we can say... is that varying degrees or states of tension seem to be involved in all our experiences, and that the most gratifying ones are those in which whatever tensions are created are also released."[8] In *Woutertje* the reader is essentially left hanging in a state of tension. Will Wouter regain his proper clothing and become a solid middle-class citizen, or will Fancy become his ultimate object of desire, whereby he will grow to be a tragic and romantic outsider-figure like Max Havelaar? The courage spoken of above appears to run out by the end of the narrative; when Multatuli puts his pen down for the last time the reader (and narrator?) remains suspended in the story-line with the quest for Wouter's jacket and cap.

What was so compelling about Wouter's story that moved a narrator to fill over 500 pages of text without a reconciliation? Because Wouter represents hope or a utopian element in Dutch society. Without the story Wouter's romantic impulses would otherwise remain unnoticed within their framework of a congealed middle-class mentality, complete with moral codes, ideology, and sense of place. How does the narrator know that these impulses exist in Wouter? If s/he cannot know simple details, place names etc., how can s/he know and

---

[7]Frank Kermode, *The Sense of an Ending: Studies in the Theory of Fiction* (New York. Oxford U P, 1967): 23.

[8]Barbara Herrnstein Smith, *Poetic Closure: A Study of How Poems End* (Chicago: U of Chicago P, 1968): 3.

understand Wouter's mind and soul? Is Fancy the narrator? One is led to believe this from the fragment that precedes the Woutertje pieces; Fancy is asked to tell (actually whisper) a story, "LIEVE FANCY, wilt ge my een sprookje vóórzeggen?"[9] When one speaks of a good story, this is more a compliment to the narrator than the author. The author lends his/her name to the book, provides it with a title, and signs the copies you buy at his/her reading. The author provides a face to the work, often in the form of a picture on the dust cover. But, the narrator tells the story; s/he places one word after the other such that it grows into narrative. It is important, especially in *Woutertje Pieterse* not to confuse the two. The narrator is a poetic spirit that makes sense of the ideas and events that go together to make up the narrative. The narrator in *Woutertje Pieterse* understands the value of an imagination willing, courageous, and diverse enough to engage in the truth of poetic expression.

Woutertje's story depicts the life of a child who exists between being educated to become a competitive subject within society, and his attempts to transcend such boundaries and limitations by means of "Fancy" and/or imagination. Thus, his desire divides into ego-drives, which strive for death, and sexual drives, which are life affirmative, as Freud discusses them in "Beyond the Pleasure Principle," "The upshot of our enquiry so far has been the drawing of a sharp distinction between "ego-instincts" and the sexual instincts, and the view that the former exercise pressure towards death and the latter towards a prolongation of life."[10] By the close (not closure) of the narrative we find Wouter's attention shifting from an object of desire that constitutes a life-affirmative attitude in "Fancy" to a death-affirmative drive depicted in his desire to re-acquire his middle-class attire. The Bible and clothing represent objects of desire that constitute an ideological, religious, and social consensus, which Wouter's mother and brother Stoffel insist he join. They signify a life of containment and formal training. According to Freud, "Death is rather a matter of

---

[9]"DEAR FANCY, would you whisper a little tale to me?" Multatuli, *Ideeën*, 7 vols. (Amsterdam: Salamander Em. Querido's Uitgeverij, 1985) 1:240.

[10]Sigmund Freud, *Beyond the Pleasure Principle,* trans. and ed. James Strachey, International Psycho-Analytical Library 4 (New York: Liveright Publishing, 1961): 38.

expediency, a manifestation of adaptation to the external conditions of life..."[11] Wouter's desire for Fancy signifies his rejection of measures to form him into a competitive, and thereby, productive member of the Dutch middle-class. Thus, Wouter's bifurcated desire is caught between life and death affirmative impulses. Poetry is to be his savior from a life of dullness and triviality, hence Fancy's interest in him.

Wouter tells the wonder tale of Kusco, Telasco, and Aztalpha, which represents a poetic protest against competition for power, wealth, and influence. It is not by coincidence that the figures in the story are aristocratic and that it takes place, "Ver van hier en lang geleden..."[12] (90) Since the basis of middle-class existence is competition for possessions, Woutertje is risking his place in society by not joining in the struggle for material gain dictated by the middle-class mentality. Actually Wouter desires to abandon one form of competition for another. The struggle for power, money, and material is inherently life-negative. Life-positive is the competition for *knowledge* as we read in Multatuli's *Ideeën*:

> ...overal is juist die brandende begeerte tot éénzyn met het onbekende, de oorzaak onzer beweging, dat is: van ons *bestaan*. Het spreekt dus vanzelf dat dit bestaan vernietigd werd, wanneer het bereiken van 't doel mogelyk ware. En deze onmogelykheid stelt alzo de derde soort van kracht daar, die ons instand houdt: opstand tegen het verbod, behoefte aan *strijd*.[13]

Subjective, self-serving, ideological modes of thought have long since taken over where formerly there existed an objective, albeit aristocratic, world order, not based on money-acquiring structures, but on personages. For example, a king is a personage, not an office;

---

[11] Freud, 40.

[12] "Far from here and long ago..."

[13] "...just that burning desire for unity with the unknown is everywhere, the cause of our movement, that is: of our *existence*. It goes without saying then that this existence would be destroyed if reaching that goal were possible. And this impossibility portrays thus the third type of force, which maintains us: rebellion against prohibition, need for *struggle*." Multatuli, *Ideeën*, 7 vols. (Amsterdam: Salamander Em. Querido's Uitgeverij, 1985) 2:266.

aristocratic government cannot be effectively depicted as machine-like with interchangeable parts, like "enlightened," constitutional governments. As we find in *Max Havelaar* and in *Vorstenschool*, there exists a positive attitude toward monarchs, especially benevolent ones, which is also reflected in *Woutertje Pieterse*, "Er bestaat dan tevens kans, nader kennis te maken met prinses Erika, bij welke gelegenheid we misschien te weten komen, dat aristocratie van verstand en hart niet uitsluitend behoeft gezocht te worden in de...lagere standen..."[14] (335) The narrator insinuates that the middle-class has no capacity for emotional sensitivity when s/he explains that not everyone can understand Femke's emotions, "Femke zou begrepen zijn geworden door lager gemeen, of door adel. 't Is met gevoel, als met het goud der speelbanken. Dat komt niet in aller handen."[15] (101) One does not think of the aristocracy as having financial troubles, nonetheless, a prince or princess does not partake in petty competition to gain his/her wealth; at least they are not depicted this way in Multatuli's texts. There exists an express difference in the type or level of competition. Compared to the struggle for truth, which is intrinsically poetic for Multatuli,[16] and breaking out of the ego-boundaries that dictate competition on a trivial level, the struggle for money and other material goods is of a lower level. Nonetheless, Wouter must learn the lowest tasks in life, i.e., recognize his "naastbij-liggende werkelijkheid" (337)

---

[14]"There exists also, then, a chance to make better acquaintance with princess Erika, by which opportunity we will perhaps come to know that aristocracy of the mind and heart does not exclusively have to be sought in the... lower classes..." As we can see "aristocratie" possesses its figurative and literal meaning. Aristocratic feelings and reason are the highest forms, which can, paradoxically, be found in the lowest classes of society. An aristocrat harbors here "aristocratic" emotions. The main point is that these emotions and this brand of reason are not found in the middle-class, except in our protagonist. This is one reason Wouter is such a utopian element.

[15]"Femke would be understood by the lower common folk, or by nobility. With feeling, it is the same as with the gold of the gambling houses. It does not come into just anybody's hands."

[16]"There is nothing more poetic than the truth. He who finds no poetry in it, shall always remain out there a miserable little poet." "Er is niets poëtischer dan de waarheid. Wie dáárin geen poëzie vindt, zal steeds 'n pover poëetje blyven daarbuiten." Multatuli, *Ideeën* 1:168.

before he can rise up to the level of "*Poëzie der Werkelijkheid.*"[17] (335) Not surprisingly the lowest tasks in life are performed in the Owetijd & Kopperlith company. The type of competition Wouter enters into in the business world is in the words of one worker there, "Allemaal wind en 'n engelse *notting.*"[18] (393)

It is interesting that the company in which Wouter learns the lowest tasks in society deals in textiles. The significance of laundry and linens in Multatuli's texts is undeniable. Femke and Vrouw Claus both work with laundry: Fancy, in the *Minnebrieven* works with clothing, washing them and mending them; in *Vorstenschool* the characters depicted with good hearts, Hanna and Landsheil, are a "naaister" (seamstress) and a "klerenmaker" (tailor) respectively. The two notions, textiles and poetics, come especially close as Albert, Hanna's fiancé, reads his latest creation as Hanna sews.[19] There is a definite relation between spiritual, emotional, and intellectual superiority, and persons who work with or make clothing. An explanation of this connection lies in the etymology of textile, which is derived from the Latin *texo,* meaning to weave, to entwine, or represent in tapestry. Interestingly, its third meaning in the *Oxford Latin Dictionary* is to construct a complex structure like a ship or "writings and other mental products."[20] Thus clothing or textiles represent an allegory of poetics and become a metaphor for Fancy's creation of narrative, "En spint de vlok tot draad/ Tot doek, waarop zij, eindloos voortbordurend,/ De loop van al wat is, te aanschouwen geeft./ En wie 't verband ontkent, is schuldig blind,/ Ter nauwernood onschuldig wie 't niet kent!"[21] (247) The complex allegory of *poëzie* becomes clear. Princess Erika, for example, represents the sublime not only signified by her aristocratic

---

[17]"most immediate reality" (337) and "*Poetics of Reality*" (335).

[18]"Nothing but wind and an English *notting*"

[19]Multatuli, *Vorstenschool* (Amsterdam: Uitgevers-Maatschappij "Elsevier," 1919): 58-60.

[20]"Texo," *Oxford Latin Dictionary,* 1982 ed.

[21]"And spins the flock into thread/into cloth, upon which she, endlessly embroidering,/ offers to behold, the course of everything that exists./And he who denies the connection, is guilty of blindness,/barely innocent he who does not know it."

heritage but also by her behavior. She is a cat-like figure difficult to pursue; as such she represents the sublime as aloof, unapproachable, undisciplined, yet noble. Opposite princess Erika stands Femke as a representation of daily existence and practical work. Furthermore, Erika has the desire to become a laundry girl like Femke (460), and Femke could have been aristocracy (309). Having felt Fancy's sting, the sublime and the practical blend in Wouter's perception (177). Together Femke, Fancy, and Erika represent a *teritum* (267 and 335), that influences Wouter in his desire for knowledge and Fancy, as well as his struggle against societal limitations. To be successful in his struggle to become *poëtisch*, Wouter must allow all three to influence him. He can receive love from all three while learning about the sublime, practicality (het gewone), and the power of imagination from the individual figures. All three are necessary for the ability to produce *poëzie*. Otherwise, as the narrator explains, the nature of Wouter's social class dictates that he remain "*onpoëtisch*" (122-123).

What prevents our narrator and author from finishing his/her "complex structure," about which we are reminded several times that it is not a novel but a story, a narration, "een geschiedenis." Are we as readers allowed to expect a reconciliation of the carefully wrought tensions in Wouter's life? It is obvious that Wouter is not pleased or satisfied with reality as he perceives it. He wishes to change what he sees, "'Later, later!' dacht hij. Later, als-i bevrijd zou zijn van schoolse en huiselijke banden. Dan zoud-i 'n werelddeel gelukkig maken. En nog een. En nóg een...'"[22] (177) Wouter's intentions are not only qualitatively noble but also in the simple fact that he wishes to make these continents happy as king — "koning van Afrika" (176) for example. However, our narrator conveys to us that pure dreaming has no place in the world and remains an illusion in the life-affirmative, reality-negative, posture of the dreamer. The person who rejects reality is certainly a utopian figure, but guiding such a figure requires that s/he remain within reality while maintaining utopian impulses of dreaming and a will toward change. We must bear in mind the motif of clothing and work with clothing; the metaphor of poetics is intertwined with the tasks of the day. After Pater Jansen praises how well Femke mends his

---

[22]"'Later, later!' he thought. Later, if he were free from the bonds of school and home. Then he would make a continent happy. And another. And yet another...'"

underwear we read the lines, "De hoogheid van Fancy versmaadde 't rangverschil tussen paters onderbroeken en de melkweg."[23] (219) As the narrator explains, the poetics of reality stands much higher than "liefelijk bontgekleurde — maar kinderachtige, onvoedzame en verderfelijke — dromerij!"[24] (335) This explains why Femke tells him to be the best in school within three months (163) and Holsma's shift from an apparently free-thinking, liberal person to one who encourages Wouter to adjust his focus from the temporally and spatially far away, to the immediate here and now:

> ik was ook zo! — ze komt grotendeels voort uit luiheid. Het is gemakkelijker zich te verbeelden dat men zweeft boven 'n berg die heel in de verte ligt, dan in werkelijkheid z'n voet op te lichten om over 'n steentje te stappen.... Vraag altijd jezelf af: 'wat wordt er *op dit ogenblik* van me gevorderd?' en gebruik niet de ingenomenheid met het vermeend hogere, als voorwendsel tot verwaarlozing van wat je lager toeschijnt. Je bent ontevreden met je tegenwoordig standpunt? Wel, maak je 'n beter standpunt waard!... Vraag jezelf bij elke gelegenheid af: wat is m'n *naastbijliggende* plicht?[25] (331)

The narrator is making a case here for literature that not only rejects reality the way it is, but one that is suitable to bring about change in that reality. The task is not to switch worlds but to change the one in front of you. Poetics suited to aid in this cannot be "verdraaide poëzie en valse romantiek."[26] (163)

---

[23]"The highness of Fancy spurned the difference in rank between father's underwear and the Milky Way."

[24]"sweetly colored — but childlike, unsubstantial and pernicious — dreaminess"

[25]"I was that way too! — it occurs for the most part due to laziness. It is easier to imagine that one is floating over a mountain that lies far off in the distance than to pick up one's foot to step over a little stone.... Always ask yourself: 'what is being demanded of me at this moment?' and do not use the satisfaction of the alleged sublime, as a pretext for neglecting what appears to you to be lower. You're dissatisfied with your present position? Well, make yourself worth a better position!... Ask yourself at every opportunity: what is my *most immediate* duty?"

[26]"Disguised poetry and false romanticism" (163)

We should recall that Wouter first encountered Fancy at the windmills near Femke's house. She did not come to him in a dream or vision. Fancy spied a capable person as Wouter rid himself of his Bible, i.e., his ideological handbook for inclusion in the middle-class as a complete and solid citizen. She spies a soul that writes a poem about bandits instead of about virtue as he was supposed to. Fancy's voice comes to Wouter out of a machine. What could present a greater metaphor of the triumph of Dutch middle-class society than the windmill? When the winds (of change for example) blow against this machine they become even more resolute in their task of grinding or sawing for profit. The windmill becomes a metaphor for the way society works in all its intricacy and machine-like qualities; one is reminded here of Pennewip's hermetic categorizations of members of the Dutch middle-class (21). Fancy had to come to Wouter out of the run-of-the-mill, practical world in order to take advantage of his "romanziekte" (9), i.e., imagination and desire to change the world; she did not want to lose him to an escapist's mode of poetics. The dream world is not Fancy's home but rather the open niches of imagination and genuine love that she finds in reality. As he listens to the sawmills working they reveal their names "Morgenstond" and "Arend," signifying a new beginning (morning hour) above the earth (eagle). Together the mills sing the name Fancy (25).

Wouter's training is quite clear; he knows what he has to learn, but our narrator is not certain how to bring this about. A reader of the *Woutertje* narrative develops the impression that the ending is being avoided or even thwarted due to indecision about what to do with Wouter. He is caught between two objects of desire that comprise the oppositions that create tension throughout the text. When Holsma communicates to Wouter that he must first become acquainted "met het állerlaagste"[27] (335), in reality he meant trade and business, the arena of struggle for what the narrator termed "*machine infernale*" (9) or money. For Wouter, regaining his clothing means being accepted again in society, which is his main concern when the narrative ceases. He cannot simply break from society: "Hij was niet grof genoeg van inborst om de draden waarmed-i zich aan de maatschappij verbonden

---

[27]"With the absolute lowest"

voelde, eenvoudig te verbreken en zich vrij te maken..."[28] (448) There is an obvious shift in the object of desire from a romantic quest for Fancy and poetics to the mundane matters of middle-class life, having the proper clothing in order to be seen on the street. The Bible, which Wouter gives up in the beginning and the jacket and hat he sells for the benefit of the Calbb family, to repay them for a parasol he broke, sandwich the multifaceted entity of Fancy, who gets repressed in Wouter's psyche. The initial line of the chapter, in which Wouter is depicted getting up for work, reads, "Fancy's luim had alzo voor ditmaal uitgestormd... en de lezer wordt nogmaals uitdrukkelijk uitgenodigd z'n verwachting op de leest van het dagelijkse te schoeien." (336) From here on Wouter is occupied with repressing his romantic impulses, "terzijdestelling van utopieën en fantastische begeerten..."[29] (336) Whenever he thinks of events or people in his life who might distract him from the hic et nunc he looks at the picture of Mercury, "die... ook geen kleren aan 't lijf had"[30] (346) hanging on the wall in the office. The desire for death manifests itself quite literally when Wouter decides he wants to commit suicide after breaking the parasol. But his spiritual death had already taken place in the office of Owetijd & Kopperlith:

> De romantiek was — niet voor altoos, waarschijnlijk — uitgeput, geknot, bedorven. Zijn worsteling tegen afdwalen begon vrucht te dragen, en de inspanning om zich met niets te bemoeien dan wat allernaast voor de hand lag, werd pijnlijker omdat hij met de hem ingegeven nietigheden z'n ziel niet voeden kon. Hij was iemand die men 't ongezond gebruik van snoeperij verbiedt, en

---

[28] "He did not have a rough enough disposition simply to break the strings, with which he felt bound to society, and make himself free."

[29] "Fancy's mood is all stormed out for now... and the reader is again expressly invited to direct his expectations along the lines of daily tasks" and "putting aside utopias and fantastic desires."

[30] "who didn't have a stich of clothing on either."

inplaats daarvan op zaagsel en zand onthaalt, of... op niets. (389-390)[31]

In short, his whole time at work is characterized by control over his wishes for romantic endeavors and free thinking, because Wouter, "aan 't breidelen van z'n begeerten zo bijzonder behoefte had."[32] (416) The Fancy part of his psychological economy is not being developed and in fact being smothered and killed off. He has all but forfeited the desire devoted to Fancy and poetics, "De bloemen zijner fantasie waren verlept en geurloos geworden." and "Wouter had sedert einige tijd het poëtizeren verleerd. Hij durfde 't niet, omdat hij reden had zich te schamen voor 't liefelijke."[33] (435) Earlier Wouter had seen Femke on the street but was so ashamed of his life style that he did not call to her. The narrator explains that Wouter would have avoided his friends Dr. Holsma and Pater Jansen as well (426). Femke could save him from the stifling and damaging atmosphere of the Kopperlith household; he runs to her after the embarrassing incident with the parasol. However, the narrator does not allow him to to see her and claims " — maar zo ver zijn we nog niet."[34] (436) The narrator does not wish to proceed further in any real sense and has injected here (another) delaying device so that the end is avoided. When Wouter breaks the parasol and the first serious thoughts of death enter his mind, the narrator refers to them as a "wenselijke uitweg" (444). Does s/he mean a way out of the narrative? Is this his/her opportunity for conclusiveness? The narrator cannot bring her/himself

---

[31]"The romanticism was — not forever, probably — exhausted, knotted up, spoiled. His struggle against going astray began to carry fruit, and the effort to not trouble himself with anything but what immediately lay at hand, became more painful because he could not feed his soul with the trivialities dictated to him. He was someone for whom the unhealthy consumption of sweets is forbidden, and instead of that is given a diet of saw dust and sand, or... nothing."

[32]"had such a great a need to bridle his desires."

[33]"The flowers of his fantasy became wilted and without aroma" and "Wouter had since some time lost his talent for poetry. He didn't dare try it because he had reasons to be ashamed of that which is sweet."

[34]"but we're not quite that far yet"

to terminate the narrative. To kill Wouter off would be to destroy a truly utopian element in the mundane world of middle-class existence.

But why should the narrator be reluctant to make just that statement: "Wouter cannot exist in our society, should we not change it to include people like him and be the better off for it?" There is a definite resistance to closure where the narrative ceases with a romantic on a rather unromantic quest, i.e., regaining his middle-class identity. D. A. Miller claims, "The text of obsession or idiosyncrasy is intrinsically interminable; as it can never be properly concluded, it can only be arbitrarily abandoned."[35] Peter King reminds us, "*Max Havelaar* was written in a few weeks, *Woutertje Pieterse* was unfinished after seventeen years."[36] Let us assume then that Woutertje did become an obsession of its author and narrator. Multatuli and his narrator were not wanting to work themselves out of the corner they had written themselves into. Either Wouter remains in his hideous looking jacket and the outsider he actually is, or he regains his clothes and returns to the Kopperliths with money for the parasol and reconciliation, in every sense of the word. Even this is made uncertain by the narrator as s/he depicts Wouter spending the money given to him by princess Erika for buying back his jacket. On the ferry to Haarlem many eyes have noticed that Wouter has money, will it get stolen? Will Wouter spend it all? Will he find the shop where he sold his jacket? At this point not even the narrator knows. If Multatuli had lived 30 years longer the Wouter-narrative would simply have been twice as long and little more than a collection of clever dilatory devices. The narrative's inconclusiveness is due to the undesired knowledge that Wouter cannot exist in middle-class society without either abandoning his desire for Fancy, or his desire to remain anchored in society. The former would doom him to an outsider's existence, in which he would physically perish, and the latter would mean a mundane existence, in which he would spiritually perish. There was no satisfying way to end the narrative. Suspended squarely between objects of desire, Wouter progresses nowhere due to the narrator's and Multatuli's undesired knowledge.

---

[35]D. A. Miller, *Narrative and Its Discontents: Problems of Closure in the Traditional Novel* (Princeton: Princeton U P, 1981): 41.

[36]King, 100.

Dutch Tenses and the Analysis of a Literary Text: The Case of Marga Minco's *De val*

Saskia Daalder and Arie Verhagen
Free University, Amsterdam

1. Introduction. In this paper we will present some aspects of the analysis of Marga Minco's fine novella *De val (The Fall)*, which came out in 1983 after many years of silence on the part of this widely admired author of well-constructed and balanced prose. Our first aim is to enrich the understanding of this novella — no doubt already quite detailed — of those interested in Minco's work. Secondarily, we wish to show that literary interpretation may take advantage of elements of linguistic analysis — the latter being our true profession.[1]

Let us start with a short overview of the novella. The all-important event of *De val* is the accident of an old lady, who falls into a manhole which has been left open and unattended, without safety gates being placed around it. The manhole is filled with boiling water and the old lady, named Frieda, suffers a horrible death. The accident is the more tragic because some forty years earlier, in the determining event of her life, Frieda was the only one of her Jewish family to escape deportation and death at the hands of the Nazis. Just as blind fate took the life of her loved ones then while sparing herself, it has now finally claimed her as a victim. The circumstances of the events then and now comprise quite a few similarities, a parallelism which is carefully exploited by Minco, as one might expect.

---

[1] The research for this paper was done within research programme LETT 88/10, Vrije Universiteit Amsterdam.

Robert S. Kirsner (ed.), *The Low Countries and Beyond,* 139-150. Lanham, MD: University Press of America, 1993.

Now for our contribution to the interpretation of *De val*, let us take as a starting point a piece of information which is mentioned in several essays on the novella (cf. Middeldorp 1981-84). Evidently, Marga Minco got the idea for her book from a newspaper report: such an accident really did occur. It is also mentioned that the lady in question was the mother of Minco's sister-in-law. These are of course interesting facts; however, no mention is made of any connection between them and the novella as one reads it. But surely this would be an interesting possibility: perhaps one need not have the external, documentary information about Minco's particular inspiration to be able to still perceive some such layer of objectivity in the text itself.

We think we are able to do just that: to present a piece of linguistic analysis of *De val* from which we may conclude that this work is indeed best interpreted as a novelization of an event whose objective outlines have some separate role within the text. This part of our analysis turns on the use of past and present tense verb forms. However, it leads to a correction of the idea that the relevant kind of objective information would be precisely a newspaper report. We will show (sections 2-3) that a more interesting instance of 'intertextuality' exists between *De val* and another type of objective, non-fictional text.

Of course the precise wording of the text forms the basis of many other aspects of the story as it is understood by a reader. Our second piece of linguistic analysis will show (sections 4-5) that the use of verbal tense in *De val* (this time the perfect tense forms) is also involved in a very important distinction between the old lady's attitude to the traumatic events of the Second World War and that of other characters in the story. Linguistic details of the description of Frieda's thoughts will be seen to reveal the nature of her undiminished obsession with remembering the old days and the minutiae of what happened.

2.   Past tense. To begin the first part of our analysis, let us state our view of the general import of the use of past tense finite verbs in Dutch. We analyze the opposition between Dutch present tense verbs and past tense verbs as an opposition between 'unmarked' forms and specifically 'marked' forms, roughly in the sense of Jakobson (cf. Jakobson 1971). That is to say that, in comparison to the present tense forms, the past tense forms have an added formal part (the endings *-te* or *-de* or a stem change) which is in each case also interpreted as an extra aspect of meaning.

We will characterize the meaning contribution of the past tense by saying that a reader or hearer, when presented with a past tense form, is to understand that any IMMEDIATE EVIDENCE for the truth of what is being said is lacking (cf. for a somewhat similar analysis, Bakker 1974). For instance, the past tense in a simple utterance like "Ze waren niet thuis" ('They were not at home') implies that for the one interpreting the utterance there will not be any immediate experience of the well-known waiting at the door and getting no answer. But, although the interpreter will not find data to confirm or to disconfirm the state of affairs mentioned by simply looking around himself, he should still be willing to entertain various aspects of this state of affairs. Sometimes he will justify such open-mindedness by the realization that truly past events cannot actually be experienced; in other cases he is aware that some thoughts may be approached most relevantly within the framework of the knowledge contained in another mind (maybe his own mind at some other moment). "Dit ging te ver!" ('This was the limit!') — a reported thought of another person. A past tense verb alerts to just such a situation of 'lack of immediate evidence.' Note that this holds whether or not a marking of the perfect (cf. sections 4-5) is present as well; we claim that clauses with 'past perfect' and those with 'simple past' involve exactly the same caution with respect to the evidence.

By contrast, the so-called present tense verbs simply do not indicate anything of the sort. They are in fact used for situations in which there is a direct experience of truth or falsity, as well as for those without; compare "dit artikel is in het Engels" ('this article is in English') with "de meeste artikelen zijn in het Engels" ('most articles are in English'). The only thing one can say about present tense forms is that they are not SPECIFICALLY associated with a message of caution concerning the evidence. In Jakobson's terminology, they are 'unmarked.'

Now *De val* displays the normal usage of past tense verbs. Past tense forms indeed often evoke situations and events that are narrated;

for the reader, they are thus not supported by any direct evidence. An example: "Frieda Borgstein werd om halfacht gewekt" ('Frieda Borgstein was awakened at half past seven') — this on the fatal day. Alternatively, such forms indicate states of affairs as they are entertained in thought by the novella's characters. The evidence for them is thus really doubly indirect: the narrator does not just relate certain events but he actually narrates the thoughts of several characters about those events. *De val* in fact weaves together apparently disparate events from a day in the life of a number of characters. First of all of the main character Frieda; she wakes up and thinks about preparing for her birthday that is to take place the next day — "Morgen nam ze een douche. Morgen kleedde ze zich netjes aan" ('Tomorrow she would take a shower. Tomorrow she would dress up'). We come to know about the ill-humored servicemen; they begin their day with the strongest possible grudge. Also about Carla, the woman from the café, who observes the two men in the early morning and later remembers her irritation about their attitude — "Ze moesten niet op de vroege morgen de boel al komen verzieken" ('They'd better not start spoiling the mood at this hour'). And we become acquainted with the staff of the old people's home where Frieda lives, all thinking of the tasks at hand and — at the last moment — unable to accompany the fragile lady on her excursion on an icy cold day to do the shopping for her birthday.

3. After-the-fact fragments in "De val." The structure of *De val* is complicated by the presence of a number of non-dialogue passages dominated not by past tense verbs but by present tense verbs. Reviewing these passages in turn, we will find they have a specific relevance.

The very first sentence of the novella reads as follows (translated, with italics added): '*It is certain* that the two servicemen of the public works department stopped off at the Salamander café first thing that Thursday morning, rather than taking the usual straight road from the central boilerhouse to the location of their job.' The next paragraph has in similar fashion: '*It may be* that they thought it was still too cold or too dark for the job they had to do.' And immediately: '*It is also possible* that it was simply due to the reaction of Baltus, who sat behind the wheel and stepped on the brake instinctively when he saw the neon lights above the counter flash on just as they drove by the café.' One notes the repetitive assessment of certainty and possibilities, prefixed in a stern and — for the reader — ominous fashion before the descriptions of the doings of the servicemen on the day of the accident. The descriptions themselves, in the subordinate clauses, are in the simple past. In the Dutch original: *"Het staat vast* dat de twee monteurs [...] eerst *aanlegden* bij De Salamander"; "*Het kan zijn* dat ze het nog te koud of te donker *vonden* [...]"; "*het is ook mogelijk* dat het *kwam* door [...]." Surely, these are unusual combinations of plain narrative and objective, after-the-fact statements.

After the first paragraphs of the novella, the objective style with present tense verbs remains in the background for a while. It turns up again on p. 33 in a rather detailed description of the underground hot water heating system and its service entrances in the street, situated near the old people's home where Frieda lives. 'The buildings of the social services department and of the municipal gas and electricity board *are located* side by side in the Uiterwaardenstraat, separated by a broad footpath [...]. Somewhat farther on the same side of the street there *is* the office of the housing department, built against the old low-rise houses. Those three buildings *are connected* to the municipal hot water heating system and they *are each provided* with a stopcock located down a manhole in the street.'

The technical description continues about the groundwater, which reaches a high level in wintertime, fills up the manholes, and gets heated to a temperature near the boiling point by the hotwater pipes. Because of certain dangers inherent in this situation, 'the entrances *must* [present tense in the original] be pumped out at regular intervals [...],' a statement which allows for an immediate return to the past tense narrative: '[...] and it *was* this chore which *had been assigned* to the servicemen for that morning.' An evocation follows, with past tense verbs, of some personal thoughts that were on their minds while they were busy with the job. It was no more than a routine task for them, and we read the explanation for that again in the present tense: 'Once the submersible pump *hangs* in the manhole, it *does* the job; the seething water *is* drained off to the sewerage all by itself. Nothing *can* go wrong as long as you *keep* an eye on things' (p. 34f).

The last sentence is in colloquial Dutch: "[z]olang je de boel in de gaten houdt." This gives the impression of an oral testimony, a statement made afterwards by the servicemen in the context of an investigation into the circumstances of the fatal accident. One may surely expect an official investigation to be carried out in the case of a death caused by what looks like gross, even culpable negligence on the part of the servicemen. A report resulting from such an investigation usually contains testimony not only from those directly responsible, but also from everybody else who was near the spot of the accident or who met with the protagonists at some time during the day. The structure of *De val* is indeed reminiscent of this: the narrative is divided up into shorter episodes, with precise time indications.[2] And such a judicial report may well state its conclusions with careful but definitive present tense phrases like those which introduced the novella: 'It is certain that [...]; it may be [...]; it is also possible [...].' Finally, if anything is typical of official reports, it is detailed, objective present tense description — as the one we just read — of the location where some event took place. Such a description is, in fact, not typically found in such newspaper reports as are said to have inspired Minco to write her novella.

The report fragments turn up again — and with strong effect — at the very moment that we expect to 'see,' through the eyes of one of the bystanders, Frieda's fatal step. On p. 69 we are witness to Frieda's own thoughts while she leaves the home to do her shopping. She is surprised by the strange clouds of steam and becomes aware of a van, almost blocking the footpath but not quite. With normal past tenses: 'She thought she had plenty of room to pass the car. There was a space of about two feet left.' At this point nine lines of comment follow, report-like sentences with present tense verbs alternating with past tense narrative sentences and clauses: '*Maybe she has misjudged the space.* Maybe it was her eyes, which she had not been able to dab dry. *There is the possibility* that she tripped over the hose lying beside the manhole, or over the manhole cover. *A combination of*

---

[2]Concerning Gerrie, a geriatric helper in the home, it is noted (p. 76): 'Later she had said that it had been like in a movie [...].' Carla from the café 'later remembered that [...]' (p. 11). The women have apparently been asked to relate their impressions of the fatal day of the events in the home and of the mood of the servicemen, respectively.

those factors cannot be excluded. The full facts of the case will never be known. In any case she has taken no more than two or three steps before she felt the ground vanishing under her feet' (p. 70). It is clear: nobody actually saw Frieda falling into the manhole, and although for the reader the calamity has been imminent all along, his knowledge in the end is no more than is contained in these reconstructing statements.

In short, the tragic story narrated in *De val* is interwoven with a number of objective assessments concerning the accident, which are like echoes from a judicial report. Asking ourselves about the significance of this construction, we may note two complementary, and mutually reinforcing, effects. From a literary perspective, the servicemen are, by opening up the hot water hell, the agents of fate, reincarnations of the death-bringing Germans. However, the present tense forms at decisive points of the text indicate that the parallelism should not be allowed to obscure the fact of the servicemen's plain personal resonsibility, their being guilty of gross negligence. Now ironically, this in turn leads back to the well-known fact that it was precisely out of a rigid sense of duty that many German officers reportedly performed the crimes of the Nazi regime. Deadly as it was, their devotion to duty was beyond reproach, and criminal proceedings could not be instituted in many cases... Fate seemingly traces its course undisturbed by the ethics of human actions.

4.   **Perfect tenses: looking back.** Let us now present an analysis of some important aspects of the use of perfect tenses in *De val*. Again, we will first provide a general characterization of these tense forms in general terms, and then demonstrate how their use can be seen as contributing to a fundamental theme of the novella.

Formally, the perfect tenses in Dutch are construed with a form of one of the auxiliaries *hebben* 'to have' and *zijn* 'to be' and, in general, the past participle of the main verb. In certain contexts involving the presence of yet another auxiliary, all non-finite verbs are infinitives and no past participle occurs in the perfect tense.

Semantically, we regard the perfect in all its forms as a marking for 'looking back': it consists of an operation on the content of the verb stem to the effect that — from an interpreter's position — this process, situation, or event is looked back upon. The focus of attention, as tense theorists call it, may be some situation resulting from what the verb stem indicates, or it may be that the point is to provide an overview or summary of a certain situation. 'Looking back' can be taken as the general, encompassing catchword (cf. Koefoed 1984).

In our view, the meaning provided by 'perfect' is completely independent from 'past.' From the point of view of grammar, there are no constraints on their combination. The two markings give rise to four possible combinations: (1) not marked 'past' and not marked 'perfect': the 'simple present;' (2) marked 'past' and not marked 'perfect': the 'simple past;' (3) not marked 'past' and marked 'perfect': the 'present perfect;' (4) marked 'past' and also marked 'perfect': the 'past perfect.'

Note that in our analysis, there is no grammatical opposition between 'past' and 'perfect,' nor can there be. The present perfect simply provides a marking for 'looking back,' while the past perfect provides the very same marking and the marking for 'lack of immediate evidence' as well. We will see that in *De val* the present and past perfect tenses indeed fulfil the same role.

5. **History in "De val": living in it vs. looking back upon it.** As we have observed in section 3, nobody is witness to Frieda's actual falling into the manhole. In the nine lines that comment on her fatal step, two clauses are in the present perfect (the first and final main clause of the paragraph). So without abandoning the viewpoint of an objective reporter, we are effectively looking back on the event.

This occurrence of perfect tense forms marks a turning point in the novella, in a way we will now explicate. Let us start by considering the final chapter. Its beginning and end picture Ben Abels, an old acquaintance of Frieda's, at the funeral. But the major part of the chapter relates Abels's recollection of the conversation he had with Hein Kessels the day before; Kessels is the man who in 1942 was supposed to help Frieda and her family escape to Switzerland. It is this conversation that reveals something about what really went wrong then (though much will still remain unclear).

In the speech of both men as reported, the present perfect is used frequently when they speak of the incident of 1942. Just a few examples, from a large number of instances (we translate literally): "Door anderen zijn wel hogere bedragen gevraagd" ('Others have been asking even higher amounts,' p. 86), "Bent u er later niet achtergekomen?" ('Have you not found out later?' p. 89), "Ze hebben me eindeloos verhoord" ('They have interrogated me endlessly,' p. 90), "Die heeft zij niet gehad" ('SHE has not had them [i.e. periods of forgetting],' p. 91). Details of the incident are also reported in non-perfect tenses (generally simple past), but Abels and Kessels use the perfect so consistently that it is quite clear what their relationship to these past events is: they are looking back on them, not able to forget but not living in them anymore either.

The position of Abels and Kessels towards the past contrasts sharply with Frieda's; her frequent and detailed recollections are largely narrated with simple past tense verbs. Frieda's position is explicitly indicated by the author at the end of the 8th chapter: 'Until the end of her days, two images would keep entering her mind, and sometimes they would overlap, as they did now: she was standing on the threshold of a room full of people and could not go in — she was standing on the threshold of her empty house and could not go out' (p. 54). But even as early as on pp. 17-19, when Frieda has just woken up, the overlap of images occurs in the text itself, as much as four times. We give one example, from the passage about Frieda making her breakfast in her room in the old people's home: 'Busy with the transparent, sticky slices of cheese, she became aware of the smell of fresh bread and fried eggs — the sun was shining through the kitchen window and cast spots of light on the table set for breakfast' (p. 19). And there are more instances of flashbacks at other places in the text, sometimes indicated by a single past perfect form. The images do not always overlap completely, but often they do (cf. the quotation from p. 54 above).

We conclude that use and non-use of perfect tense forms in the novella serve to differentiate two contrasting positions with respect to the same past events: one, Frieda's, in which the past is still being lived in; the other, Abels's and Kessels's, in which the past is looked back upon. Furthermore, we note that perfect forms do not only occur in the reported speech of Abels and Kessels; at some points in the final chapter, the thoughts of Abels, as he recollects the conversation with Kessels, are reported by the author by means of perfect tenses as well. Some examples: "Hoe heb ik hem herkend, dacht hij" ('How have I recognized him, he thought,' p. 87), "Toen [...] had hij gezien dat hij mankte" ('Then he [Abels] had seen that he [Kessels] limped,' p. 92). In this way, not only the contents of the conversation display a perspective of looking back, but also the way in which it is narrated. The truth about the 1942 incident is thus conveyed in hindsight on two levels: Abels en Kessels are looking back at the absurd events of 1942, and the reader is looking back at them talking about it.

In fact, the latter perspective prevails in all four chapters following Frieda's falling into the manhole; it is in this respect that we stated earlier that the use of perfect tense forms on p. 70 marks a turning point. In chapter 13, many sentences in the past perfect look back upon events coinciding with or just preceding Frieda's fall, or upon that event itself. In the first paragraph, they help specify the contents of the suggested objective report ("deze keer had niemand het oversteken van Frieda gezien," 'this time nobody had seen Frieda crossing,' p. 72); in the remainder of the chapter, it is the thoughts and behavior of other characters that are looked back upon. This pattern continues in chapter 14: each character has her or his story told, so to speak. Chapters 13 and 14 are 'dramatized' testimonies: the details of each story are embedded in texts portions which as a whole look back on the fatal event, witness the repetition of past perfect forms.[3]

Chapter 15 shows the same mechanism. The only difference is that the perspective here is not eyewitness testimony but Abels's personal recollection (on the day of the funeral) of his experience of Frieda's fall. He is the only person in whom Frieda had taken a personal interest in the period after the war (cf. p. 47), and he is also nearest to the position of the author (these aspects are of course related). This perspective is one of looking back too, albeit more personally involved.

---

[3]In some places, this aspect of 'dramatized' testimony becomes very clear; cf. note 2.

Generalizing over these observations, we may say that after Frieda's death, there remains only looking back: both on her life and death, and on the life and death of her husband and children. In a sense, she had continued their lives also (cf. p. 20: 'As long as she lived, [...] she kept them present; with that idea she justified her existence'). Frieda could not take the position of looking back on the past events of her life, but Kessels, Abels, the author, and we, the readers, can. The linguistic conclusion is that we have to give a similar interpretation to the perfect tense forms both in the narrated text and in the dialogues in the final chapters. Consequently, the meaning of 'perfect' must indeed be taken to be exhaustively characterized by our description; there is no 'systemic' relation (opposition or otherwise) between the perfect and the past tense forms.[4]

Concluding our analysis of *De val* as a work of literary art, we note the following. In the passages where Frieda's point of view is chosen, the details of life then and now are described in an unusually unitary form, showing Frieda's somewhat hazy picture of reality changing. Other characters also wonder about the causes of the catastrophic events but in them there is an overriding sense of hindsight and things past. The richer for it is the reader, who is gradually presented with the detailed temporal knowledge of participants and witnesses and also with the moving possibility of a state of mind in which recollections are not really different from experiences.

---

[4] The logic of this position is straightforward. The marking 'perfect' has the same interpretation when combined with 'past' as when combined with 'present'; therefore the meaning of 'perfect' cannot be determined as being in some way opposed to past, nor as being similar. Either position would make it difficult to explain combinations of 'perfect' and 'past': on the former view, opposite meanings would be used simultaneously, while the latter view would entail a claim of redundancy. In that sense, no systemic relation between 'perfect' and 'past' enters into the determination of either.

References

Bakker, D. M. 1974. "Werkwoordstijden en taalhandeling." *Handelingen van het 33e Nederlands filologencongres,* 169-176. (Repr. in *De macht van het woord. Een selectie uit het taalkundige werk* by D. M. Bakker, 20-28. Amsterdam: VU Uitgeverij, 1988.)

Jakobson, R. 1971. "Shifters, categories, and the Russian verb." *Selected Writings* by R. Jakobson, 2, 130-147. The Hague and Paris: Mouton.

Koefoed, G. 1984. "...om te ontkomen aan de tijd." *Van periferie naar kern* ed. by G. J. de Haan et al., 141-153. Dordrecht: Foris.

Middeldorp, A. 1981-84. "Marga Minco." *Kritisch lexicon van de Nederlandstalige literatuur na 1945,* Minco 1-9. Alphen aan de Rijn: Samson, 1980.

Minco, M. 1983. *De val.* Amsterdam: Bert Bakker.

The Pink Pages of Petit Larousse:
Marnix Gijsen's "Art of Quotation"

Marcel Janssens
Catholic University of Leuven, Belgium

1. In these high-days of intertextuality, the study of literary quotations is very popular. Although this kind of literary research was not invented yesterday, it is currently undertaken in a more sophisticated and specialized way than ever before. An epoch-making book on our subject matter was Herman Meier's *Das Zitat in der Erzählkunst. Zur Geschichte und Poetik des europäischen Romans*, published in 1961, one of the very great books in the history of comparative literature, was written after the Second World War. A French scholar, Antoine Compagnon, published an encyclopedic standard work, *La seconde main ou le travail de la citation,* in 1979. In recent years, the Belgian scholar Paul Claes has been working out both theoretical concepts and practical analyses with regard to the noble art of quotation in several books, such as *Het netwerk en de nevelvlek* (1979) and *Echo's echo's. De kunst van de allusie* (1988). Last year a vast international bibliography of intertextual research, including quotation and allusion, was published by Udo J. Hebel in his book *Intertextuality, Allusion, and Quotation. An International Bibliography of Critical Studies* (1989). In a word: intertextual research appears to be the pet subject of literary studies everywhere nowadays and, more specifically, the study of the appearance, the forms, and the functions of quotations in literary texts can be said to be the very heart of it.

2. In this paper I will comment very briefly on personal research done recently on quotations in Marnix Gijsen's narrative prose.

Marnix Gijsen, or Jan-Albert Goris, is one of the first prose writers in Flemish literature who took a genuine doctor's degree (including a doctoral thesis) at one of our Faculties of Arts. In 1925 he received his Ph.D. in "Sciences morales et historiques" at the University of Leuven with a thesis on the rise of modern capitalism in Antwerp. *[Etude sur les colonies marchandes méridionales (Portugais, Espagnols, Italiens) à Anvers de 1488 à 1567. Contribution à l'histoire des débuts du capitalisme moderne.]* With Marnix Gijsen, a very learned prose writer — with all the skills and learning of the Faculty of Arts — enters our literary scene, explicitly and prominently. We had not had that many examples of this kind before and, although I do not pretend that literature is better when produced by someone having a Ph.D., having studied somewhat and having read a lot can be very profitable for an author. (As I will say further on, having read TOO much may lead a writer into quoting too much, as is overtly the case with Marnix Gijsen.)

Marnix Gijsen belongs to an entire generation of educated people who liked to exhibit their vast cultural knowledge in their essays and critiques, as well as their narratives. Raymond Brulez, for instance, also campaigned against the original sin of the Flemish novel — folklore — abusing primarily French quotations. And Raymond Herreman, admitting that he did not know one foreign language properly, candidly confessed that "the pink pages of Larousse" were the very treasure-house of his beloved quotations. These pink pages of Petit Larousse must have been a gold mine for Marnix Gijsen, too, of course, next to a vast amount of acquired cultural literacy. We will encounter the pink Larousse pages more than once in my paper, but I will refrain from quoting all the quotations.

The art of quotation is no longer exceptional in contemporary Dutch and Flemish literature. Undoubtedly, Gijsen is the most showy *citateraar* of his generation and his ostentatious use of quotations and allusions can hardly be exaggerated. But younger writers — such as Hugo Claus, Willy Roggeman, Daniël Robberechts, Paul de Wispelaere, Walter van den Broeck, Monika van Paemel or Maarten 't Hart, and Willem Brakman, and so many other prose writers whom you might call "postmodern intertextuals" — exhibit similar abilities, proceeding however not quite similarly, using more sophisticated techniques of intertextual appropriations. As Hugo Claus said in a 1965 interview with H. U. Jessurun d'Oliveira, "No writer falls out of a tree. We write books after having read books, don't we?" Perhaps he already knew John Dos Passos, saying at that moment, "We are drugged with literature so that we can never live at all of ourselves." Marnix Gijsen said in an interview in 1974, "I do not write for peasants. I write for snobs with a certain culture." You may remember that Winston Churchill once said that reading quotation books can be very profitable for uneducated people: What wonderful things will a man with Marnix Gijsen's learning do with the pink pages of Petit Larousse? When you compare his own procedures with the intertextual games of present day writers, adaptors and rewriters, you might even call his "art of quotation" somewhat naively showy. Intertextual patchworks of manifest or, preferably, hidden quotations are being woven now in a much more skilful way than Marnix Gijsen — with all his candid pride of an erudite scholar and diplomat — can ever have dreamt of.

3. I will now try to restore one or two rooms of Marnix Gijsen's "imaginary library" by means of numerous quotations of literary, popular, and scholarly books, of the bible, of books on art history, of songs and films, and so many other sources. Quotations constitute the most striking feature of his erudite narrative prose, but they are by no means the only entrance to his "imaginary library." Next to the innumerable quotations, many allusions and other references must be taken into account.

3.1. Quotations are generally marked in Gijsen's prose, but much remains cryptic, as if the narrator were playing hide-and-seek with the reader who, as a matter of fact, should be a bit more than a farmer, preferably even a kind of literary snob with a certain culture, in order to be in a position to play the game properly. I must say that lots of alien materials have not been identified as such. I confess that, for instance, I had to rely on other people's knowledge in order to identify an awkward French quotation like "suffisance matamoresque" and "crevaison grenouillère" as being taken from the Flemish painter James Ensor. In all the hiding and the seeking, it is the reader who is often the loser.

The game gets even more complicated when Marnix Gijsen quotes Marnix Gijsen without any warning at all, for instance from his poems into his novels or from his autobiographical texts or essays into his narrative prose. In these cases the game is only to be played by extremely expert insiders with a strong memory who manage to recognize literature within literature without the support of quotation marks.

The reader is supposed to perform with equal perspicacity in the case of so-called lexical quotations: proper names of writers or of characters (Hamlet, Fortinbras, for instance) may evoke the context of a particular text or of a whole work they belong to or stand for. Such lexical quotations, which are meant for the expert reader, occur abundantly. They are like very tiny hat-racks where the reader is expected to hang a set of induced meanings, if at least he wants to be taken seriously and to get the shade of irony or the various semantic levels involved in the lexical quotation. Some cultural literacy is required, for instance, for a reader to grasp the meaning of "the fulfilment of the desires of our local and age-old Philemon and Baucis of Chelsea." But for Marnix Gijsens, that is a quite normal speech act.

3.2. Another means of giving a flavour of scholarly learning or irony to a text is the lexical allusion in the forms of a periphrasis, a synonym, or just a name, thereby evoking a vast context. When the lexical allusion only points at accidental or peripheral features of the contexts involved, it may be extremely difficult to recognize them. In Gijsen's American novel *De vleespotten van Egypte,* the European intellectual Andreas says about the American lady Mrs. Dobson: "(She is) drunk but nevertheless callipygos." "Callipygos" is another name of the goddess Venus "with the beautiful buttocks." The ironic flavour of the allusion can only be enjoyed by a reader who catches a glimpse of that mouthful of Greek.

Lexical allusions are linked to particular words or names; textual allusions, moreover, refer to a text as a whole. In *Klaaglied om Agnes,* for instance, the myth of Orpheus and Eurydice mirrors the tragical love story of the first-person narrator and Agnes.

On the whole, it may be even more painful to detect allusions since they are not marked like quotations. The exquisite tricks of allusion are usually shown in the areas of very learned cultural understanding, especially in the stories of Marnix Gijsen who appears to have turned that game of periphrastic and synonymous allusions into a personal device, even a mannerism.

3.3. When the boundaries between quotation and allusion are not that clear, it is even more difficult to distinguish between allusion and mere reference. Names of historical persons or of artists can be classified as mere references, at least when they are not linked to a quotation or a lexical allusion. The name Rubens, for instance, is nothing more than a somewhat easy reference in most cases, especially with regard to the measures and volumes of "Rubensian women," mostly in America. It is a little bit boring to find out that Marnix Gijsen, our "doctor doctissimus" in the fine art of periphastic allusion, indulges in abusing the cliché "Rubensian" when he depicts women, as usual, in a by no means flattering way. This irony neutralizes the platitude a little bit, but he turns that game with commonplaces into a trick that does not work any more in the long run.

4. I must limit this presentation of intertextual procedures to the use of literary quotations, allusions and references, the number of which runs up to more than 40% of the intertextual materials.

4.1. Gijsen himself had an impressive reading culture and a well-trained memory. Some main characters of his novels, or at least the narrators, have a Ph.D. like himself. Dr. Robijns, the main character of *De vleespotten van Egypte,* has written a doctoral thesis on modern history in Europe, and finds his academic culture confronted with the barbarism of the American intellectuals, just as Marnix Gijsen himself did, living in the States for some 25 years. Andreas, in the same novel, is another alter ego: a Belgian intellectual in the States, with a tough reading culture, affectionate, pedantic, a poseur. He quotes the first song of the Illiad in Greek and the first chapter of Genesis in Hebrew. When he looks at Mrs. Dobson with the nice buttocks, naked and drunk at the end of a party, he quotes a famous line of Jean Racine's *Phèdre* in order to protect himself from the vulgarity of that scene. He starts an academic discussion with the same Rubensian Mrs. Dobson on the costumes of wild and civilised people. The way the exhibition of learning and literacy functions in similar scenes is 100% Marnix Gijsen.

The characters Robijns and Andreas show that the demonstration of learning occurs in the narrator's and the character's text alike.

4.2. Literary references are taken from a dozen literatures, above all from French literature, a bit less from classical literature, not too often from Dutch literature, but also from German, Anglo-Saxon, even Russian, Italian, Spanish, Scandinavan, Chinese, Japanese, or Babylonian sources. Among them all, Voltaire has the highest score. Even the American Mr. Dobson says: "I live in Voltaire's century" — and that could have been an appropriate motto for this presentation.

Marnix Gijsen once said, in an interview with Lidy van Marissing, "I read Homer, the Odyssee, every day." I trust this is not a pedantic overstatement. In any case, the first line of the Odyssee, in Greek of course, "Anda moi enepe Musa polutropoon," is quoted several times. It is given to the reader as a sort of stamped signature with the inscription "I, Marnix Gijsen."

4.3. When a writer indulges so frequently in the mannerisms of quotation, he must inevitably repeat the same things. As a matter of fact, Marnix Gijsen repeats the same texts, sometimes in slightly altered forms, including the same platitudes. This habit turns out to be slightly irritating in the long run, especially when the things quoted show nothing more than some sort of trivial academic pursuit: "Roma locuta, causa finita; de minimis non curat praetor; Tu Marcellus eris; cogito ergo sum; In paradisum deducant te angeli; Jedem Tierchen sein Pläsierchen; das Land der Griechen mit der Seele suchend; Madame Bovary, c'est moi; l'état, c'est moi; Money is to the clergy what sex is to the layman." Such commonplaces, but also more precious sayings or other intellectual ornaments or exquisite jewelry of a "Schöngeist" which he recalls continuously, show that — after all — his intellectual and textual dwellings were not as well furnished as you might conclude at first sight.

5. In conclusion let me add a few words on the various ways these quotations function in Gijsen's prose.

5.1. As Herman Meier said, quotations are like raisins in a cake. Marnix Gijsen adores exhibiting cultural literacy. References of all kinds are undoubtely meant to form a striking topographic map of his knowledge. I even suspect him of having invented quotations, since sometimes he says that he does not remember exactly, or that he forgot who said what. In another case he introduces the famous saying of a well-known author but omits to say what the celebrity said. In most cases, quotations are both exemplum and argument and, above all, mere display of learning.

This amount of learning enhances the elitist nature of this narrative prose. It makes possible an alliance of intellectual superiority between the narrator and the reader. Such a display of superiority on behalf of "literary snobs," as Gijsen himself stated ironically, even looks like a gesture of impertinence. In *Het paard Ugo*, the first-person-narrator says to his superior, the Belgian Consul-general in New York, "Everything in the pink pages of Petit Larousse belongs to my culture, I said somewhat uneasily about my impertinence," and the Voltairian uncle Felix in *Telemachus in het dorp* also distinguishes himself from other people by quoting the pink pages of Petit Larousse.

5.2. The second function of the art of quoting is characterization. Tell me whom and how you quote and I will tell you who you are. That goes both for the self-presentation of the narrators and for the characters who, as we have said, are mostly an alter ego of the narrator or of the writer. That goes even for the self-esteem of the reader who constantly feels challenged to join the club of narrators and characters.

5.3. In the third place, the art of quotation is an instrument both of self-defense and aggression, above all in Gijsen's American novels. The most precious treasures of Europe are imported into the States as a Greek or Roman armour against American barbarians. The two novels in which references to European culture are displayed most frequently are the American stories *De vleespotten van Egypte* and *Het paard Ugo*. There is nothing astonishing about this. It is an aspect of a strategy of self-defence and superiority which easily turns into impertinence.

5.4. Last but not least, this impertinence must have some psychological roots. Marnix Gijsen not only criticizes conventional wisdom and petrified sayings and hackneyed quotations — exhibiting intellectual superiority in neutralizing banality with an overdose of banality — he needs these tricks to compensate for a certain innate uneasiness in social contacts. "We have no secret incantations or magical remedies to protect ourselves any more," he wrote in *Er gebeurt nooit iets,* "We have to rely on irony, literary quotations, the magic of a poem, parody." Irony, quotations, parody, sarcasm: these are weapons or screens by means of which he can exorcise his inability to communicate or to behave properly in social contexts, compensating for that failure by hiding himself behind a mask of learning. Impotence transformed into impertinence: such could be the underlying psychological mechanism of the display of literacy. To quote may have been a flight forward towards a level where he could be untouchable. To quote is anticipated self-defence and therefore already aggressive. In this strategy of self-protection, quotations are like an intertext of barbed wire around the over-protected garden of the ego.

References

Ben-Porat, Ziva. "The poetics of literary allusion." *PTL: A Journal for Descriptive Poetics and Theory of Literature* 1 (1976), 105-128.
Boheemen, Christel van. "Intertextualiteit. Een inleiding." *Forum der Letteren* 22 (1981), 242-249.
Broich, Ulrich and Manfred Pfister. *Intertextualität. Figuren. Funktionen, Anglistische Fallstudien.* Tübingen. Max Niemeyer Verlag, 1985.
Claes, Paul. *De mot zit in de mythe. Hugo Claus en de oudheid.* Amsterdam. De Bezige Bij, 1984.
_____. *Claus-reading.* Antwerpen. Manteau, 1984.
_____. *Echo's echo's. De kunst van de allusie.* Amsterdam. De Bezig Bij, 1988.
_____. *Het netwerk en de nevelvlek. Semiotische studies.* (Argo-Studies-1) Leuven. Acco, 1979.
Compagnon, Antoine. *La seconde main ou le travail de la citation.* Paris. Le Seuil, 1989.

Gijsen, Marnix. *Verzameld werk.* Amsterdam, Meulenhoff's Gravenhage/Rotterdam. Nijgh & Van Ditmar, 1977 (6 volumes)
Hebel, Udo J. *Intertextuality, Allusion, and Quotation. An International Bibliography of Critical Studies.* (Bibliographics and Indexes in World Literature, Number 18) New York, London. Greenwood Press, 1989.
Jessurun d'Oliveira, H. U. *Scheppen riep hij gaat van Au.* Amsterdam. Polak & Van Gennep, 1965.
Marissing, Lidy van. *28 interviews.* Amsterdam. Meulenhoff, 1971.
Meier, Herman. *Das Zitat in der Erzählkunst. Zur Geschichte und Poetik des europäischen Romans.* Stuttgart. J. B. Metzlersche Verlagsbuchhandlung, 1961.
Roggeman, Willem M. "Gesprek met Marnix Gijsen." *De Vlaamse Gids* 58 (1974) nr. 11, 4-15.
Weisgerber, Jean. "Propos sur la citation, ses formes et ses fonctions dans la littérature contemporaine." In *Ecritures à M.-J. Lefebvre.* Bruxelles. Editions de l'Université de Bruxelles, 1983, 281-294. Also in Weisgerber, Jean, *Avant garde/ modernisme, als hulde uitgegeven door Michel Bartosik e.a.* Brussel. V. U. B. Press, 1989, 225-237.

Nooteboom and Postmodernism

Christa Johnson
University of California, Los Angeles and Stanford University

Still not widely accepted, Postmodernism has become a veritable curse-word for many scholars. Like many terms in the humanities, it often runs the risk of simply becoming trendy — an undifferentiating slogan for "anything goes." Many have alluded to a new quiescent mood of a so-called Post-histoire and Postmodernism that has characterized Western European politics and culture since the 1970s. In such descriptions, Postmodernism is depicted as the result of the fizzled-out utopian impulses and revolutionary energies of the tumultuous 1960s: a period of political inertia, only recently ruptured by the events in Eastern Europe. This inertia or Postmodern mood characteristic of contemporary culture putatively extends to all reaches of life and letters. It is not my purpose here, however, to assert or demonstrate the correctness of one particular theory about Postmodern culture; rather, I will attempt to outline some tendencies observed and identified by Jean Baudrillard and Frédéric Jameson that serve well for describing certain cultural phenomena as reflected in literature. For my analysis, I will use Cees Nooteboom's 1980 novel *Rituals* which, in my view, proves itself a telling example, indeed.[1] In order to clarify and come to a better understanding about what I see as Postmodern in this work, I will contrast it to what I view as its Modern tendencies.

---

[1] For the purpose of fluidity, I have used the excellent English translation by Adrienne Dixon for all citations.

Robert S. Kirsner (ed.), *The Low Countries and Beyond*, 161-169. Lanham, MD: University Press of America, 1993.

Frederic Jameson has said that most Postmodernisms emerge as specific reactions against the established forms of high Modernism (111). Those formerly subversive styles — from abstract Expressionist art to the Modernist poetry of Pound, Eliot, Wallace Stevens; the style of Frank Lloyd Wright, or Stravinsky, Joyce, Proust — are marked by feelings of tragedy, suffering, fragmentation, and alienation. What is important in understanding these examples as Modern works is that they still have a framework to which they refer, they are still considered reactions to certain canonized models — and were felt to be scandalous or shocking in their time. "The new impulse of Postmodernism, on the other hand, is given not in itself, but in the very Modernism it seeks to displace" (Jameson 112). Postmodernism no longer has a framework of its own: in this phenomenon the sign has lost its referent.

Frederic Jameson has developed the notion of "pastiche." Many great Modernist styles, he maintains, use the technique of parody in their work (113-4). Parody, however, targets a work and capitalizes on any uniqueness of styles; also, it mirrors the idiosyncrasies and eccentricities of the work to produce reflections which mock the original. The implication, here, is that a work can still hold something unique, but this idea of originality is precisely what distinguishes Modern parody from Jameson's Postmodern pastiche — for pastiche is the moment of "a neutral practice of mimicry, without parody's ulterior motive, without the satirical impulse, without laughter, without that still latent feeling that there exists something *normal*.... Pastiche is blank parody that has lost its sense of humor" (Jameson 114).

Jameson's notion of pastiche is in many ways similar to the world of simulacra that Jean Baudrillard has described. Because of the lost referent, culture is now dominated by simulations, by signs and images, by commodities that refer to each other and lack any real use value, any authentic interaction. In an effort to extend the Marxist critique of capitalism to areas that are beyond the scope of the theory of the mode of production, Baudrillard has developed a theory to describe the proliferation of communications through the media. He contends that in a sense, what Walter Benjamin wrote about "the age of mechanical reproduction" applies to all reaches of life: objects and discourses have no firm origin, no referent, no ground or foundation. This phenomenon is described as a "floating signifier," a linguistic formulation of the same kind of interaction between people and objects, resulting in an unauthenticity of life as things blur into what Baudrillard has coined as an "unreflecting screen of communication" (123).

Now, after having defined "floating signifier," "simulacra," and "pastiche," I would like to briefly define my understanding of "Post-histoire" before I approach an analysis of Nooteboom. Post-histoire, with regard to memory, is the disappearance or erasure of history, "[t]he fragmentation of time into a series of perpetual presents" (Jameson 125). Things from the past have lost their association with the past, that is, with the time in which they were produced or experienced.

Turning now to Nooteboom's *Rituals,* we can see that the opening motto immediately raises questions of meaning, and of aesthetic and social realities. The motto is a quotation from German Realist author Theodore Fontane: "Und allen Plänen gegenüber begleitet mich die Frage: 'Was soll der Unsinn?'; eine Frage, die überhaupt ganz und gar von mir Besitz zu nehmen droht" (1). The reader's attention is focused on "nonsense," yet because it can still be described — as nonsense — it may still be considered Modern as its impulse is to try to make sense out of the nonsense. The speaker, here too, senses the threat. But since it points to a total overcoming, Postmodernism is present as well. Thus, this quote, by its position in the text, identifies the novel from the beginning as a threshold experience — between Modern and Postmodern.

The symptoms of the crisis of Modern culture permeate *Rituals* and account for the text's general depressive mood — melancholia pervades the novel. Depicting life as a mere series of rituals, Nooteboom shows metaphorically how even highly significant events become ritualistic, repetitious, and detached from any authentic experience: rituals like the reading of business reports and the news; writing horoscopes in *Het Parool*; making love to women; memorizing things; Arnold Taad's walks with the dog, his reading hour, his eating goulash, and his drinking whiskey. Yet this world of endless and meaningless ritual is once again pastiche as even death loses significance:

Perhaps the daily death was so immensely sad because no one was really dying at all. There was only a number of barely connected snapshots at which nobody would ever look. This unchangingly and relentlessly identical, meaningless cycle never bothered him during the daytime, because this kind of death did not really belong to that life. (6)

Stylistic innovation is no longer possible, all that is left is to imitate dead styles, to repeat in meaningless ceremony. In this Baudrillardian world of simulacra, no "real" objects — in the sense of obvious facts, substances, realities, or use-values — exist any longer (Baudrillard 126). Moreover, it is important that this absolute indifference, equivalence, and interchangeability, this meaningless cycle "never bothered him" (6). Inni has lost both the emotion of sadness and humor. Life is described as merely a number of barely connected snapshots: a snapshot, an instantaneous photograph which tries to capture an instant — a brief moment in time — in images barely connected. This is reminiscent of avant-garde montage photography; although in montage, there is still a frame, a borderline that coheres the pieces. However, these "barely connected" pieces are on the verge of losing their relationship to each other. They are "snapshots at which nobody would ever look" (6). Thus, this lack of connectedness is accompanied by a lack of emotions not only on Inni's part — it is not only the alienation of fragmentation, but a second degree of such an alienation, a lack of general emotional response — a Postmodern mode of experience.

Genuine tears can still be shed as long as one can understand and identify a threat and anxiety of change, which is a Modern impulse; however, the unfathomable dread of the takeover of the sign is undeniable: "Six years previously... he had wept.... And for the same reason. Dark premonitions, and an unfathomable dread of changing something, anything, in his life, if only by a mere sign or ceremony" (1). Still able to examine his position, Inni is not yet completely engulfed, yet the uncontrollable movement of signs anticipates the Postmodern condition and Inni's anxiety about the signs and ceremonies indicates the fatality of the Postmodern whirlpool of signs.

Just like Aunt Therese flies past nature when she comes into contact with it as if it were a "hostile element" (23), Inni and Zita unauthentically perform a natural act, described as mere "lust machines": "Inni and Zita thus became two perfect lust machines, attractive to the eye, ornaments to the city, dream apparitions..." (4). As machines, they have not only lost any connection with the authentic experience, but their experience has also been objectified to the point that they function as automatons. They produce lust as a Postmodern mass product, failing to feel anything authentic about each other or interact in any authentic manner. They produce images; through mere reproduction and repetition, they produce copies of the original experience, and become photo images of themselves. The photo images symbolically adorn the city, also becoming aesthetic signs. Spread out across the metropolis, their images transform into "dream apparitions" as they are reduced to the optical aesthetic sign of themselves.

News reports of, for example, Kennedy's assassination, the stock market, the Dow Jones's average, and dates, are interwoven through the novel; these "snapshots" flow through the storyline without abrupt interruptions or direct associations. Inni's daily horoscope demonstrates precisely the phenomenon Baudrillard describes as a "communication surface." Predicting his own fate, Inni writes about Zita's leaving him for the Italian, and his suicide attempt before these events actually happen. He thus sets up his own story and then lives through it in a hyperreal experience. These *ersatz*-horoscopes present a circularity of the flow of information underscored by the novel's structure: it begins with an "Intermezzo" going back and forth in time as Inni remembers and predicts particular situations and occurrences. Inni also uses plagiarized material to write his horoscopes: he culls his information from previously written predictions. This simulation is different from a fiction or a lie: it not only presents an absence as a presence — the imaginary as the real — but it also undermines any contrast to the real, for it absorbs the real within itself. Instead of a "real" economy of commodities that becomes somehow bypassed by an "unreal" myriad of advertising images, we can now only discern a hyperreality, a world of self-referential signs. The arbitrary sign, the horoscope about what is to happen in the future (Inni's own suicide), simultaneously determines future events that are then devalued by his failed suicide. Not only does his suicide failure become a sign without referring to the original or future story, but he performs it without emotion. His farcical suicide attempt is absorbed into the continued chain of events. Moreover, the notion of suicide itself becomes a sign. For Baudrillard death is an act that defies the world of simulacra, models and codes, signifying the reversibility of signs; however, intentional death, i.e. suicide, does not reverse the process of signs — it is yet but another sign for an intention.

The metaphor of time as an amorphous mass that drags along (20) suggests one more symptom of this imaginary and symbolic universe: "He was unable to estimate the time, measure it, divide it up" (21). "One thing was certain," reflects Inni, "the time he had lived was finished, but now... this amorphous thing containing both his memory and his lack of memory continued to accompany him as mysteriously and, even in reverse direction, as immeasurable as the universe about which there was so much discussion these days" (21). Inni has trouble with his memory precisely because it is no longer a part of him, but is, rather, absorbed into the amorphous mass of time. "Memory is like a dog that lies down where it pleases" (1). Inni's memories are blurred shadows; consequently, he tries desperately to memorize his life "so that in these recurring nocturnal last moments he could at least have watched an orderly film instead of all those loose fragments without the cohesion you might have expected of a life just ended" (6). This sense of time is analogous to Walter Benjamin's notion of chronological and allegorical time, albeit in reverse. The protagonist attempts to unify the loose fragments and force a coherent subject, but the fragments remain loose snapshots. Inni's lack of memory shaping an amorphous mass of time thus demonstrates the moment of Post-histoire — "the fragmentation of time into a series of perpetual presents" (Jameson 125).

The presentation of the "sign" of memory causes Inni to reflect on the function of memory. At each significant moment in one's life, he recalls, one ought to have someone who forces one to describe exactly that first experience at the moment itself in order to preserve the memory (30). But Inni has a problem with his memory: "What made exercising his memory difficult was not only the fact that his apparatus was so limited... but also that... the available supports and footholds needed for a trip to the underworld of the past were beginning to disappear" (21). "Thousands of whiskeys he had drunk since. Malt, bourbon, rye, the best and the worst, straight, with water, with soda, with ginger ale. And sometimes, suddenly, that sensation would come to him again. Smoke — yes, and hazelnut" (30). Thus in the absence of anything to fix the original experience in memory, Inni may succumb to the world of signs — the world of thousands of meaningless whiskeys. Yet through words, through story-telling, the memory is preserved.

This displacement of image and object is evident in the fact that Inni falls in love with Zita's photo before he sees her, yet "he did not know who betrayed whom, the woman in the photograph, the woman who stood before it, or the other way around" (11). Zita is standing in front of the photograph of herself when Inni realizes that if he wants to get to know her, he must approach the woman standing in front of the photograph, but it is the photograph he "had at once been sucked toward.... Power emanated from it" (11). The image was no longer a reflection of Zita: "It seemed as if that face, which could never really belong to a live human, had existed for thousands of years, independent of all else and completely absorbed in itself — an equilibrium" (11-2). Since Inni falls in love with the photograph and not really Zita herself, it is through photography that his love must die: "Zita saw her Italian [lover], slept with him, let herself be photographed by him. And each time another photo was taken, another fleck of Inni dissolved into the air of Amsterdam. The new love was the crematorium of the old" (13).

The picture of Zita suddenly appears in front of Inni while he is making love to another woman, Lyda: "As he half-raised himself and Lyda began to grunt softly under him, he suddenly looked into Zita's eyes. Paper eyes, but still Zita's. It was the photograph from *Taboo*, spread over two pages" (10). Inni reflects on his relationship with Zita, asking himself if she has ever looked at him with love. He focuses on the photograph which is personified as a rebuffing mask: "He looked more and more intently at the paper face that every second changed further into an unfamiliar, rebuffing mask" (10-11). The signified, that is Zita, and her image or her signifier, exchange roles as they intermingle in a dreamlike blur. Inni, too, is completely absorbed: "And so he had entered her world without ever becoming a member of it, and he had wrought damage in it while refreshing himself on the perfect equilibrium" (12). This intermingling is further underscored through the narrator's play with words: "[Zita. Inni.] Zinnies, Itas, Inizitas, Zinnininitas, Itizitas..." (2).

Inni's first encounter with Lyda can be described as a hyperreal experience. "I'm all green inside" (8), she tells Inni. Lyda is large, white, soft, and full. She has silver-gray sprayed hair up in a momentous hairdo, large vast white breasts, a wide mouth into which a river of green creme-de-menthe soda liquid disappears, and she is more than a head taller than Inni (9-11). This immense stature of artificiality begins to make its imprint on Inni: her silver hair-spray rubs off and is everywhere. "The stuff was everywhere, on his face, his chest, her face, everywhere!" (11). The silver-gray stuff, like the silver used in X-ray and photo production, smears everywhere as the entire scene becomes reminiscent of a black and white film. Inni himself is reduced symbolically to a half developed photograph as he runs to nature, to the pond in the city park, to remove "the outward sign of his removal from Zita's life.... But he does not succeed" (11). Absorbed into the signs of communication, he "saw his silver figure walk past the mirror" (11).

Finally, Philip Taads also becomes engulfed in the signifier. Although the Japanese tea ceremony is an attempt to create meaning through ritual, it is also defined as a reminder of one's insignificance in relationship to the world; furthermore, attached to an object: the tea cup from which Philip performs his last ceremony. The tea ceremony means everything to Philip as he wishes to escape from the meaninglessness of the world by means of this ritual. When the right time comes, he performs the last ceremony, breaking the object linked to the idea of his transcendence into the *Weltall*. Significantly, he drowns himself, swallowed by the signifier in a kind of sea of green tea.

In conclusion, the two features on which I have dwelt here — Postmodern trends of the blurred silver screen of communication or "pastiche," and themes of avant-garde fragmentation and alienation — represent two salient issues in contemporary literary analysis today. Nooteboom's *Rituals* lends itself well to the illustration of how these features are reflected in literature. Since Inni swears into "this life" at the end (144), the Postmodern trends in this novel can be read as managing to reinforce the logic of consumer capitalism itself, for "whatever it was — the long wear and tear, the painstaking mutual consummation as if it were a perpetual meal, all those long Amsterdam nights of body migrations and sudden visions destined for an empty film reel — all of this together... was about to disappear, and it would never come back. Never" (7).

References

Baudrillard, Jean. "The Ecstasy of Communication." *The Anti-Aesthetic: Essays on Postmodern Culture.* Ed. Hal Foster. Seattle: Bay Press, 1983. 126-34.
Benjamin, Walter. "The Work of Art in the Age of Mechanical Reproduction." *Illuminations.* Trans. Harry Zohn. Ed. Hannah Arendt. New York: Schocken Books, 1969.
Huyssen, Andreas, and Klaus R. Scherpe, eds. *Postmoderne: Zeichen eines kulturellen Wandels.* Hamburg: Rowohlt, 1986.
Jameson, Frederic. "Postmodernism and Consumer Society." In: *The Anti-Aesthetic: Essays on Postmodern Culture.* Ed. Hal Foster. Seattle: Bay Press, 1983. 111-25.
Nooteboom, Cees. *Rituelen.* Amsterdam: Uitgeverij De Arbeiderspers, 1980. Trans. Adrienne Dixon. *Rituals.* Baton Rouge: Louisiana State UP, 1983.

The Work of Marga Minco: A Wrangle of Time and Space

Johan P. Snapper
University of California at Berkeley

> Das Haus ansehn. Es ist still, niemand geht ein und aus, man wartet ein wenig, auf der Haus-Seite, dann auf der Seite gegenüber, nichts, solche Häuser sind so viel weiser als die Menschen, die sie anstarren.
> — Kafka
> (quoted by Marga Minco at the beginning of *Een leeg huis*)

In this paper I will focus attention on one of the primary motifs in Marga Minco's work: the collusion of time and space. While the temporal and spatial elements play an equally discernible role in Minco's entire *oeuvre*, I am limiting my discussion to those works which deal with the holocaust, because they represent a thematically unified body. They also make up the bulk of her writings.

Marga Minco's first and most popular work, *Het bittere kruid*, 1957 (*Bitter Herbs*, 1960) is generally considered one of the most successful post-war Dutch novels. In the past thirty-three years it has appeared in over 30 editions, sold nearly 400 thousand copies, and has been published in English, German, French, Spanish, Norwegian, Swedish, Welsh, and Hungarian. The autobiographical novel, narrated

---

Robert S. Kirsner (ed.), *The Low Countries and Beyond,* 171-179. Lanham, MD: University Press of America, 1993.

in the first person singular, chronicles the experiences of the youngest daughter of a Jewish family during the Second World War in 22 separate but related stories. It is a simple, sober account of WHAT happened TO WHOM, WHEN, and WHERE. Remarkably, the question WHY the holocaust took place is almost ignored and even the plot, WHAT exactly happened, is described with peculiarly vague matter-of-factness. By surpressing her own feelings about these horrible experiences, Minco records what appears to be detached recollections of events, coolly expressed in terms of time and space.

Emphasizing the importance of space, the narrator in *Bitter Herbs* gives a detailed account of where the family lives before and after each involuntary move, from Breda to Amersfoort to Amsterdam. From here the road or the railroad tracks lead to a hidden address for the only survivor and to a concentration camp for the rest of the family. We are presented with vivid descriptions of the crowded and deserted streets where they live, and the houses that gradually grow empty. We get to know each new dwelling in some detail, especially the doors and windows that in turn lead to other rooms or to a world outside that is both beckoning and threatening. The novel recounts the violent intrusion and forced abandonment of the family home at different times in different places, causing an inevitable estrangement from one's community, and, because of the need to assume another identity, ultimately from oneself.

The second novel, *Een leeg huis,* 1966 (*An Empty House,* 1990), also largely autobiographical, is again narrated by the familiar only survivor of a Dutch Jewish family that did not return from the concentration camps. It differs from *Bitter Herbs* by being placed in a post-war setting, and consists of three parts, each identified with a specific day, month, and year: Thursday, June 28th, 1945 (in Amsterdam); Tuesday, March 25th, 1947 (in France); and Friday, April 21st, 1950 (Back in Amsterdam). Together these crucial days span a five year period pursuant to the five war years chronicled in *Bitter Herbs,* turning *An Empty House* novel into a kind of sequal.

An Empty House is the story of Sepha, who goes into hiding in a house on the Kloverniersburgwal in Amsterdam, where she spends the hunger winter of 1944 with a fellow undergrounder, Mark. For firewood they literally wreck an empty house nextdoor. Right after the liberation Sepha travels to a farm in Friesland in order to recover and fatten up. After 4 weeks she hitchhikes back to Amsterdam, meeting up with a fellow-hitchhiker, also Jewish, by the name of Yona, who in many ways turns out to be her alter-ego. Yona, who has lost her entire family in extermination camps, is obsessed with the past. This is primarily reflected in her preoccupation with her family home. Sepha wants to forget the past, but Yona cannot. Partly through Yona's vivid recollections of her childhood home — which bears a striking resemblance to Sepha's — she is confronted with her OWN past. Minco accomplishes this by way of flashback and flashbacks within flashbacks, usually right in the middle of a thought, conversation, or description. The only way that the reader can figure out that s/he is now in another timespan is by the sudden, if often subtle, change in tense. But not the logical shift from present to past, but from past to present. Minco turns things around. She tells the story proper in the narrative past and interrupts with flashbacks that are presented in the present tense. The effect of his linguistic technique is considerable. By telling the main story in the traditional narrative past, Minco assigns not only a beginning, but also an end to the main plot; whereas the stubborn past by virtue of its present tense appears to have no end whatsoever. The relentless intrusion into the plot on the part of the past means that the past is always there and will always be there. So is Minco's emblematic house. *The Empty House* is ultimately the story about an ever-present past holding two young women captive in the prison-like houses of their childhood past. At the end of the story, after learning that Yona has committed suicide by jumping from a train — always a profound metaphor for Minco, as we shall see — Sepha visits Yona's room, and examines her personal effects, as if to try to understand her better. Upon leaving, she locks the room, taking the key with her. When she is back on the street on her way home, Sepha stops on the bridge — another significant leitmotif in Minco's work — and takes a final look at Yona's attic room, this time from the outside, studying the windows with the black shutter and contemplating the protruding hoisting beam above it, like domestic relics of a ravaged life and epoch.

In a collection of short stories entitled *De andere kant,* 1959 (*The Other Side*), four of the twelve stories deal with the subject of Jewish persecution in the war. We will see that here again the Minconian wrangle of time and space dominates the narrative. I will briefly concentrate on some of these elements before concluding with a more elaborate analysis of this motif in the novel *De glazen brug*, 1986 (*The Glass Bridge*, 1988).

"Het dorp van mijn moeder" ('The Village of my Mother') recounts the odyssey of the narrator-daughter to the birthplace of her mother, somewhere in Groningen. Both her parents are incarcerated in the deportation camp of Westerbork from where they will later be transferred to a concentration camp. The visit to the village represents a last ditch effort to save her parents by obtaining her mother's baptismal certificate, that may prove that her mother was not Jewish. The journey with its detailed emphasis on travel and places is typically Minco and the outcome of the mission is foreshadowed by the gloom of the journey. Armed with false identification papers, the girl boards a train that travels past the ominous deportation camp — she can see it from the train window — then takes a bus over bumpy, sandy roads and arrives at the village, where the streets as well as the houses are in disrepair, usually an omen of impending danger for Minco. After a long walk through the streets, she reaches the parsonage. The journey turns out to be a failure, for they cannot find her mother's name in the church records, and the highly-principled church elders refuse to furnish a false certificate. Minco works this out through her focus on the surroundings that evoke the curses of time and space. While the girl is waiting, for instance, two objects draw her attention, a large armoire with heavy copper lock that she (wrongly) assumes contains the baptismal certificates; and an obtrusive Frisian clock that at first ticks caustically ("vinnig") and that later has problems ticking altogether in a room filled with the heavy cow manure stench of the self-righteous elders.

The story ends with a kind of postscript that draws upon the pungent travel motif that unites place and time. Back at home, the daughter receives an unsigned postcard from her father, presumably thrown from the fateful train. In an ironic message that is typical of Minco's understated sense of tragedy, it says: "We are en route to the border. Mother is fine. The train is very full."

Unlike the previous two narratives, the story "De dag mijn zuster trouwde" ('The Day My Sister Married') emphasizes the temporal element in the TITLE, but its primary focus is on place, specifically on the house in Amersfoort where the uprooted family was forced to live in 1942. The story, which, significantly, begins with an alarm clock and an open window, is Sepha's moving account of her sister's wedding. At her mother's insistence the occasion seems to be a traditional celebration with gaiety and a full house of relatives, as if everything were normal. But the way Minco handles the plot, the collective pretense does not work. Consider the clues: the yellow stars of David that mark their coats, the star-shaped flowers of the bridal bouquet, and the screech of a tomcat perched on the fence (!) between their house and the neighbor's that sounds like a human scream. For Sepha the cry functions as a premonition that the family may never return to this house. Taken together these clues serve to unmask the deception that belies their neurotic claim to normalcy. Even more poignant is the procession through the streets. The way the family surrounds the bride and groom in the synagogue reminds the narrator of a game they used to play as children: "In Holland staat een huis" in which the man chooses a wife, she, a child, then a maid, etc. until at the end of the game all the principals cheerfully burn the house to the ground: "En dan steken we 't huis in brand." And indeed, the song is prophetic, for the newly formed family is arrested in a pogrom and the home of the two newlyweds is destroyed almost before it began. In "The Day My Sister Married" Minco has once again unleashed the wrangling forces of time and space to pronounce their cataclysmic sentence upon the innocent.

The story "Het adres" ('The Adress') once again zeroes in on the domestic aspect of the Minconian tragedy. But here too, the author provides an unexpected twist. This time the titular address belongs not to the prey, but to the predator. It is again the story of Minco's proverbial surviving Jewish daughter, this time visiting the house of a woman who had exploited the narrator's family during the war. The woman, an acquaintance, had "generously" offered to "store" the family's prized silverware, paintings, china, and other articles personal possessions in her own home during the war in order to keep them away from the enemy — a theme that first appears in *Bitter Herbs* and recurs time and again. It is after the war and the (nameless) sole surviver sets out to reclaim the family belongings. The woman, wearing the vest belonging to the visitor's mother, expresses surprise that anyone of the family had "come back," but she nevertheless refuses to let her in and she physically blocks the door. On a second visit the woman is not home, but her little daughter lets her in. The two daughters are alone. The visitor immediately recognizes her family heirlooms prominently displayed on the walls and tables of the house. But she feels like a stranger and oppressed by the foul smell that pervades the atmosphere — both familiar motifs, as we have seen in the story "The Village." Telling herself that relics of her past mean little outside of their original context, she decides to leave empty-handed. In this story time and space are once again in collusion. Unable to retrieve the remnants of her past life and home she leaves the address where the holocaust still lives, and catches the train back to her own apartment. But here, too, the war still lingers, as the ugly tatters of blackout paper still hanging down from her windows clearly suggest. With the clinking of the silver spoons still ringing in her ears — like the chiming of a clock — she decides to forget this address of shame.

The story "De terugkeer" ('The Return') has yet a different twist. It is a complex account of the post-war survival not of a single child, but of the parents. The story concentrates on the travails of Mr. and Mrs. Goldstijn, who are orphaned by the extermination of their children. The narrative covers four wrangling time periods and their corresponding settings. And, unlike Minco's earlier work in this regard, each of these stations seems to beg the unanswerable question of the "why" of their plight. This is especially the case with Mr. Goldstijn, whom Minco portrays as wandering within the intertwining mazes of time and place, unable to find his way out. Although the story begins 8 years after the war, with the couple living in a strange house in a strange city, the numerous flashbacks to earlier periods dominate the present. We see the man surveying the streets of Amsterdam, visiting familiar buildings, like the old synagogue — now a warehouse — and, of course, the family house, now occupied by anonymous strangers. Everything is irreversibly altered. As he crosses the proverbial Minconian bridge the old man studies his old house from rooftop to the doorstep — like Sepha in the novel *An Empty House* — and concludes that he himself is the real stranger in the old familiar street — a realization that underscores Minco's oft-repeated theme that the present and the future after the war are even more difficult for the Jews than the years of hiding during the war. Here again all of time is dominated by an ever-present past. The bridge appears a second time. In the park where Mr. Goldstijn used to spend so much time with his children before the war and where he now frequently wanders about. They are both surprised, for neither is where she is expected to be. He is supposed to be at work; she at home. Unbeknown to him, she too is scouting out the old city — also all by herself. But he also knows that HER reconnaissance differs from his. Putting it somewhat diffently, HER bridge symbolizes an attempt to step out of the painful past into the present no matter how difficult; whereas his own bridge is a desperate search for a distant idyllic past that is forever gone. What remains for Minco is the war and the antisemitic forces that shaped it. That horrible past is permanently engraved on the streets, on the old synagogues; and the on the facades, the steps, the doors and windows of the houses. It is a past that registers and re-registers itself deep within the souls of the victims. The tragedy of the Minconian past is further heightened by a prophetic dimension, and as such has an active life of its own. This is the function of the frame with which the story begins and ends. While in bed and unable to sleep, Goldstijn hears disquieting sounds coming from the neighbor's shed. The new neighbor who seems to be working, is keeping him awake by whistling the familiar tune of an old nazi S.A. song he recalls from the war ("Die Fahnen hoch, die Reihen fest geschlossen, SA marchiert"). For Mr. Goldstijn the new neighbor is an old nazi collaborator who has only recently been released from prison. When Mr. Goldstijn looks at his watch, he sees that is 1:30 a.m. But, no matter what the clock says, for Mr. Goldstijn the war is not over and, in a profound sense, it is both earlier and therefore also later than it is.

Let me conclude with some remarks about Minco's last and best novel *De glazen brug,* 1986 (*The Glass Bridge,* 1990) which is the story about a young woman, Stella, who spends the war years in hiding under the name of Maria Roselier, and who 20 years later visits the distant village where her original namesake lived and died. Most of the work consists of flashbacks to the war years, with particular focus on Stella's many changes of address, her relationship to the streets, the houses and the rooms where she lived; and especially her solitary escape via the roof during a raid in which most of her remaining friends and relatives were captured. As in the earlier works, *The Glass Bridge* abounds in the interacting motifs of time and place. Once again we recognize "travel" as a particularly striking metaphor, not only referring to a change in location, but also from one era to another, or even from life to death. Minco's vehicles of change include walking, hitchhiking, riding bicycles, cars, buses, trams, and ferries, and especially the ever-present fateful train. And their function more often than not is that of a bridge between separate places, periods, and conditions. In no work is this clearer than in *The Glass Bridge,* where Minco has constructed a titular bridge out of these treacherous building blocks of change. The image of the glass bridge represents a double recollection by Stella, introduced in the form of a flashback. It is the first winter in Amsterdam, and Stella and her father have gone out to sellsome family possessions in order to be able to buy false identification papers for her. Not far from their house, they come upon an arched bridge that Stella recalls in almost magical terms. It is transparent and so uniformly covered with ice that it reflects the sky. After carefully crossing the bridge, Stella slides down on the other side, just as she used to do as a little girl with her father on a bridge near their native Breda. But, unlike the old days, this time he does not follow her. She still sees his hand clutched around the railing, his eyes filled with tears. Equally vivid to her is the image of the tree that was snapped in two and trapped in the ice of the canal behind the wind-blown figure of her father. The picture of the bridge with the backdrop of the dead tree, clearly a prophetic image of separation, has never left Stella, no matter how hard she tries to drive it out with other memories of her father and herself.

The Minconian bridge no longer bridges, but separates. It does not explain life; it simply depicts the horrible reality of time and space, in which the road ahead remains treacherously slippery and the clock is running rampant. There is perhaps a flicker of hope in the paradoxical bridge. Minco does not elaborate, she only leaves us with a final picture. When twenty four years later Stella at long last reaches the village of Avezeel where the girl whose identity she had taken over had lived, she is taken to the bridge from which the original Maria had jumped to save her life, but which instead hastened her tragic premature death. Yet it was this very jump from the bridge that also saved the life of Stella, the new Maria Roselier.

In the last scene of the novella the complex travel motif is introduced for the last time. Stella is leaving Avezeel as she had arrived: alone. This time she is portrayed standing on the bridge of the ferry, her hands clutched around the railing, her travel bag at her feet, the burdensome weight of the past on her back, hesitantly facing the road toward an uncertain future. The picture depicts the Minconian world in a nutshell.

References

Minco, Marga. 1957. *Het bittere kruid: een kleine kroniek; met tekeningen van Herman Dijkstra.* Den Haag: Bert Bakker/Daamen.
_____. 1960. *Bitter Herbs: a Chronicle.* Translated by Roy Edwards. London: Oxford University Press.
_____. 1959. *De andere kant.* Den Haag: Bert Bakker.
_____. 1966. *Een leeg huis.* Den Haag: Bert Bakker/Daamen.
_____. 1990. *An Empty House.* Translated by Margaret Clegg. London: Peter Owen.
_____. 1986. *De glazen brug.* Amsterdam: Bert Bakker.
_____. 1988. *The Glass Bridge.* Translated by Stacey Knecht. London: Peter Owen.
Middeldorp, A. 1981. *Over het proza van Marga Minco.* Amsterdam: Wetenschappelijke Uitgeverij
Kroon, Dirk, ed. 1982. *Over Marga Minco: Beschouwingen en interviews.* Den Haag: BZZTôH.

Gospel and Religion in the Poetry of Ida Gerhardt

Jacques van der Elst
Potchefstroom University for Christian Higher Education, South Africa

1. **Introductory.** Ida Gerhardt (born 1905), a student of J. H. Leopold and, like him, a classical scholar, made her debut in 1940 with a volume of poems called *Kosmos*. She has been awarded a variety of literary prizes, including the very distinguished P. C. Hooft Prize. In 1980 a third edition of her collected poems was published by Athenaeum Polak and Van Gennep in Amsterdam. Her latest volume, *De Adelaarsvarens,* was published in 1989.

2. **Innate spiritual capacity ("religie"), religion, and gospel.** The most striking feature of her poetry is possibly the handling of the religious, including worship, evangelism, and even a Protestant predilection. Gerhardt warns against an over-simplified view of the religious subject matter in her poetry: "Ze willen me wel eens rangschikken onder de Protestantse dichters: dat maakt me razend" (Gerhardt, 1980:30).[1] She possibly means by this that she does use Scriptural givens, but that these givens are not necessarily handled with an evangelistic view in mind. The aim of the present paper is to indicate that Gerhardt's poetry reaches much further than the religious or the evangelical, while not excluding these qualities.

A distinction should be made with regard to the concepts *religious/evangelizing* and *worshipful.* The term *religious* is used here in

---

[1] "They keep insisting on categorizing me among the Protestant poets. That drives me up a wall."

Robert S. Kirsner (ed.), *The Low Countries and Beyond,* 181-196. Lanham, MD: University Press of America, 1993

the sense of god-fearing, devout, or pious. For the purposes of this paper I regard *evangelizing* as a synonym for *religious,* with the difference that evangelizing, in complementarity to religious, carries a certain connotation of intention: the intention to convert. Gospel or the evangelical has to do with the conscious spreading of the message of redemption through Christ's death on the Cross. When a poem simply has as its intention the spreading of the Gospel, then it can become superficial, like a piece of Christian reading matter.

Innate spiritual capacity is a more comprehensive term and in reality includes the religious and evangelizing. It ties in with the fact that each individual is in essence capable of worship, has a capacity for religion, in the sense that he believes in another reality, not necessarily a transcendental reality, which would mostly be better and more ideal than his own reality. A. Roland Holst's symbolistic poetry reveals a religious link to such another world, an elysium detached from time and space. It is an elysium which might reveal similarities with Christianity and gospel but which is emphatically not Christian/religious or evangelizing. This innate spiritual capacity in general has to do with man's inherent tendency to create for himself "something," an ideal, which he regards as holy and untouchable. Where the Christian/religious artist has been inspired divinely or Biblically, and wants to testify to an Ultimate Truth, one's innate spiritual capacity has to do with, as in the case of Holst, self-projected worlds beyond the worldly dispensation of time and space.

3.   Easter poems. Whether one refers to worship, religion, or gospel, all three concepts have in the course of the centuries been important driving forces in poetry. The manifestation and accentuation of these concepts and their meaning for the production of text will be discussed subsequently in a number of poems with a similar theme, that of the Resurrection: the Easter poems.

3.1   Nel Benschop. A good example of religious/evangelizing literature is the Easter poem by Nel Benschop "Een open hand uit de hemel" from the volume *Een open hand naar de hemel* (1976:5).

> Een stille, wonderlijke morgen:
> Wachters, die waken bij't gesloten graf

waar Christus' moede lichaam werd geborgen;
ze wachten, half in slaap, de morgen af.
Dan, plotseling, begint de grond te beven,
een bliksemflits schiet door de donk're lucht;
de dood wordt overwonnen door het Leven,
de wachters slaan verbijsterd op de vlucht.
Geen oog ziet Christus uit het rotsgraf komen,
geen oor heeft 't rollen van de steen gehoord,
geen hart heeft van dit wonder durven dromen,
Gods samenzijn met hem wordt niet gestoord.

En Petrus ziet de opgerolde doeken,
Johannes staat er stil-aanbiddend bij.
Dan, als de Heer Zijn jong'ren gaat bezoeken
vertoont Hij hun Zijn handen en Zijn zij.

En elke keer als wij zijn dood gedenken
en drinken van de wijn en eten 't brood,
mogen wij aan die stille morgen denken
toen Christus is verrezen uit de dood.
Vol van erbarmen tot ons neergebogen
neemt Hij de last van onze zonden af.
En in zijn licht zie ik met nieuwe ogen
een open hand, een open hart, een open graf...

An open hand directed at heaven

A serene, tranquil morning:
Guards hover over the closed grave
where Christ's broken body was laid;
they wait, half asleep, for day to break.
Then, of a sudden, the earth starts heaving,
a shaft of lightning tears the dark sky
death is vanquished by Life,
the guards stand transfixed, some flee.
No human eye sees Christ emerging from the grave,
no ear hears the thunder of the stone heaved aside,
no heart has dared to dream of the wonder,

God's nearness to Him is not disturbed.

And Peter sees the rolled ceremeonts,
John stands by in prayer,
then, when the Lord appears to the disciples,
He shows his hands and his pierced side.

And whenever we commemorate his death
and drink of the wine and eat of the bread,
we are enjoined to think once more of the quiet morn
when Christ vanquished death.
He bent down to us with compassion
and took away the burden of sins.
and in his Light I see with new eyes
an opened hand, an opened heart, an opened grave...

Perhaps the limiting factor of the poem is the fact that the reader is offered practically no option of choice. With this kind of poem, according to Van der Ent (1982:43), the reader is faced with a forced choice: "...kan ik dit meevoelen en nazeggen of niet?" and he continues with "...de godsdienstige gevoelens zijn te specifiek. Wanneer het gedicht geen ruimte laat voor de ervaring van de lezer, wanneer deze verplicht is precies na te voelen wat daar is geschreven, verzet hij zich snel tegen deze poëzie. Lezers kunnen zich niet herkennen, of een beetje, of niet helemaal."[2]

This kind of poem is, in literary terms, indigestible. The element of surprise is missing from this confessional outpouring in rhyming lines. It is in reality a paraphrase of the events of Resurrection, with an eventual reference to participation in Holy Communion. It is a kind of religious propaganda. It ties in with the above-mentioned dilemma of religious and evangelizing lyrical poetry. This is not meant to indicate, however, that Nel Benschop had pretensions with her work. She typified her own poems as "meditations in rhyme," and the message to

---

[2] "...could I empathize with this and repeat it, or not?" and "...the religious feelings are too specific. When the poem leaves no room for the experience of the reader, when the reader is forced to feel exactly in terms of what has been written, he soon resists the poetry. Readers cannot recognize themselves in this — or only slightly, or not at all."

be got from her popularity, attested to by the fact that tens of thousands of her volumes are sold, is that there is a need among believers for this kind of poetry.

3.2 Izak de Villiers. The Afrikaans poem "Gebed vir Paasmôre" ('A Prayer for Easter Morning') (1974:21) by Izak de Villiers has a corresponding theme. There are aspects which count in the favour of the poem, as De Villiers' poem reaches out further than Benschop's poem. The English translation of the poem reads as follows:[3]

> Risen Saviour
> The church bells have a new ring this morning.
> They are Easter chimes,
> Chiming across the valley
> Over the city
> Through the world.
> The Lord has risen,
> Yes, He has truly risen.
>
> With all Christians all over the world, all the Lord's children,
> I want to pray to You, o Conqueror!
> With bells I want to rejoice
> over the miracle of a grave in a garden
> which opened never to close again.
>
> A path has been trodden through the vale of death.
> You have trodden it.
> Leaving tracks of blood.
> The path runs right through death
> into eternal life.
> And I shall follow it, if You call me.
> I have risen with You, Lord Jesus
> For my heart has changed already.
> I have touched You
> And You have touched me
> And so I shall never die.

---

[3] The original Afrikaans version is found in the *Appendix* to this paper.

Because You live
I live.
I rejoice over You, Lord Jesus.
I rejoice with the bells of Easter.
I rejoice in this morning
About a new morn
when the bells will not be stilled
and morning will nevermore fade
into evening.

Amen.

3.3 Comparison. In comparison with Benschop's poem, the following should be seen as favoring the De Villiers's poem, both in terms of form and content. First, the poem as prayer has a dramatic impact — the concern here is a dialogue with God. The free verse form supports the dialogic aspect of the poem. Second, there is also a temporal variation of the *then* of Easter to the *now* of the poet. The *I* of the poem hears that the sound of the Easter bell is different *today*. There is also a reference to the future: "this morning" brings the "new morning." Third, the concern is also strongly with the confessional *I* as against a somewhat removed collective *us* in Nel Benschop's poem. Although objectivation is more successfully attained in De Villiers's poem, the narrowing direct recognition of the religious and the evangelizing is still present. The reader and empathizer with the poem cannot engage creatively with the poem. Ultimately it is still poetry which confirms too much. Good poetry has to inspire, stimulate, release, and open up, and perhaps rather set questions than answer questions, and become a network of interrelations rippling outwards.

4. Ida Gerhardt. The poem "Pasen" by Ida Gerhardt (1988:535), sharing the same theme as other two works we have discussed, is very possibly such a poem:

```
1    Een diep verdriet dat ons is aangedaan
2    kan soms, na bittere tranen, onverwacht
3    gelenigd zijn. Ik kwam langs Zalk gegaan,
4    op Paasmorgen, zeer vroeg nog op den dag.
5    Waar onderdijks een stukje moestuin lag
```

6   met boerse rijtjes primula verfraaid,
7   zag ik, zondags getooid, een kindje staan.
8   Het wees en wees en keek mij stralend aan.
9   De maartse regen had het 's nachts gedaan:
10 daar stond zijn doopnaam, in sterkers gezaaid.

Easter

A deep sadness which has been inflicted
on us can at times, after bitter tears,
be ameliorated. I came along Zalk
on Easter morning, very early in the day.
Where, in the lee of the dike a scrap of vegetable garden
nestled, prettied with rustic rows of primula
I saw a small child in Sunday best
who pointed and pointed and looked at me with shining face.
The March rain had done this during the night:
His baptismal name was there, sown in garden cress.

What is striking is that while Christian-religious elements are present (there are references to Christmas, to Easter, to baptism), the poem alludes further than the MERELY religious and thereby reveals an interesting complexity.

The universally human given of grief that harrows is elevated to an experience early in the morning — a kind of motif of dawning? — in a pastoral setting in Zalk, a small rural area. In the environment something magical and worshipful emerges: a child with a shining expression on its face which alludes to the primitive forces of impregnation and germination: the garden cress, the herb which spells out his name (line 10) possibly sown by a parent who wished to elicit from a child a sense of surprise and wonder about natural events. The garden cress is an herbal plant which can be sown throughout the year. Apart from its being used in salads, it also has healing qualities and deters snakes. De Vries (1974:117) also mentions that the herb can be symbolic for stability and strength. Perhaps one could go even further with the symbolism of the garden cress, as the link with stars (from the

Dutch name *sterkers*) is not excluded, and this opens up an association with universe, heaven, earth, light, eternity, and resurrection (the cress has been sowed and has germinated). Tightly woven into the texture of the poem there are stirrings of the great Christian events of Resurrection and Baptism.

One of Gerhardt's most enthralling Easter poems is "De afdaling" (198:593) from the volume *Het Sterreschip*. The poem by implication contains the full account of the Christian events: crucifixion, the descent to hell (the grave), resurrection, and the vision of the final ascent to heaven, all anachronistically situated in a true Dutch landscape.

1	Op de Elisabeth van Maasbracht
2	heb ik gevaren, drie nachten drie dagen;
3	trappen van water daalden wij af.
4	Veertig meter gaat het omlaag
5	vanaf Maastricht tot Grave.
6	Met de Elisabeth van Maasbracht.
7	Sterk is het ancestrale, het water:
8	trappen van water dalen er af
9	tot in de dood en zijn krochten omlaag,
10	's nachts, als de dromen ontwaken.
11	Op de Elisabeth van Maasbracht —
12	schaduwen, raadselen, wolkengevaarten;
13	trappen van raadselen daalde ik af:
14	zeventig jaren ben ik gesmaad
15	door wie een naam met mij dragen.
16	Met de Elisabeth van Maasbracht
17	rijzend en dalend nog laat in de sluizen
18	— trappen van water daalde zij af —
19	meerden wij. Het was stil op de kade,
20	wit was om de lantarens de mist.
21	"Als alle tranen zijn afgewist"
22	staat er in de Openbaring.

The Descent

I have voyaged on the Elisabeth of Maasbracht
for three days and three nights;
we went down a watery stairway.
From Maastricht to Grave it
was forty metres — down, down.

With the Elisabeth of Maasbracht.
The ancestral force, the water is strong:
we slide down stairways of water
down to death and to its hidden underworlds
at night, when dreams rise up.

On the Elisabeth of Maasbracht —
shadows, riddles, threatening clouds;
down stairways of riddles I descend:
for seventy years I have been disdained
by such who share a name with me.

On the Elisabeth of Maasbracht
which rides up and down in the locks
— stairways of water down which to descend —
we anchored. It was quiet on the quay
and the lanterns shone white in the fog.

"When all tears have been washed away,"
it says in Revelations.

On a concrete, realistic level, the poem concerns a barge with the name *Elisabeth van Maasbracht* which moves down the river by means of a series of locks (line 3) from Maastricht to Grave (it represents a fall of 40 meters, as mentioned in the poem — line 4).

But the title of the poem has certain implications. It contains a reference to Christ's descent into hell which is extended by way of further data. The THREE days and THREE nights (line 2) supply the ASSOCIATION with the story of RESURRECTION and, along with it, the place-name Grave (line 5), which may contain an allusion to the grave. Accordingly, the resurrectional givens are complete.

A trip across WATER — the image of water as primitive force figures strongly in Gerhardt's poetry — becomes a spiritualized voyage. The first stanza contains something more of reality: the second stanza represents something of night, of death, of forces, and of dreams — an image of deepening fear and anxiety. Van der Zeijde (1985:260) calls this a disquieting world, a world of night, where the forces of darkness are overpowering and threatening. There are various associations with hell: In this regard "Krochten" (line 9) is a typifying word; cf. Van Dale's gloss of it (1970:1042) as a hidden underworld space, often a hiding place of creatures shying away from light, "also of application to hell."

The third stanza, with its allusions to "shadows, riddles, threatening clouds" (line 12) contains a further individualization: the steps of water (the locks) are now steps in a RIDDLE — along which I still HAVE TO proceed, with an added autobiographical reference, to personal harm done by others, one's own family, bearing the same SURNAME, in general people with evil intent. The poem does not become mired in personal and individualized forms, however — from the personal there is a movement to the universal levels of hope and redemption. The conclusion contains something of an image of peace — the SILENCE — the whiteness of the fog which is visible around the light shed by the lanterns (line 20).

At the end there is a Biblical word of consolation which is by implication the promise of the kingdom of peace of Revelation 21:4:

> And God shall wipe away all tears from their eyes; and there shall be no more death, neither sorrow, nor crying, neither shall there be any more pain: for the former things are passed away.

With the discussion of the four Easter poems it has become clear that Gerhardt, in contrast to Benschop and De Villiers, has moved much further in the poetic experience of Easter than merely providing a Scriptural or paraphrased résumé of the story of the Resurrection. Benschop and De Villiers's versions (the latter to a lesser extent) are too explicitly Christian and persuasively evangelizing. Gerhardt has serious objections to this kind of explicit poetry. Van der Zeijde (1985:259) says the following: "Van hieruit is het ook begrijpelik dat, en waarom, Ida nooit heeft gehouden van de zogenaamde 'christelijke poëzie.' Allereerst, omdat die christelijke poëzie bijna altijd zeer zwakke poëzie is: niet zelden een enkele vondst en de rest is erbij gesleept. Maar het is misschien vooral het expliciet karakter waaraan zij zich stoot: te expliciet en juist daardoor inadequaat."[4]

As has emerged above, Gerhardt uses the Christian elements as a source of allusion, just as she frequently uses the Greek-classical world as a field of reference and allusion. Often she gains access to the religious suggestion of "gene zijde" ('the beyond, the hereafter') via Classical Antiquity. All this coheres with her religious acceptance of the primitive force of poetry. In her poetics there is always again the thought that verse has a kind of superhuman power and can do with her what it likes. She sometimes calls herself an instrument.

In the poem "Dichterspreuken II" (1988:591) ('Poetic proverbs') she deals with the "detachment of the heart" ("onthechting des harten") of being a poet — something which is reminiscent of Nijhoff's "De pen op papier." This "detachment" can be briefly illuminated by way of the poem "Voltooiing" (1988:528), in which something is said of the primitive force of creating poetry:

> Diep in die kern van het vers,
> daar waar de strengen ontstaan,
> hoort het al niet meer aan mij,
> breken de krachten zich baan;
> steigeren, vinden bestand.
> Machtig in rijmen en rand,
> hoor! stem en branding gaan aan:
> werking van trek en van tij.

---

[4]"From this it can be understood that, and why, Ida never liked the so-called 'Christian poetry.' In the first place because Christian poetry is almost always very bad poetry: not infrequently one single insight with the rest dragged into it. But it is perhaps mostly its explicit character which repels her: too explicit and for that reason inadequate."

Diep in de kern van het vers
scheurt het zich naakt van mij vrij.

Consummation

Deep in the core of the verse,
there where the sinews come into being,
there it does not belong to me any more,
and the forces escape from their set paths;
they rear up, find their feet.
Mighty in rhyming and edge,
Listen! voice and surf boom on:
the action of ebb and of flow
Deep in the core of the verse
it tears itself from me in blood and nakedness.

This primal instigation of poetry is finally conveyed in intensified form in "In den beginne" (1988:430), with the reference to the creation story, the faith in an indefinable source of energy with "quiet nuclei" to which she, as poet, can only give the hard SHELL to cover it: "zet ik de mantelen aan" ('I add the shells...').

ik zet mijn verzen als een schelpdier aan
in diepten waar geen sterveling mij kent,
ik adem in en uit, en zij ontstaan
uit stille kernen, in het element
dat was van den beginne. Altijd blijft
het grote stromen in mij overgaan.
Ik ben alleen. Een maatgang schrijft en schrijft:
ademende zet ik de mantelen aan.

In the beginning

I offer my verses crawling like a crustacean
in depths where no being knows me,
I breathe in and out, and verses come into
being in still nuclei, in the element that has

been there since the beginning. Forever strong
streams keep rushing through me.
I am alone. A regular force writes and writes:
in deep-held breath I add the shells.

Truly good poetry is double-layered. "Lees maar er staat niet wat er staat," the well-known quote from "Awater" by Nijhoff (1964:216),[5] is especially applicable to Gerhardt's poetry. The essence of her verse, as is the case with the Easter poems, does not merely lie in what is said, but much rather in what is suggested. The difference between the religious poems of Benschop and De Villiers on the one hand and the work of Gerhardt on the other is essentially contained in the word of Van der Zeijde (1985:278).

> Er is een uitspraak over poëzie die luidt dat verzen 'bestaan uit woorden en hun stilten.' Ik versta dit als: woorden met de pauzes daartussen, en met de gedachten en gevoelens waarmee die pauzes zijn gevuld. Een vers dat die stilten niet heeft, is vrees ik helemaal geen vers. Maar bij de poëzie van Ida Gerhardt geldt in vele gevallen nog iets anders. Hetgeen NIET gezegd wordt — met geen enkel woord —, is daar niet zelden juist de essentie van het vers.[6]

5. **In conclusion.** Man's innate spiritual capacity may be the primal source of poetry, but when it becomes religion within the limiting meaning of religiosity or gospel, this can have a narrowing effect on the reception and eventual interpretation of the poetry itself. A religio-spiritual impact in the wider sense of the word — not necessarily with the exclusion of the evangelical — can allow poetry to reach out much further, and this is the case with Gerhardt's lyrics. She moves without excluding the gospels, across the frontiers of the gospels to the world

---

[5] Literally: "Just read, it doesn't say what it says."

[6] "There is a statement about poetry to the effect that verse 'consists of words and their silences.' I understand this to mean: words with pauses in between, and with the feelings and thoughts with which these pauses are filled. Verse which does not have these silences is, I am afraid, not verse at all. But in Ida Gerhardt's poetry something more comes into play very often. There, what is NOT said at all — by any means — is not seldom the very essence of the verse."

of the universally human, and vice versa. This provides her poetry with its universal impact.

The Easter poems by Nel Benschop and Izak de Villiers, on the other hand, have limited value within the reception and referential frameworks of Christians and people who are converted to Christianity, and as such are means to an end. Gerhardt's Easter poems, in both their reception and experience, are also aesthetic objects whose range of impact stretches much further than merely confession and mediating towards evangelization and conversion.

Gerhardt's poetry conforms to and confirms the plea by Van der Ent (1982:45): "Ik voer een pleidooi voor het moeilijkste genre van de lyriek. Zowel aan de dichter als aan de lezer stelt zij [i.e. religious poetry] de hoogste eisen. Aan de lezer, omdat hij zich moet losmaken van allerlei vooroordelen. Aan de dichter, omdat hij een religieuse dimensie moet aanbrengen IN HET GODSDIENSTIGE. Kan dat? Ja, dat kan."[7]

Finally such a finding about Gerhardt's poetry is perhaps also applicable to an approach to all ideologically-directed poetry. An overemphasis on ideology in lyrical poetry, to the detriment of the more universal values, can do no other than to lead to a more negative evaluation or characterization of a poem or even an oeuvre of a poet.

---

[7]"I would like to plead for the most difficult genre of lyricism. To both poet and reader [the religious lyric] presents the most stringent demands. To the reader, because he has to detach himself from all kinds of prejudices. To the poet, because he must bring a genuinely religiously aware dimension to the FORMALLY RELIGIOUS. Can this be done? Yes it can."

Appendix

Gebed vir Paasmôre (I. L. de Villiers)

Verrese Heiland
Die kerkklokke lui vanoggend anders
Hulle is Paasklokke.
Hulle lui oor die vallei.
Hulle lui oor die stad.
Hulle lui oor die wereld.
Die Here het opgestaan!
Ja, Hy het waarlik opgestaan!

Saam met Christene oor die wereld, al u kinders,
wil ek aanbid, Oorwinnaar!
Saam met die klokke wil ik juig
oor die wonder van 'n graf in 'n tuin
wat oopgegaan het om nooit weer toe te gaan nie.

Daar's 'n pad getrap deur die dal van die dood.
U het dit uitgetrap.
U het bloedspore getrap.
Die pad gaan deur die dood
na die ewige lewe.
Ek gaan die pad volg as u my roep.
Ek het saam met U opgestaan, Here Jesus.
Hierbinne in my hart is dit al anders.
Ek was met U in aanraking.
U het my aangeraak.
Ek sal nooit sterf nie.

Want U leef!
U leef!
Ek juig oor U, Here Jesus.
Ek juig saam met die Paasklokke.
Ek juig in hierdie môre,
oor 'n nuwe môre
wanneer die klokke nie sal ophou nie, wat sal môre bly
en nooit sal aand word nie.

Amen.

References

Benschop, N. 1976. *Een open hand naar de hemel.* Kampen: Kok.
De Villiers, I. L. 1974. *Manna oor die duine.* Kaapstad: Tafelberg.
De Vries, A. 1974. *Dictionary of Symbols.* Amsterdam/London: North Holland Publishing Company.
Gerhardt, I. 1980. *Nu ik hier iets zeggen mag.* Amsterdam: Polak & Van Gennep.
_____. 1988. *Verzamelde gedichten.* Amsterdam: Athenaeum — Polak & Van Gennep.
_____. 1989. *De adelaarsvarens.* Amsterdam: Athenaeum — Polak & Van Gennep.
Jansen, E. 1988. "De reiskameraad op het spoor" (55-74) in *Woorde open die beskouing.* Durban: Butterworths.
Nijhoff, M. 1964. *Verzamelde gedichten.* Den Haag: Bert Bakker/Daamen.
Van Dale. *Groot Woordenboek der Nederlandse taal.* 1970 's-Gravenhage: M. Nijhoff.
Van der Ent, H. 1982. *Literatuur en christelijk perspektief.* 's-Gravenhage: Boekencentrum. pp. 144.
Van der Zeijde, M. H. 1985. *De wereld van het vers. Over het werk van Ida Gerhardt.* Amsterdam: Athenaeum — Polak & Van Gennep.

Politics in Frank Martinus Arion's *Nobele Wilden*

Manfred Wolf
San Francisco Sate University

Frank Martinus Arion is a Curaçaoan writer whose novel in Dutch, *Nobele Wilden,* is curiously European. His characters think about the West Indies, but they do so mainly from afar: the book is set in France, in Lourdes. It has none of the features of most other West Indian fiction, no accounts of song-making, no description of the music that permeates island life, no rendering of that talk-for-its-own sake so common in the Caribbean, no depiction of island dialect; on the contrary, it is an indoors kind of book, reflective and often epistolary, its tone urbane and its conversations polished and cerebral. What this novel provides is not a new understanding of West Indian life but a perspective on its political possibilities — or the lack of them.

The title of Arion's novel, too, is oddly European. The Noble Savage, after all, is a European concept, and it's odd that a black writer should use it without apparent irony. But with obvious approval, *Nobele Wilden* cites Rousseau's fondness for the warmth of primitive people, and it calls noble savages the revolutionaries of our time, especially the young people, whatever their color, who "after all also live in the Third World, where feeling and warmth still dominate. Together they have taken the way back — back to noble human nature."[1]

---

[1] Frank Martinus Arion, *Nobele Wilden* (Amsterdam, De Bezige Bij, 1979), p. 460. The English translation of this passage is mine. Subsequent references are indicated by page numbers in the text.

Robert S. Kirsner (ed.), *The Low Countries and Beyond,* 197-203. Lanham, MD: University Press of America, 1993.

This warmth is remembered by the novel's main character, Julien Bizet Constant, and his two former lovers, Mabille and Ursula, from their participation in the Parisian student uprising of 1968; but their political activity is not rekindled in the Seventies, the time in which the book is set. And while Mabille — now back in Martinique and writing to Julien, who has become the Roman Catholic bishop of Lourdes — retains her political commitment, she and everyone else are gripped by disillusionment and despair. In this disillusionment with early idealism, the book is again reminiscent of a 1970s European mood.

But European though the novel is, the concern for what should be done about the Caribbean, for what the future of these islands holds, binds Arion to such black West Indian writers as George Lamming (from Barbados), Earl Lovelace (from Trinidad), and Michael Thelwell (from Jamaica). In *Nobele Wilden* that question is especially pertinent because Julien comes from Martinique, which is, as so many tourist brochures proudly proclaim, an overseas department of France. The famous Trinidadian V. S. Naipaul remarked in his 1962 essay on Martinique in *The Middle Passage* that the overwhelming French character of the island has an ominous underside: "Assimilation has not made Martinique an integral part of prosperous France, but has reduced the island to a helpless colony where now more than ever the commission agent is king."[2]

And while Arion has a hearty dislike for Naipaul (he calls him *ingebeeld,* "conceited"), they appear to be in complete agreement about the deplorable conditions on Martinique. Julien is frequently enraged at French treatment, past, present, and presumably future, of its far-flung department.

It is precisely when the larger question is narrowed down to its political core — What kind of revolution would do the most good? — that the answer in this novel is bafflingly absent. And this is what makes *Nobele Wilden* both an exasperating and a compellingly honest book. Everything in the novel — from the radical epistles of Mabille to

---

[2] V. S. Naipaul, *The Middle Passage* (New York, Vintage Books, Random House, 1962), p. 199. Subsequent references are indicated by page numbers in the text.

the bitter childhood memories of Julien — leads us to expect an answer. But no real answer emerges.

The problem for Julien is that he knows that his visions cannot be made real. His admiration for the "primitive first inhabitants, the Indians" (54) cannot bring into being some semblance of their society now. He can think of nothing that would create it or the independent Martinique he dreams of. More important, in the post-War industrial world, such a primitive community, if it could exist, would be a prescription for poverty and full scale emigration. Hence the novel rejects this Romantic dream but continues to yearn for it.

This yearning is nourished by the loving nostalgia bestowed on the Parisian events of May - June 1968. Though the novel is skeptical of the achievements of '68, it endorses the emotional explosion, the hardy mix of youthful zest for the new and disdain for the old. The uprising's chief slogans are invoked reverentially — Power to the Imagination, To Express Oneself is to Seek Power — and the book's opening and closing sections are called Imagination to Power and The Power of Imagination. But as everyone knows, although the explosion of '68 seemed to threaten the old order, it actually strengthened Gaullism well into the age of Pompidou and Giscard d'Estaing. *Nobele Wilden* came out in 1979, so Arion could not know that the Fifth Republic would continue to thrive in the Eighties, even with a socialist President. But it has.

Much of what Arion did know found its way into Julien's conflicts. Checkmated by thought, Julien is incapable of action. Having become a Catholic bishop, living as he does in enemy territory in Lourdes, he has been able to give his island a vague moral support and money only.

It is Christianity that competes for Julien's allegiance. Or to phrase it differently: Julien is nothing if not ambivalent. Christianity (and Bernadette) in Lourdes are as real and unreal to him as revolution in Martinique. Both are ideals; both are endlessly questioned; neither is embraced wholly. And he is not alone in his ambivalence: even his revolutionary friend, Mabille, questions revolutionary means and wonders whether the search for violence could mean nothing more than a desire to persuade oneself of one's own authenticity (81).

In addition to doubting the revolution, Mabille has questions too about the role of women in the movement and the private behavior of revolutionary people. Clearly the "mental decolonization" (84) she has in mind will have to come first, and even Mabille does little more than "study Frantz Fanon more meticulously than before" (84). A process of education, involving a more Caribbean consciousness (85) is needed, for clearly the French, by making the inhabitants feel French, have managed to alienate them from themselves. This sentiment is in accord with Fanon's idea that the majority uses culture to repress the minority by forcing the minority to identify with the dominant class and suppress their anger or have it turn to self-hatred, but even the radical Mabille lacks Fanon's fierceness.

This kind of caution and this kind of mildness make all the characters — and the reader — doubt that anything can be done — or that much of anything is possible. Because Mabille has more fervor than anyone else, Julien admires her greatly, but doesn't know whether she is on the right course:

> Mabille! Het soort zwarte vrouwen dat blanke mannen bedoelen als zij het over Negerinnen hebben, al was zij van Hindoestaanse afkomst: Vurig, onberekenbaar. Geen "adorable chat," zoals Baudelaire van Jeanne Duval heeft geschreven, maar een ontzettend kattige minnares. En toch lief. Toch lief. Opofferingsgezind.... Mabille die hem bewonderde zolang ze hem kon zien als de man die in de aanwezigheid van duizenden Fransen kon opstaan en maken dat iedereen z'n smoel hield, zoals zij het zei, om naar een zwarte Martiniquaan te luisteren. Mabille... Zou het hem ooit gelukken te bewijzen, dat zijn manier beter was dan iedere andere? Maar wat was dan zijn manier? Verdomme (179).[3]

---

[3]"Mabille! The sort of black women that white men mean when they talk about Negresses, though she was of Hindustani descent: Fiery, unpredictable. No 'adorable chat,' as Baudelaire wrote of Jeanne Duval, but a tremendously catty lover. And still sweet. Still sweet. Self-effacing.... Mabille who admired him as long as she could see him as the man

That is just the point. Julien doesn't know what his own way is and remains revolutionary in name only — or rather, since as a priest he must keep it a secret, in thought only, or in vague sentiment. The black bishop of Lourdes can only continue as a peace-loving, doubting, tormented cleric with a vague sense of the resemblance between the remote superstitious region of France and his West Indian home and a great fondness for Fidel and Cuba. Sometimes he'll even doubt that he wants Martinique liberated.

Not only are his confusions political and religious, they are sexual as well. Before his return to the monastery, Julien makes love to any number of women but always with a self-tormenting lack of enjoyment. His self-consciousness has become a disease and is no different from that of the white culture he attacks for its desire to control reality with words. Any revolutionary act would have to be undertaken by a personality less divided than Julien's, less ambivalent and less complicated.

Julien is the opposite of the natural man — self-conscious, repressed, overly deliberate, sin-obsessed. His introspectiveness and oversensitivity make it unlikely that he could ever live in the more natural world he seeks. Two cultures within him are at war and their clash paralyzes him. He is temperamentally incapable of experiencing the world he craves, and yet he can only reject what in cultural style he seems better suited to, the bourgeois world of the whites. For to become middle class is a form of capitulation to whiteness and an abandonment of a dimly remembered African past.

These contradictions are fascinating, but because the novel promises a political answer and provides none, and because it appears to lose itself in endless talk, it is emotionally disappointing. And yet its failure to find a political answer and its main character's refuge in thought and counterthought finally do constitute a political statement of sorts.

---

who in the presence of thousands of Frenchmen could get up and see to it that everyone shut up, as he said, in order to listen to a black Martinican. Mabille... Would he ever succeed in proving that his way was better than anyone else's? But what was his way? Damn it."

It is that no satisfactory answer for Martinique is available, for to quote the "ingebeelde" Naipaul again: "Scarcely any development is possible, for no Martiniquan industry could compete with a French one; and without her connection with France Martinique would be lost" (199). And even if Naipaul is wrong, if Martinique could gain from independence, then more broadly it still remains true that if the West Indies should not mimic white nations, their black models are certainly gone. But in the modern world to refuse to become industrialized and middle class is to consign oneself to poverty and weakness. The dilemma is insoluble, and not surprisingly *Nobele Wilden* preaches in some of its content what in all of its form it rejects. For the novel itself, its manner, its over-reflectiveness, its endless talk about possibilities, its quest for salvation — detracts from the *un*ambiguousness of any revolutionary credo. The book may crave a revolutionary blueprint but it is too honest to offer one, for no revolution is likely to accomplish anything, though the status quo is unbearable. The triumph of the West Indians is their rejection of a white middle class world; the tragedy is that this rejection consigns them to second-rate status as nations and despair as individuals. Revolution cannot solve the dilemma.

But if the revolution is not possible, at least there is the revolutionary. Perhaps the one consolation in this rather bleak picture is that somehow the noble savages, the hippies, the students, the rebels, have arrived in Europe and hence have raised European consciousness to the point where colonialism is seen for what it is and the oneness of all beings and of life itself can be celebrated. Looked at in this way, it makes sense for the novel to be as European as it is — while the noble savages haven't appeared to do the West Indies much good, they certainly changed the face of Europe, and at the very least have brought a sympathy and an understanding to countries and cultures that were once hell-bent on domination and enslavement. In that sense, the Imagination, like Bernadette's vision, may have come to power after all.

This is a change in consciousness rather than in reality, a psychological victory rather than a political one. In the final analysis, *Nobele Wilden* sees beyond the Rousseauistic paradox that the old innocent way, or the imagined old way, can be restored by sophisticated people. This is its fundamental honesty — it knows that no such restoration is possible. Julien's sentiments may remain occasionally Rousseauistic, but his character and the action (or rather, the non-action) of the book deny any real back to nature or back to Africa notion. In its vacillations and contradictions, the novel reflects the conflict in which the West Indies are trapped: struggling to avoid Europeanization, they still cannot remain where they unhappily are.

And indeed, the novel makes it clear that Julien's ambivalence, his paralyzing inability to act, mirrors a larger Third World fact: to beat poverty is to despoil the environment, to live in the modern world is to become middle-class, and to flourish as a twentieth century nation is to give up any dream of the noble savage.

Nederlandkunde

New Perspectives on the Second World War in Dutch Historiography

Bob de Graaff
Institute for Netherlands History, The Hague

Shortly after the end of the Second World War, many former members of the Resistance were concerned that the experience of the Occupation might eventually come to be forgotten.[1] With hindsight this fear can be easily dismissed. After some signs of repression of the wartime past in the 1950s, the war has reemerged as a popular issue of formidable dimensions. Books, films, and TV programs on the war can be counted by the hundreds if not thousands.[2]

The continuing preoccupation with the history of the Netherlands during the Second World War seems to defy the general notion that present day society is unconcerned with history. One reason for this interest has been the need for self-justification, the need to demon-

---

[1] For instance, Th. Delleman, *Opdat wij niet vergeten. De bijdrage van de gereformeerde kerken, van haar voorgangers en leden, in het verzet tegen het nationaal-socialisme en de Duitse tyrannie,* Kampen 1949, Egbert Barten, "Toenemende vrijheid. De verwerking van de Tweede Wereldoorlog in de Nederlandse speelfilm," D. H. Schram/C. Geljon (eds.), *Overal sporen. De verwerking van de Tweede Wereldoorlog in literatuur en kunst,* Amsterdam 1990, 224.

[2] Dick Schram, "Taal behoudt de feiten. De verwerking van de Tweede Wereldoorlog in de literatuur," Schram/Geljon (ed.), *Overal sporen. De verwerking van de Tweede Wereldoorlog in literatuur en kunst,* Amsterdam 1990, 94; Anne de Vries, "De oorlog komt steeds dichterbij. De Tweede Wereldoorlog in het kinderboek," ibidem 146; Louk Tilanus, "Monumenten. Het herdenken in brons en steen van de jaren 1940-45," ibidem, 68; Wim Ramaker, Ben van Bohemen, *Sta een ogenblik stil... Monumentenboek 1940-1945,* Kampen 1980.

Robert S. Kirsner (ed.), *The Low Countries and Beyond,* 207-218. Lanham, MD: University Press of America, 1993.

strate that the Netherlands did not behave as badly during the war as had been alleged, that the country did have its good side. Compared to other nations, Holland had been rather easily defeated by the German troops. Organized resistance was relatively insignificant and made a slow start compared with, for instance, Belgium and France.[3] A higher percentage of Jews were deported from the Netherlands than from any other West European nation.[4] To repress these unwelcome facts, chauvinism and a cult of resistance had been bolstered.[5] But this repression had succeeded only partially and only temporarily.

The implicit or explicit feeling of guilt about these matters led to the conviction that, if war ever were to reappear, the Dutch would have to score a better mark.[6] After the Second World War even people who had been born during it or afterwards began to consider the possibility that they or their progeny might someday have to resist another, future occupier or collaborating regime or so-called proto-fascist tendencies.[7] In 1971, for instance, Willem Sandberg, Peter van Straaten, and Lucebert warned against a national census by means of a poster with the words "voordat je 't weet is het weer zover; dan draagt de een een zweep, een ander een jodenster" ('before you realize it, matters have come so far; one carries a whip, the other wears a star'). People born after the war did not want to be as tongue-tied as so many parents were after the Second World War when their children asked: why did not you do something?[8] For the postwar generations the war became "a character test" they never had to pass,

---

[3] Bob de Graaff, "Collaboratie en verzet: een vergelijkend perspectief," J. P. B. Jonker, A. E. Kersten, G. van der Plaat (ed.), *Vijftig jaar na de inval. Geschiedschrijving en de Tweede Wereldoorlog,* Den Haag 1990.

[4] J. C. H. Blom, *Crisis, bezetting en herstel. Tien studies over Nederland 1930-1950,* Den Haag 1989, 134; L. de Jong, *Drie voordrachten aan de Harvard Universiteit,* 's-Gravenhage 1989, 29.

[5] "Veertig jaar na 'veertig'," *Militaire Spectator,* Vol. 149 (May 1980), 193.

[6] For instance, A. Coolen a.o., *Vrij Volk,* Amsterdam 1945, 22.

[7] Blom, *Crisis,* 151.

[8] Kees Schaepman/Ageeth Scherphuis, "Vrij," *Vrij Nederland,* June 17, 1989.

a Day of Judgement they had missed.[9] And the question "What would I do faced with the choice between collaboration and resistance?" was all too easily answered in the affirmative. As the title of a history of the former illegal newspaper *Trouw* read: *Verzet verjaart niet* ('There is no limitation to Resistance').[10]

In the postwar era, resistance has become more than just a moral obligation. Resistance and collaboration have also become metaphors for change, innovation, self-liberation, and underground culture on the one hand, and resistance to change and lack of morals on the other. In more general terms, the period of the Occupation has become a metaphor for human existence. By reading about the war, looking at paintings, or watching movies on this theme, the general public expects to see love and hatred, self-sacrifice and treason, hope and anxiety; in short: life and death in their most extreme or purest forms.

It would be rather unhistorical to expect that this interest in the Second World War will never decline. Inevitably it will, and perhaps this moment has already arrived. There is evidence that the interest reached its apex in the first half of the 1980s: The number of pension applications to the Stichting 1940-1945 rose from 125 in 1970 to over 300 a year in the first half of the 1980s. The peak-years of production of literary works and movies about the Second World War were the 1980s.[11] In 1981 a permanent Comité Nationale Bevrijding (Committee of National Liberation) was established. In the same year, May 5th was reestablished as a yearly national holiday. In 1983, the Commemorative Centre Westerbork was opened at the site of the former concentration camp. During the 1980s Resistance museums were opened in Amsterdam, Leeuwarden, and Gouda.

---

[9]Abraham de Swaan, "Een huisaltaar voor het oorlogsverleden," *NRC Handelsblad*, December 24, 1988; Jacques Klöters, "De geest van het verzet en het cabaret," Schram/Geljon (ed), *Overal sporen*, 205.

[10]J. G. A. Thijs, *Verzet verjaart niet. Momenten uit de veertigjarige geschiedenis van het dagblad Trouw*, Amsterdam 1983.

[11]D. Schram, "Taal behoudt," 94; Egbert Barten, "Toenemende vrijheid," 215, 231.

But after 1985 there were indications of a decline. Since 1986 no major films have had the war as a theme. After a colossal growth until 1985, the services rendered to the general public by the RIOD, the Rijksinstituut voor Oorlogsdocumentatie (State Institute for War Documentation), have declined while the services rendered for scientific research have grown.[12] The 1989 remake of *De Bezetting* ('The Occupation'), the television series which had been responsible for empty streets in the early 1960s, attracted a smaller audience than had been expected.[13] With the release and death of the Two of Breda a rallying point for postwartime resistance disappeared.

On the other hand, predictions that a turning point was near in the interest for the Second World War may have proven almost as fallacious as prophesies of Judgement Day. There are a host of events to prove that, contrary to earlier expectations, interest in the Second World War was still growing in the late 1980s. New generations have appealed for help and understanding of their war-related problems. The children of resistance fighters, the second generation Jews, the so-called camp children of Indonesia, the children of German, Japanese, and Canadian soldiers, and the children and even grandchildren of collaborators have only recently come to the fore.[14] At least for some time to come, the popular interest in the Second World War, even if it is on the decline, will be quite considerable. It may take another major upheaval before the Second World War is surpassed as a point of reference.

---

[12]*Jaarverslagen RIOD 1986 en 1987.*

[13]Anneke Visser, "Rapporten over deportatie joden werden door Radio Oranje niet verwerkt," *NRC Handelsblad,* March 8, 1990; Hans Steketee, "P. Tania neemt kijker op de knie en vertelt," *NRC Handelsblad,* April 12, 1990.

[14]"Uitkering bepleit voor tweede generatie oorlogsslachtoffers," *NRC Handelsblad,* October 6, 1988; "Nood onder tweede generatie joden," *NRC Handelsblad,* January 25, 1990; "Vereniging van kampkinderen kritiseert hulpverleners," *NRC Handelsblad,* October 30, 1989; Frits Abrahams, "Verboden kinderen," *NRC Handelsblad,* May 6, 1989; "Kinderen 'foute' ouders nog steeds gestraft. De volgende generatie dient zich aan: de NSB-kleinkinderen," *De Volkskrant,* April 7, 1990.

In the 1980s, the growing moral and emotional interest in the war was looked upon by professional historians with mixed feelings.[15] The relation between "goed" en "fout" ('good' and 'bad') has — according to them — unduly dominated Second World War historiography. They wanted to abstain from explicit moralizing. They wanted to analyse wartime history instead of describing it. Their pleas were implicitly or explicitly a reaction against the writings of the leading Dutch historian on World War II until the late 1980s, Louis de Jong.

The mistaken conception of the general public that academic history should give moral verdicts and should be helpful in a commemorative and a therapeutic sense had not been countered by De Jong. On the contrary, he identified himself to a large extent with the former Resistance.[16] Never shy with the media, he defended Bastiaans' therapeutic centre in Oegstgeest as the proper treatment for war victims. When he was to be given civil honours, De Jong refused them, explaining that immediately after the war former resistance fighters had acted similarly. When he had found evidence that the politician Willem Aantjes had been a member of the SS, De Jong played a role that could hardly be described as different from that of an attorney-general. It was only at the end of his multivolume series on the Netherlands in the Second World War, when describing the situation in Indonesia, that the expectations as to De Jong's role of advocate of the wartime victims collided with his as usual black-and-white dichotomized history.[17]

---

[15] J. Bank, *Oorlogsverleden in Nederland,* Baarn 1983; J. C. H. Blom, *In de ban van goed en fout,* Amsterdam 1983; J. Jansen van Galen, "De heilige oorlog. Vier historici in debat over hoe zij èn de oorlog door de publieke opinie achtervolgd worden. '40-'45 als 'heerlijke' escape," *Haagse Post,* May 7, 1988.

[16] De Jong, "Anti-Nazi Resistance in the Netherlands," *European Resistance Movements I,* Oxford 1960, 138, 149.

[17] Max Pam, *De onderzoekers van de oorlog. Het Rijksinstituut voor Oorlogsdocumentatie en het werk van dr. L. de Jong,* The Hague 1989, 83-86; "Blijvend verzet tegen werk van dr. L. de Jong," *Rotterdams Nieuwsblad,* November 18, 1988.

During the 1980s, however, professional historians came to realize that they should not only be spellbinders but also spellbreakers,[18] that they differ from participants, judges, therapists, and occasional speakers. Amateur historians like E. H. Brongers and L. Elfferich on the other hand have served the reading public with stories that seem to confirm the worst suspicions one always had regarding the actual events.[19]

In both scholarly historiography and the arts there has been a change from a clear-cut presentation of the Resistance of 'the good guys' against the occupier to a more problematizing attitude, in which collaboration also takes its place. It seems though that the historians are not ahead of the artists. Writing about real persons and real situations, they have felt less freedom to disengage themselves from the monolythically presented categories of collaboration and resistance. Children's books about the war pay more attention to the ambiguities and concessions of people in wartime than most of the historical literature does. And whereas in novels on the war, collaboration became the main theme in the 1980s, it is still a minor theme in history-writing. There is a general feeling among scholars that the analytical study of the occupation period is still in its infancy.[20] At the same time, however, there is a general recognition that some changes have occurred. Let us examine a few of these.

First, the description of the period of the Occupation as a break in the continuity in 20th century Dutch history has been challenged. The attack on discontinuity was forcibly launched in 1980 at a

---

[18]Ralph White, "Introduction," S. Hawes/R. White (ed) *Resistance in Europe, 1939-1945; based on the proceedings of a symposium held at the University of Salford, March 1973*, Harmondsworth 1976, 1.

[19]E. H. Brongers, *De slag om de residentie 1940*, Baarn 1968; idem, *De oorlog in mei '40*, Utrecht etc. 1969;[3] idem, *Grebbelinie 1940: verslag van een wanhopige strijd*, Baarn 1982;[7] L. Elfferich, *Eindelijk de waarheid nabij: analyses en emoties naar aanleiding van het bombardement op Rotterdam*, Den Haag 1983; idem, *Rotterdam werd verraden*, Rotterdam 1990.

[20]P. Romijn, "Herbeleving en herinterpretatie: recente literatuur over Nederland en de Tweede Wereldoorlog," *BMGN* Jg. 102 (1987), 224; D. Schram, C. Geljon, "Woord vooraf," Schram/Geljon (eds.), *Overal sporen*, 3.

conference of the Nederlands Historisch Genootschap on the period 1944-1950.[21] Since then, the period 1944-1950 has received considerable attention.

Second, the focus of attention has shifted somewhat from the Resistance to the population at large. Both amateur and professional historians have paid more attention to daily life and labors: the families who had people in hiding (onderduikers), the forced laborers, the Hungerwinter of 1944-1945.

Finally, some efforts have been made to place the history of the Occupation and its historiography in an international comparative perspective.[22]

Given these developments in the 1980s, what should be the research objectives to pursue in the 90's? Firstly, there is a need for quantification. There is, for instance, very little information on the social background of collaborators.[23] Efforts to systematically quantify the German exploitation of the Dutch economy have only recently begun.[24] The demythologizing effects of quantative studies were well illustrated by Gerard Trienekens' dissertation on wartime food policy.[25] Contrary to popular opinion, which held that the food situation had been extremely bad during the entire Occupation, this thesis showed that only after September 1944 was there a real change for the worse. Without quantification it will be very difficult to make the necessary valid comparisons with other occupied nations from which

---

[21]*Bijdragen en Mededelingen betreffende de geschiedenis der Nederlanden*, vol. 96 (1981), no. 2.

[22]Blom, *Crisis* and De Graaff, "Collaboratie en verzet."

[23]For information on the social background of resistance fighters see Bob de Graaff/ Lidwien Marcus, *Kinderwagens en korsetten. Een onderzoek naar de sociale achtergrond en de rol van vrouwen in het verzet 1940-1945*, Amsterdam 1980.

[24]R. T. Griffiths, "The exploitation of the Dutch economy, 1940-1945," Jonkers a.o., *Vijftig jaar.*

[25]Gerard Trienekens, *Tussen ons volk en de honger. De voedselvoorziening, 1940-1945*, Utrecht 1985.

information can be obtained about the unicity or similarity of situations and developments in the Netherlands during the Occupation.

Furthermore, it is crucial to devote more research time and manpower to the study of the wartime economy. Very little has been done in this field so far.[26] Interesting studies can and should be made not only at the level of the national economy but also in the field of company histories.

More attention should also be paid to the phenomenon of collaboration. Little on this subject has been done by professional Dutch historians, and amateur publications have often encountered either judicial disapproval[27] or public condemnation.[28] Only in a few cases did such work meet with a benignly tacit reception.[29] But professional historians themselves cannot afford to stay comfortably aloof. In contrast to their Belgian colleagues, Dutch historians are hardly hampered by the authorities in obtaining the written sources they need. And they should make use of the opportunities presented by former collaborators and their children to disclose these individuals' experiences.[30]

Let me remark here that in making this plea for the study of collaboration, I am not arguing that we should simply "rake up the past" or tarnish reputations just for the fun of it. Rather, I want to discover why and how people came to collaborate. I want to find out

---

[26]An interesting start has been made by J. L. van Zanden/R. T. Griffiths, *Economische geschiedenis van Nederland in de 20e eeuw*, Utrecht 1989 and Griffith, "The Exploitation."

[27]F. Dekkers, *Eindhoven, 1933-1945; kroniek van Nederlands lichtstad in de schaduw van het Derde Rijk*, Haarlem 1982; B. Huizing/K. Aartsma, *De zwarte politie 1940-1945*, Weesp 1986.

[28]Adriaan Venema, *Schrijvers, uitgevers en hun collaboratie*.

[29]Koos Groen, *Landverraad. De berechting van collaborateurs in Nederland*, Weesp 1984; Venema, A., *Kunsthandel in Nederland, 1940-1945*, Amsterdam 1986.

[30]See, for instance, I. P. Spruit, *Onder de vleugels van de partij. Kind van de Führer*, Bussum 1983; Boudewijn van Houten, *Fout. Lebensbericht meines Vaters*, Antwerpen/Amsterdam 1987; Duke Blaauwendraad-Doorduijn, *Niemandsland*, Amsterdam 1989.

how much room people had to manoeuvre in the wartime situation, to establish the intersections and intertwinements between collaboration and resistance, and to determine which categories benefitted from collaboration. Studies of collaboration should not only be directed at the political collaborators, but also at administrative, judicial, and police collaboration.

There is one field where the study of collaboration is making headway: the biography. Until recently there was hardly any biographical tradition in the Dutch historiography of the Second World War. In general, the Dutch are not known for either their praise or their scorn of individuals. With a few exceptions, praise has been directed to the nameless: those who died in the prime of their lives and those who had risked their lives during the war but were destined to fall into oblivion after the Liberation.

In the past few years, however, it has been realized that the fate of one single person may better illustrate the history of World War II than the aggregated histories of thousands. There has been a wave of biographies of fascists and collaborators,[31] and in some of these biographies shades of collaboration have been introduced. Some of the "bad guys" turn out not to have been entirely bad. It is, by contrast, surprising how small the number of biographies of resistance fighters is, considering how much longer the Resistance has been studied.[32] It now seems as if the resisters suffer relatively more under the weight

---

[31] Jan Meijers, *Mussert, een politiek leven,* Amsterdam 1984; Gjalt Reindert Zondergeld, *Een kleine troep vervuld van haat. Arnold Meijer & het Nationaal Front,* Houten 1986; Frans Dekkers, *King Kong. Leven, dood en opstanding van een verrader,* Amsterdam 1986; G. J. G. de Gier, *Alfred Haighton. Financier van het fascisme,* Amsterdam 1988, H. J. Neumann, *Arthur Seyss-Inquart. Het leven van een Duits onderkoning in Nederland,* 1989; Bart van der Boom, *Kees van Geelkerken — De rechterhand van Mussert,* 1990; Bart Middelburg/René ter Steege, *Riphagen,* Amsterdam 1990.

[32] Albert Helman, *De levensgeschiedenis van Gerrit-Jan van der Veen 1902-1944,* Baarn 1977² (1946); Eddy de Roever, *Sphinx. Het verhaal van Jos Gemmeke: een fascinerende vrouw. Haar persoonlijke strijd tegen de Duitse bezetter als verzetsvrouw en gedrop geheim agente, 1940-1945,* Baarn 1987; Jan van Lieshout, *De aal van Oranje. Een biografie van pater "Lodewijk" Bleijs (1906-1945),* Venlo 1988; Anita van Ommeren/Ageeth Scherphuis, *"Die man had moeten blijven leven": Gerrit Jan van der Veen en het verzet,* Amsterdam 1988; J. W. Regenhardt, *Het gemaskerde leven van Eduard Veterman,* Amsterdam 1990.

of the nameless. We still know very little about the turns it took to become a member of the Resistance. Biographies not only can give us hints about general patterns of development during the war but are also eminently suited as a means of communication between the more professionalized historian and the general public. Through their attention to individual virtues and failings, they might humanize the description of collaboration and resistance which, in the Netherlands, seem to have become superhuman categories, one being godlike and the other devilish.

Just as academic historians should not leave the study of collaboration wholly to the amateurs, neither should they totally abandon regional and local studies. Almost every self-respecting town or village has its own commemorative study of the years 1940-1945. Mostly they are written by locals and they resemble chronicles. But interesting scientific local and regional studies can be written.[33] Not only can these local studies modify the insights gained at the national level, but probably even more fruitful findings can be reached by comparing the differences in impact the occupation had in different localities. Furthermore, it is amazing that major cities like Amsterdam, Rotterdam, and The Hague are still without wartime histories.

Turning now to a different matter, let me suggest that in recent years the continuity-thesis has been viewed too much from a single perspective. Since the 1980 conference of the Nederlands Historisch Genootschap on the period 1944-1950, the adherents of this position have adopted a backward-looking point of view, stating that developments in the late forties and the fifties either were not very different from those in the thirties or that they simply built upon them. Implicitly these scholars suggest that it would be possible to write a history of the Netherlands in the 20th century with the occupation period left out. In this view, only the colonial and foreign policy show remarkable breaks that can be ascribed to the experiences of the wartime. It seems almost paradoxical that the adherents of the continuity thesis have stressed the discontinuity of the occupation time to such an extent that it seems completely alien: five years to be struck

---

[33]For instance, C. Hilbrink, *De illegalen. Illegaliteit in Twente & het aangrenzende Salland 1940-1945*, 's-Gravenhage 1989.

from Dutch history. Such an analysis differs, for instance, from the historiography of the French Vichy-regime, which emphasizes the very continuity between developments in the thirties and the early forties:[34] a position that can understandably be a little less comfortable. For example, did the way in which authority had been fostered and displayed in the Netherlands in the 1930s predestine the easy acceptance of an authoritarian regime in the early 1940s?[35] Had the collaboration of the Jewish Council during the war had a predecessor in the awestricken attitude towards the government of the Committee for Jewish Refugees in the 1930s?[36] Was the unitarian approach of, for instance, the Nederlandse Unie continuous with attempts in the 1930s to do away with compartmentalization and pillarization (hokjesgeest en verzuiling)?[37]

Finally, I should add a few words on the use of values and morals, since this issue has come to be so hotly debated. As long as research is not hampered by moral prejudice nothing is wrong. The question whether moral judgement should be given in the presentation of the research findings is very much one of expediency. Proponents of more or less moral judgement in the presentation of research findings should not too easily condemn each other. On the one hand nobody can be blamed for vomiting his disgust as soon as he writes the word 'Auschwitz.' On the other hand it should not be ill-taken if historians can dismiss with moral judgement as long as their findings are not tainted with the ideas and the vocabulary of the former prosecutors, torturers, and so on.

---

[34]R. O. Paxton, *Vichy France. Old Guard and New Order 1940-1944*, New York 1972; H. R. Kedward, *Resistance in Vichy France. A Study of Ideas and Motivation in the Southern Zone 1940-1942*, Oxford 1978, 22-64.

[35]W. ten Have, "Gezag in een vacuüm? 1940 en 1945," Jonkers a.o. (ed.), *Vijftig jaar*, 178-185.

[36]L. de Jong, *Het Koninkrijk der Nederlanden in de Tweede Wereldoorlog I*, The Hague 1969, 523-524.

[37]B. G. J. de Graaff, "Bloms kleine oorlog. Om betekenis en belang van de bezettingstijd," *De Gids* Jg. 148 (1985), 556.

It may be expected that professional historians will continue to be confronted with a growing divergence between the interests of the general public and their own professional standards. Instead of making the best of both worlds, they will lose both if they do not choose for their own profession. Hopefully they will succeed in incorporating the period of 1940-1945 into the longer time frame of the 20th century and in referring further to developments in other nations, in line with recent research trends.

Myth and Understanding: Recent Controversy about Dutch Historiography on the Netherlands-Indonesian Conflict

Peter Romijn
The Netherlands State Institute for War Documentation

1. **Introduction.** This paper will deal with the historiography of the decolonization of the former Dutch East Indies, now Indonesia. In particular, I will relate how in recent years the most prominent Dutch historian of the Second World War, Professor Louis de Jong, found himself in the middle of a raging public controversy after publishing five impressive volumes on Dutch colonial history.[1] Initially, the dispute concerned the appraisal of Dutch colonial rule. Later, it came to focus upon the justification given to armed efforts by the Dutch to regain control of the colony after the Japanese occupation during World War II. Passionate discussions of De Jong's volumes appeared in newspapers and learned journals, on television screens, and even in courtrooms. As a way of protesting this work of history, some veterans refused to attend ceremonies that were part of Dutch War Memorial Day. A controversial commander in the colonial war allegedly died of anger after reading the most disputed part of the book; his burial was staged as another demonstration against the distinguished historian.

All this suggests an immense gap in understanding between De Jong and the most concerned parts of his audience, i.e. the former

---

[1]Jong, L. de *Het Koninkrijk der Nederlanden in de Tweede Wereldoorlog,* Vols. 11 A, *Nederlands Indië* 1 and 12, *Epiloog,* (The Hague, 1984 and 1988). In 1991, a final volume of De Jong's series was published, edited by an independent committee of historians: Bank, J. Th.M. and Romijn, P. *Het Koninkrijk der Nederlanden in de Tweede Wereldoorlog,* volume 14 *Reacties* (The Hague: 1991). This volume contains a large selection of reviews from the historical and general press, among which the reviews mentioned in this paper.

Robert S. Kirsner (ed.), *The Low Countries and Beyond,* 219-229. Lanham, MD: University Press of America, 1993.

East-Indies colonial elite, as well as the veterans of the colonial war. In the present paper I will discuss the conflicting elements in the historical representation of this traumatizing part of our past. I will not deal with different schools of historical analysis on this subject, but will rather demonstrate how professional historiography was forced to confront a prevalent and powerful myth. In doing so, I am indebted to John Hellmann who, in his book *American Myth and the Legacy of Vietnam*, showed how myths about the past enable particular groups to deal with historical experiences in a socially desirable way. Myths can give lasting interpretation and meaning to past experience, providing a historical narrative that reconciles conflicting elements beyond a framework of pure analytical thought.[2]

First, I should remind you that the Dutch retreat as a colonial power from Indonesia was generated by the Second World War. Indonesian independence was only accomplished after another five years of political and military struggle. After the liberation of the Netherlands, in 1945, most Dutch considered the loss of the colony's rich resources an immediate threat to post-war recovery. Consequently, about 135,000 soldiers, volunteers, and conscripts, were sent overseas, in addition to the colonial forces. The outcome is well-known: during the five years to follow, Dutch troops were engaged in an exhausting guerrilla war against Indonesian nationalists. More than 3,000 Dutch soldiers were killed in action; the number of Indonesian victims is estimated to be much higher. Meanwhile, the Government's diplomacy failed to secure international support for its return to colonial power. By 1950, Dutch abandonment of Indonesia was a fact, although for years to come it proved to be very hard to come to terms with this.

2. Contents of the controversy. Before outlining the historical controversy, I should mention the huge prestige that De Jong enjoys among the Dutch public as an important factor. Through his state-sponsored publications, as well as in radio and televised broadcasts on

---

[2]See Hellmann, J., *American Myth and the Legacy of Vietnam* (New York, 1986). In using the expression "myth" I do not intend to suggest that myths are necessarily untrue. (Neither does the word "history" necessarily imply a degree of truthfulness.) I only want to stress the social and psychological implications of such cohesive sets of values and interpretations.

the subject, he has been teaching wartime history to a huge public that was eager to read and to listen. Discussing the Second World War in a very captivating way, De Jong usually provides examples of good and bad behavior, both of individuals and of collective bodies. His moral standards rest on a firm "national" point of view, as well as on equally firm humanist convictions. To the general public, his interpretation is "official history" and words of reproof from his mouth perhaps count heavier than those of a professional judge; his emotional involvement adds to this effect.

De Jong's first "colonial" volume was a prologue to the Pacific War, and broadly outlined the history of the Dutch colonial presence. Professional historians received it with mixed feelings.[3] At the same time, however, it drew loud criticism from members of the former Dutch community in Indonesia, now living in Holland. Many of them once belonged to the administrative elite. They argued that De Jong had treated Dutch rule in an unfair and prejudiced way, paying too much attention to emerging Indonesian nationalism and its repression by the colonial Government.[4] They argued that colonial rule had been relatively progressive, stressing especially the fields of administration and elementary education. De Jong's critics maintained that his interpretation was not a new one. They branded it as the socialist and anti-colonial point of view which, in their opinion, had inspired nationalism in Indonesia and had also been responsible for the Dutch Government's decision to abandon the country. A committee was formed to fight for "historical rehabilitation of the Netherlands East Indies." This committee engaged the Netherlands State in a number

---

[3] De Jong's adviser, Professor I. J. Brugmans, himself a member of the former colonial community, criticized the author's point of view, a critique that the author cited in his preface to Volume 11A. Brugmans debated in the *Tijdschrift voor Geschiedenis* with a long-time opponent on the theme of Dutch colonial rule, Professor W. F. Wertheim (Vols. XVIIIC (1985), 215-221 and IC (1986), 50-52. For other reviews, see Locher-Scholten, E. B. in *Bijdragen en Mededelingen betreffende de Geschiedenis der Nederlanden,* CI (1985) 265-268, and Drooglever, P. J. *Bijdragen van het Koninklijk Instituut voor Taal-, Land-en Volkenkunde,* CXXIV (1986) 251-356. In addition, Professor P. W. Klein criticized De Jong for his view on pre-war Japanese society (*NRC Handelsblad,* 31 October 1984)

[4] Compare: Fasseur, C., "Het verleden tot last. Nederland, de Tweede Wereldoorlog en de dekolonisatie van Indonesië" in: Barnouw, N. D. J., et al., (eds.). *1940-1945: Onverwerkt Verleden?* (Utrecht, 1985), 137.

of lawsuits, intending to force the state to assign a different historian to write a "less prejudiced" history of the former colony.

In addition to this, veterans of the colonial war rallied against De Jong before the volume dealing with this war was even in print. As was his practice, De Jong had asked experts on the subject to comment on his draft manuscript. Among them were veterans who were particularly enraged about a paragraph on atrocities committed by Dutch forces, atrocities which De Jong in the title of the paragraph bluntly had called *oorlogsmisdrijven* 'war crimes'. They became alarmed that they were coming under collective suspicion[5] and leaked the draft-paragraph to the press, mobilizing support in conservative political circles,[6] as well as in the mass-media. They asked De Jong to change his text radically and downplay what they considered to be isolated incidents on the Dutch side while stressing atrocities committed by the other side. Meanwhile, they urged the Minister of Education to prevent the publication of the book if De Jong did not make these changes.

3. **The colonial myth.** The public criticism of De Jong's "colonial volumes" was characterized by two elements. The first was the justification of Dutch colonial rule in the Indies and, consequently, the vindication of the military and political struggle to reinstate this rule after the Japanese intermezzo. The second was the failure or, in some cases, the unwillingness to see the most important political issue at hand: the nature, appeal, and growth of Indonesian nationalism, particularly in connection with the indigenous elites who were involved in governing the country and mobilizing the population. Among many Dutch who shared the colonial heritage, a vision prevailed of an essentially enlightened and progressive Dutch rule which had been destroyed by the Japanese who, sensing their imminent defeat, had planted the seed of malevolent nationalism in Indonesia.

---

[5]The theme of atrocities had come under public attention before, although it had been played down in government reports of 1947 and 1969. These left nobody content, hence discussion remained open to public debate.

[6]Among these was the former Prime Minister Piet de Jong (no kin!), who had been responsible for the publication of the modified 1969-report on atrocities in the Indies.

This point of view had been promoted in an authoritative volume on Dutch colonial achievement dating from 1961[7] entitled, *Balans van beleid* 'Evaluation of Policy'.[8] As a contribution to historical evaluation, it dealt with twentieth century developments primarily in a sociological, economic and anthropological fashion. It contained not altogether undeserved praise for the achievements of the government in Batavia[9] and its agents, European as well as Asian. But by stressing the importance of gradual advancement, it played down the political dynamics of the rise of nationalism and the vigorous repression of it by the same Government. This added to what might be called the "Myth of Good Rule," which enabled those who had contributed to it to look back in a mood that might be characterized as *post facto* self-confidence, which is a balm to all political loss. Thus, during the colonial war and afterwards, Indonesian nationalism was not very profoundly understood. Although the study of Dutch-Indonesian relations had developed considerably since the late 1960s, reaching high scholarly levels, it is obvious that new interpretations did not have much impact upon traditional views among the "colonial" public that adhered to the "Myth of Good Rule."

To this myth, veterans added an appendage which I shall call the "Myth of Righteous War." It is worthwhile to study the circumstances in which it originated. The soldiers that were sent overseas in 1945-49 had just experienced the brutal German occupation of the Netherlands. Many had been drafted for forced labor in Germany, which they had largely evaded at great personal risk. They had seen total war and its consequences in numerous ways, some as members of the resistance movement, most as victimized civilians. Their motives to go to Indonesia ranged from a patriotic sense of duty, to sheer lack of social connections, perhaps of imagination also, which might have allowed

---

[7]The bilateral political climate between Indonesia and the Netherlands at the time had been poisoned by the unsolved problem of the decolonization of the remaining Dutch territory in the Indies, New Guinea (presently Irian Barat). In 1961, both countries found themselves on the verge of a new armed conflict.

[8]Baudet, H., and Brugmans, I. J. *Balans van beleid. Terugblik op de laatste halve eeuw van Nederlands Indië* (Assen, 1961).

[9]Batavia, presently Jakarta, was the seat of the colonial Government

them to evade conscription. As a collective body, they shared basic ideological convictions that were imbedded in the colonial heritage. These postulated a specific Dutch mission in the Indies: continuing the fight against evil dictatorship after the German capitulation in order to bring progress and prosperity overseas. Political field instruction for the expeditionary force played very heavily upon these thoughts, stressing that the Indonesians themselves were not yet "mature" enough for independence.

Generally, Dutch soldiers did not arrive in very jingoistic spirits in the country most of them only knew from school tales or family stories. They were most pleased when they could bring their general assumption of "helping the good people" into practice, for instance by providing technical and medical assistance and by sharing their food, just like the liberating allied troops had done in Holland. These were the images the common soldiers liked as much as the propaganda staffs did. Their experience of the conflict would be tainted, however, by the ever-deterioriating political and military situation. The troops witnessed the failure to find a political resolution. Meanwhile, the violence of guerrilla and counter-guerrilla warfare grew from bad to worse. Two large-scale military operations against the Republican side temporarily lessened the growing frustration of the troops. These backfired, however, when the military discovered that they could not wipe out the enemy because the United Nations had forced the Netherlands Government to negotiate with the Republican leaders about the transfer of Sovereignty.

The troops returning home were utterly disgusted, especially because the fighting had grown very violent while the settlement was being negotiated. They could not boast of the fulfillment of their mission as they had conceived it at the onset. Consequently, they did not feel very proud and did not receive much of a homecoming celebration;[10] they were merely happy to have returned safely. At once they had to adjust to the strict discipline of postwar society, then engaged in a huge reconstruction effort. Being inadequately and

---

[10]The first troops to return paraded, were addressed and decorated, but the bulk were demobilized in quite an unceremonial way. Many received the "Service Medal for Order and Peace" from the mailman.

incompletely educated, owing to the course of world history, they had to acquire skills to earn themselves a decent place in that society. And, mind you, impoverished Holland simply could not provide for anything like the GI Bill of Rights. Veterans did not have the luxury of contemplating the lost war which they had fought, let alone the question of whether or not it had been a just war.

Later, most of the veterans would probably admit that they had managed to find themselves a place in society, even if was not the one they had dreamed of. Their individual efforts should not be underestimated, and most probably, more than their actual service performance, these contributed to their collective pride. This very pride was hurt in the late Sixties and afterwards, up to De Jong's publications, by allegations of systematic misconduct and war crimes.

Two important developments coincided with this. The first was the growing concern in the Western World about the U.S. presence in Vietnam, which also focused on the theme of atrocities. The veterans were on the defensive once again, facing questions of younger generations, such as whether or not they had behaved just like Lt. Calley at My Lai. The second factor had to do with the veterans growing older. As they neared the end of their professional lives, they tended to contemplate the past, discovering that for them as a body there remained much to be desired, both in material and nonmaterial senses. Since the early 1970s, many welfare provisions for different groups victimized by the Second World War had been enlarged significantly; the veterans now started to clamor for equal treatment.

The key word would be *erkenning* 'recognition': they asked society to honor their past efforts and to recognize their present needs.[11] De Jong's book was supposed to give them the recognition they felt they deserved, just like any other patriotic group he previously had dealt with. The turmoil it aroused suggests that the veterans had acquired a collective idea of their experiences, what I called the "Myth

---

[11]"Dienstvervulling onder buitengewone en zeer moeilijke omstandigheden. De verantwoordelijkheid van de overheid voor de specifieke problematiek van oud-militairen Indiëgangers. Eindadvies van de Vertrouwensman Oud-militairen Indiëgangers drs. D. F. van der Mei" (Den Haag, februari 1989), 15-18.

of Righteous War," which enabled them to look back with a satisfactory amount of self-respect. This representation of the past was generated in a period in which society as a whole wanted to forget the Dutch colonial failure. The first evaluations of the conflict that became available were official popular and illustrated histories of separate regiments or brigades. The second evaluations were collections of reports by journalists and novelists who, as war-correspondents, provided the home front with optimistic views, stating the boys overseas were fine and that their presence certainly had a purpose. Their books often steamed of hard-boiled language and of heavy resentment towards the politicians at home, who were supposed to have messed it all up. The slogan that was supposed to offer consolation resounded with the echo of all official dealings with lost wars: "It has not been in vain."

I should add that, exactly as in the U.S. after Vietnam, Dutch society refused to deal with the theme. In Holland, however, this phenomenon lasted much longer. In the 1950s and 1960s almost without an exception, popular culture reflected this attitude: novels of adventure, movies, or tv-series did not address the colonial war. This contrasted sharply with the attention the colonial past got as a whole. Hence, the "Myth of Righteous War" was allowed to shape itself undisturbed in the veterans' minds and was not subjected to public evaluation until the late 1960s and after. When De Jongs' volume on the war appeared, so did reflections like the below, attributed to General S. H. Spoor, Commander-in-Chief of the Dutch Army in the Indies, by his former adjutant:

> We've lost a battle. We've had to endure losses, but we did not lose ourselves. Nobody can ever deny to us the fact that we were in combat together (and against each other) for a cause that we had to fight for and that we considered a just cause. The mistakes and the crimes some of us committed were terrible. But warfare without crimes, torture, rape, mutilation and death does not exist. We liberated people, fed children, took care of

the wounded who, on our behalf, have known different and better times, because we were there. It has not been in vain.[12]

4. Conclusion. Comments like these were proposed as an alternative for De Jong's image of the conflict, an alternative that would maintain rather than insult the veterans' pride. This alternative reconciles different perspectives of the war, beginning with military rhetoric borrowed from Charles De Gaulle, followed by an essentially relativist self-accusation and, quite illogically, concluding in a sentimental and desperate effort at justification. This, in a nutshell, is the myth of "Righteous War." For most of the veterans, it provided the conciliatory idea that participating in this war had not been without a purpose after all. It also was perceived as a means to secure both material and nonmaterial *erkenning* for those who had been in the "forgotten war." They were not content when newspaper editors or talk show hosts showed understanding and sympathy for their position but simultaneously maintained that it would be impossible to deny that atrocities had occurred on a more than incidental scale.

De Jong's book was offensive to these veterans not only because veterans — as Paul Fussel remarked — always are convinced that "the real war never will get into the books."[13] More important is the point that De Jong — in contrast to his policy in his previous volumes on the Netherlands during the occupation — denied a higher purpose to the Dutch colonial war-effort, because it was destined to fail. In this respect, he could not offer the consolation to his readers in the way that the myth of "Righteous War" did. This is demonstrated once more by the outcome of the conflict between De Jong and his critics. The author did not back down on his overall view of Dutch colonial rule, and the committee's efforts to secure the production of a revised version of his colonial history utterly failed in the courtroom. With

---

[12]Smulders, R. M. *Een stem uit het veld. Herinneringen van de ritmeester-adjudant van generaal S.H. Spoor* (Amsterdam, 1988), 143. I should add that this citation also was directed towards Republican representatives present (which makes the addition "and against each other" comprehensible, but the text as a whole is addressed to the Dutch soldiers).

[13]For an eloquent defense of this view, see Paul Fussel *Wartime. Understanding and Behavior in the Second World War* (New York/Oxford, 1989), 267 et infra.

respect to the veteran's criticism, however, the author did announce publicly that he had erred.[14] He changed the phrase "war crimes" into "excessive use of violence," stressing that atrocities on the Dutch side had been examples of "counter-terror." He also placed more responsibility upon the Dutch Government for its failure to reach a faster solution. Additionally, he invited an expert on behalf of his critics to add a paragraph to the volume, containing a dissenting evaluation of the subject. To his most fervent critics, however, all this was not enough, for the damage had already been done: their myth had been challenged.

De Jong's critics urgently wanted him, as the Dutch "national historian," to support the historical myth that had enabled them to come to terms with a traumatizing past. In this respect, it is significant that after the colonial volumes appeared, some critics shifted their attention to secondary education, advising that younger generations be taught more respect for the Dutch colonial achievement in Indonesia.[15] Such a desire, in my view, puts undue strain on the relationship which exits between historians and their public. It underscores the general point that the product of professional historical research — however unpleasant it may be — should not be changed simply to make it easier for certain groups to deal with traumatizing past events. Nevertheless, the controversy I have discussed also suggests that historians should incorporate a sound set of didactic notions into their research and writing. Historians need to become better acquainted with the way in which particular social groups deal with historical experience, how myths about the past are constructed, and the role that such myths play in reconciling conflicts. Taking these factors into account, we as historians may yet succeed in meeting the

---

[14]De Jong announced this in an interview with the newspaper that had been the voice of his fiercest critics, *De Telegraaf*, 28 April 1988, under the headline: "Dr. Loe de Jong: ik ben kortzichtig geweest" ('Dr. Louis De Jong: "I've been shortsighted"'). For an appraisal of De Jong's retreat by Professor Jan Bank, see *De Volkskrant*, 28 April 1988, "Koloniaal-militaire lobby brengt De Jong enigszins uit zijn evenwicht" ('Lobby of political and colonial circles makes De Jong lose his equilibrium somewhat').

[15](Algemeen Pedagogisch Studiecentrum) *Oorlog en verzet in Nederlands-Indië 1941-1949 en de voorlichting aan na-oorlogse generaties* (Amsterdam, 1989).

professional standards of our discipline, as well as the social demand for our research.

Afrikaans

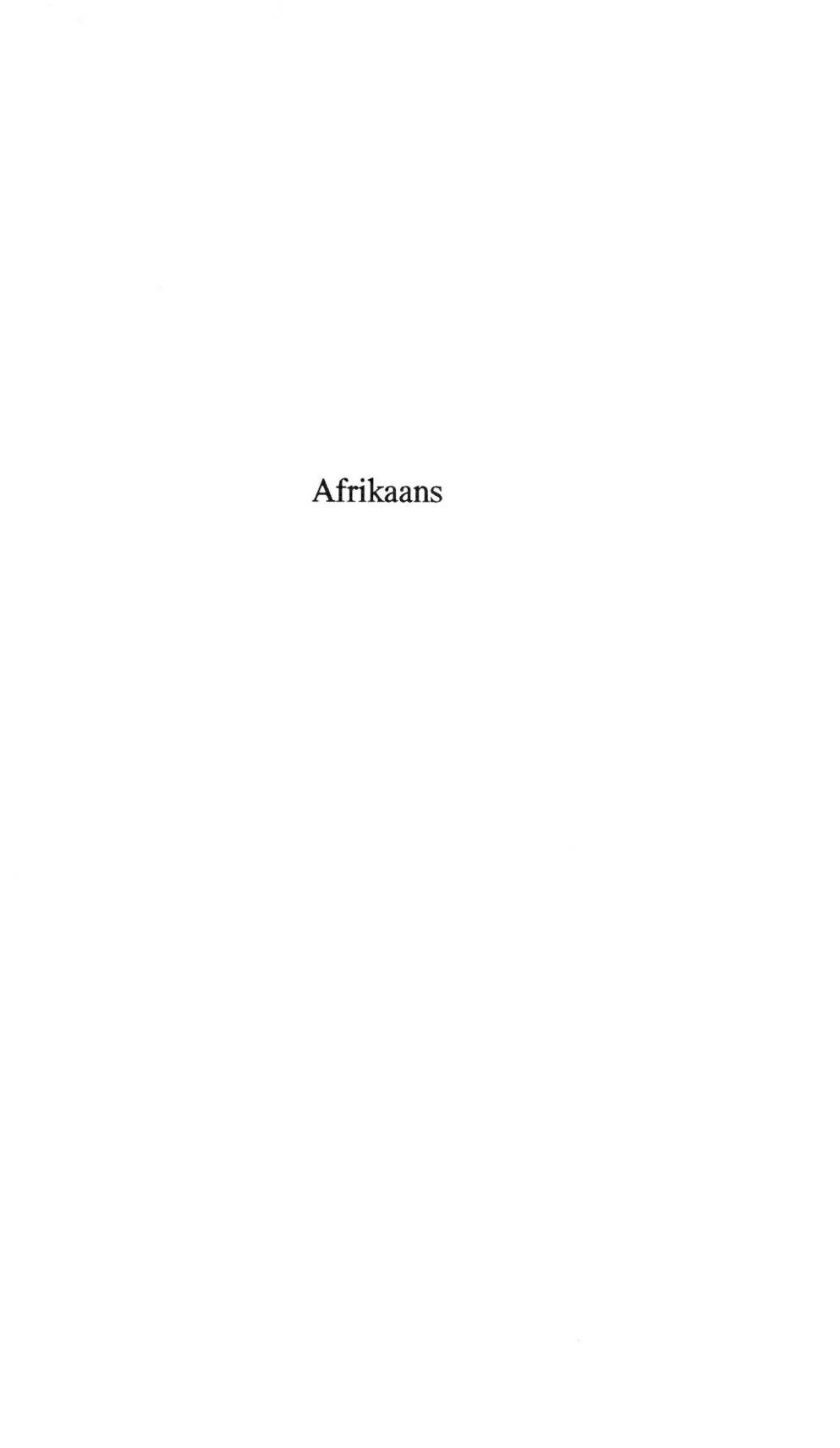

From "Verbasterde Hollans" to "Dochtertaal van het Nederlands" to "Afrikataal": Afrikaner Linguistic Mythology in Flux

Paul T. Roberge
University of North Carolina, Chapel Hill

This paper deals with linguistic myth and linguistic mythology.[1] By a linguistic myth, I mean a narrative account told about the history of a language to ennoble its origins, legitimize its position in the social order, and provide arguments for its restoration, preservation, or elaboration. By linguistic mythology, I mean a cluster of such myths that reinforce one another and jointly define a linguistic group's sense of historicity. For example, Afrikaner linguistic mythology has evinced two enduring themes. The first is the survival of an extraterritorial vernacular in the face of stigmatization within the speech community and the anglicization policies initiated first under Lord Charles Somerset during the early years of British occupation (1814-26) and again, following the Anglo-Boer War, under Lord Alfred Milner, British High Commissioner for South Africa (1897-1905). The second theme is captured by the epithet "the world's youngest literary language." The focal point of this theme is the rapid elaboration of Afrikaans into a cultural language in the face of prestigious Nederlands and all-encompassing English. Both themes involve strong motifs of victimization, historical struggle, heroism, and ultimate triumph.

---

[1] Primary research for this essay was supported by a Humanities Fellowship from the Rockefeller Foundation. The author bears sole responsibility for the views expressed herein.

Robert S. Kirsner (ed.), *The Low Countries and Beyond*, 233-245. Lanham, MD: University Press of America, 1993.

In his penetrating study of Afrikaner political mythology, Leonard Thompson (1985:69) observes that the South African social order rests on a core assumption. The core assumption is that races are the fundamental divisions of humanity, and different races possess inherently different cultural as well as physical qualities. While race is the primary category through which differences among humans are mediated, other categories play a role; and one of the most fundamental categories of Afrikaner identity is language. Language is an exponent of its speakers' particularity, nationhood, and distinction; it bestows upon them a sense of social and cultural unity; it must be protected from outside interference and preserved at all costs (cf. Crapanzano 1985:30-34). It is intimately linked with other cultural spheres (such as morality, law, art, science, and economy), and culture along with race, history, and fatherland, are the defining characteristics of a People. Language is constitutive of a symbolic universe; its attendant mythology is deeply embedded in public consciousness and reinforced in civil ritual.

It has been pointed out often enough that the Afrikaner nationalist movement has effectively exploited language for political ends. Within Afrikanerdom language has long served as a mobilizing issue. To the outside world, Afrikaner nationalists have insisted that they will be able to maintain their national identity — and language — only as long as they control their own political destiny in South Africa. The French historian Marianne Cornevin (1980) examines the latter claim in her investigation of false historical premises and myths upon which apartheid is based. As seen from the inside, the formative period of the Afrikaner people is to be distinguished from European colonization in other parts of the world:

> The striking feature of [the] "Dutch period," which lasted from Jan van Riebeeck's landing on 6 April 1652 to the demise of the Dutch East India Company in 1795, is the very small number of colonists who settled on African soil and became "white Africans" or Afrikaners speaking a new language called Afrikaans, in comparison with the colonists who settled in North America some decades earlier (1607 in Virginia, 1620 in Massachusetts) and became "Americans" (while continuing to speak English) (Cornevin 1980:54).

Cornevin goes on to discuss how official South African publications have invoked the "evolution of a new language significantly named Afrikaans" as a historical argument that supposedly "justifies" the white homeland in Southern Africa (1980:65):

> One of the weaknesses of this argument is that it applies only to the Afrikaners and not to the entire white nation. While undoubtedly respectable, it would certainly be much more so if white Afrikaans-speakers (the Afrikaners) did justice to "brown" Afrikaans-speakers (the coloureds); FOR THE LATTER'S ANCESTORS WERE LARGELY RESPONSIBLE FOR CHANGING THE DUTCH SPOKEN BY THE FIRST SEVENTEENTH-CENTURY SETTLERS INTO A NEW LANGUAGE [my emphasis]. But despite the almost religious reverence the Afrikaners feel for their language, the coloureds are victims of apartheid.

The extent to which politicians in South Africa have made use of falsified versions of history is well documented, and comment on the validity of the proffered historical argument is superfluous. The mechanisms by which Dutch evolved into Afrikaans at the Cape of Good Hope are part of a highly technical and controversial debate among linguists; they are not of direct concern here. What is of concern is the assessment of a specific linguistic myth; namely, that language genesis was a function of ethnogenesis.

For participants in the First Language (Patriot) Movement (1875-98) this "ontogenetic myth" appears to have been relatively vague except to the extent that they delineated a scant creation story implicit in the aphorism "Di Taal is di Volk en di Volk is di Taal." By the end of the Second Language Movement (1903-19) the ontogenetic myth had more fully crystallized. Perhaps the most unabashed diachronic pronouncement to this effect is that of Willem Postma (1912:625), who made the bald assertion that the birth of the Afrikaans language coincided with the birth of the Afrikaner People in the early years of the eighteenth century. With the appearance of S. P. E. Boshoff's *Volk en Taal van Suid-Afrika* (1921), the ontogenetic myth acquired scientific credibility. Boshoff contextualized the genesis of Afrikaans in the following terms:

Op die bodem van die nuwe vaderland het 'n nuwe volkseenheid tot stand gekom, waarvan die grootste gedeelte afkomstig was uit "die laghe lande bider see." Dié volk moes hom in 'n hoë droogland aanpas, hom inburger in 'n subtropiese bergland so verskillend moontlik van die oorspronklike stamland met sy polders, kanale, en gragte. Seelui en vissers, werklui en handelaars moes saai- en veeboere word, en hulle bestaan was afhankelik sowel van die diensbaarmaking van die bodem as van die verowering van die land self teenoor inboorlingstamme en wilde diere. Die woordeskat van Europese groeptale moes gewysig word in ooreenstemming met die nuwe bodem en die nuwe lewensbedrywe. Lokale en sosiale taalgrense van vroeër moes verval; maar nuwe groeptale moes weer ontstaan (1921:6-7).[2]

Notice the recurring motifs here: the new fatherland, the formation of a new ethnic group, the adoption of new ways of life, adaptation to new physical surroundings, and an environment inherently conducive to formation of a new language.[3]

The ontogenetic myth has involved several closely related elements. Accordingly, Afrikaans evolved from Dutch through an acceleration of the "normal" (i.e., internal) mechanisms of linguistic change. It is seen as a European language but at the same time one that is not a direct export from the metropole. That a European language could be autochthonous in Africa was hailed by P. J. Nienaber (1959:3) as one of the "miracles" of Afrikaans: "In die hele geskiedenis is daar nie nog 'n geval bekend waar 'n Germaanse taal LANGS GEWONE WEË [my emphasis] so radikaal en in so kort spanne

---

[2]"On the soil of the new fatherland a new national entity had originated, the largest part of which had come from 'the low lands near the sea.' This nation had to accommodate itself to a high and arid land, to adapt itself to a subtropical mountainous territory as different as it could be from the original country of origin with its polders and canals. Sailors and fishermen, workers and traders had to become farmers and cattlemen, and their existence depended upon both the cultivation of the soil and the conquest of the country itself from native tribes and wild animals. The vocabulary of European languages had to be altered in accord with the new soil and the new ways of living. Earlier local and social linguistic barriers had to fall away; but new languages had to originate again."

[3]Similarly, Pienaar (1946:1), Venter (1959:13).

tyds tot 'n selfstandige taal verander het nie. In 1652 land Jan van Riebeeck met sy amptenare in Tafelbaai; teen 1725 kan ons reeds praat van Afrikaans."[4] H. J. J. M. van der Merwe propagated a fundamentalist version of the ontogenetic myth that looks to inherent tendencies toward change in Netherlandic and denies any non-European influences beyond some peripheral lexis. In a commemorative volume published by the FAK[5] in 1974, he adumbrated a genealogy that positioned Afrikaans as a sister node with Modern Dutch on the Netherlandic branch of the Germanic *Stammbaum* (1974:33):

> Wanneer Jan van Riebeeck in 1651 Nederland verlaat om 'n verversingspos aan die Kaap te kom stig, was daar reeds ver gevorder met 'n algemene taal vir Nederland. Van Riebeeck en sy koloniste was dus die draers van die 17E-EEUSE NEDERLANDS [emphasis in original], wat voortgespruit het uit 'n eeuelange ontwikkeling. Hierdie ontwikkeling het voortgeduur na 1652: in Nederland het dit NORMAALWEG [my emphasis] ontwikkel tot Nieu-Nederlands; die NORMALE [my emphasis] ontwikkeling het ook in Suid-Afrika voortgegaan, maar as gevolg van bepaalde faktore, het dit al hoe meer begin afwyk van sy suster in Nederland... en tog het Afrikaans nooit sy Germaans-Dietse identiteit verloor nie — daarvoor is sy oerwortels te stewig in die Germaanse grond gevestig.[6]

---

[4]"In all of history no case had been known in which a Germanic language — following normal pathways — changed so radically and in such a short period of time into an independent language. In 1652 Jan van Riebeeck landed with his officials in Table Bay; by 1725 we can already speak of [there being] Afrikaans."

[5]Federasie van Afrikaanse Kultuurvereniginge, or "Federation of Afrikaans Cultural Organizations."

[6]"When Jan van Riebeeck left Holland in 1651 to found a refreshment station on the Cape, much progress had already been made towards the creation of a common language for the country. Van Riebeeck and his colonists were therefore the bearers of 17th-century Dutch, which had arisen after a development lasting centuries. This development continued after 1652; in Holland it took its normal course, leading to the development of Modern Dutch; the normal development also continued in South-Africa, but as a consequence of certain factors, the language began to deviate from its sister in Holland... and yet Afrikaans never lost its Germanic-Netherlandic identity. Its original roots were too firmly planted in Germanic soil for that to happen."

The ontogenetic myth has always included a racist ingredient, and one can readily discern this in pronouncements that assert the purity of Afrikaans from non-European influences. To linguists these are too well known to require mention.

Initially, Afrikaner nationalist mythology imbued the ontogenetic myth with a strong neo-Calvinist element. In the late nineteenth century S. J. du Toit, a minister of the NGK and founder of the Genootskap van Regte Afrikaners (1875), cultivated a mythology that fused Afrikaner history, the Cape Dutch Vernacular, and Calvinist theology. The central concept was that God Himself placed the Afrikaners in Africa and gave them the Afrikaans language (cf. also Postma 1912:627). He entrusted them with a mission to spread Christian civilization to Africa. C. J. Langenhoven's exclamation upon the recognition of Afrikaans as the second official language of the Union of South Africa (1925) implies the fulfillment of a divine promise: "Regtig, die saak is van die Here, en dis wonderlik in ons oë, te wonderlik om ons eie ervaring te glo."[7] Even after constitutional recognition of Afrikaans in lieu of Dutch, some writers continued to propagate the idea of language being the hallmark of a Chosen People. In an essay commemorating language heros as the bearers of the "miracle" of Afrikaans, H. Venter (1959:12), like du Toit before him, sought to ground language and linguistic differentiation in the ordinances of God's creation. Afrikaans was created by and for the Afrikaner: "Dit is die enigste taal wat deur die gees van die mens wat God die Here gestel het met 'n spesifieke roeping, gevorm kon word" (1959:13).[8]

By the end of the Second World War, the ontogenetic myth had become more or less codified. In a series of radio talks compiled for and broadcast by the South African Broadcasting Corporation, Roy Macnab explained to English-speaking South Africans that "a language WILL change as it comes to fulfill a totally new role, to express a new

---

[7]Cited from Nienaber 1959:3. "Verily, it is the Lord's doing, and it is wonderful in our eyes, too wonderful for us to believe our own experience."

[8]"It is the only language which could be formed by the spirit of man upon whom the Lord God has imposed a specific calling."

people in a new environment, cut off from its original sources" (1973:8). Thus,

> [By 1691] the Cape Dutch, the Boers, the Afrikaners... were well and truly in existence.... Here, then, were the first *[sic!]* 1,000 South Africans and on their own now, living in surroundings totally different from those of Europe.... Their language gradually came to reflect their new life in its idioms and sayings, which were born of their experience of Africa and made sense nowhere except in Africa. So it became a language of Africa, Afrikaans, and because the people who spoke it were largely country people, it developed a pastoral flavour, redolent with the tang and texture of the African soil (1973:9).

Macnab's statement is remarkable for its apparent ignorance of quite respectable Afrikaner linguistic scholarship available at the time. Instead, it reaches back to Boshoff 1921 for its conception of language genesis. The souvenir *Gedenkboek* of the Afrikaans language festival held in Bloemfontein in 1975 carries an essay by a standard ten pupil in a section bearing the rubric "Die Stem van ons Jeug." The young woman writes (p. 24):

> Die boom [Afrikaans] kon nou vir homself sorg. Die doringbos [English] kon die lig nie meer keer nie en só gaan ons met die triomf van ons Taal die toekoms tegemoet in vaste vertroue op die nuwe vertaling van die Bybel, wat met ons praat in ons eie, geliefde moedertaal.
>
> > "die één einigste witmanstaal wat in Suid-Afrika gemaak is en nie oor die seewater klaar gekom het nie..."
> >   Afrikaans![9]

---

[9]"The tree [Afrikaans] could now take care of itself. The thorn bush [English] could no longer turn away the light and thus, with the triumph of our Language we go forward into the future, trusting upon the new translation of the Bible, which talks with us in our own beloved mother tongue.

This touchingly innocent tribute to the mother tongue pushes all the right buttons. The strophe from Langenhoven's well-known poem frames the essay and conveys the racial element; the image of a tree too large to be strangled by the thorn bush calls to mind the *taalstryd* and the survival of a dramatic crisis; the burden of the neo-Calvinist element is effectively borne by the juxtaposition of the future with the 1933 Bible translation.

Like other myths, the ontogenetic myth is dynamic. Notwithstanding codification, individual elements have been susceptible to change with changing circumstances. To an urbanized and secularized generation of Afrikaners born after the Second World War, the old symbols no longer hold the same meaning. Contemporary formulations of the ontogenetic myth have generally been more secular (e.g., Macnab 1973, Kok et al., eds., 1974), while others, such as the *Gedenkboek* essay, still bear the mark. Of particular interest is how Afrikaner leaders had to reconcile the ontogenetic myth with the fact that the "purest," most advanced forms of Afrikaans have been widely equated with the varieties of its black speakers (chiefly, though not exclusively, the "Coloureds"), who today constitute virtually half of the Afrikaans speech community.

No linguist who has examined all the evidence concerning the origin and development of Afrikaans could fail to note that during the nineteenth century educated colonists tended to regard the Cape Dutch Vernacular as the language of "Hottentots" and of only the lowest strata of Whites. The Dutch-born clergyman Arnoldus Pannevis, whom Afrikaners would later revere as one of their *taalhelde* and even as "vader van die Afrikaanse taal" described the Cape Dutch Vernacular as "'n soort van verbasterde Hollans [*sic*]" (November 7, 1874). This is virtually the same terminology he had earlier applied to Virgin Islands Dutch Creole ("bastaard-Hollandsch") in a letter of September 7, 1872.[10] Association of the Cape Dutch Vernacular with its black

---

'the one single white language which was made in South Africa and which did not come ready-made over the ocean...'
Afrikaans!"

[10]Cited from Nienaber, ed., (1968:30, 45).

speakers clearly presented something of an image problem for its white advocates, for there can be no doubt that this perception was widely held. The problem was made all the more acute by the prevailing belief in mainstream linguistics of the era that "mixed" languages were developmentally less advanced and epiphenomenal.

Advocates of the Cape Dutch Vernacular had staked their case for recognition on the premise that Dutch was linguistically so far removed that it had become a virtual foreign language for Afrikaners. If Afrikaans, as they preferred to call this vernacular, were to win a place among the world's cultural languages, some theme other than ethnogenesis and linguistic distance would have to be exploited. In these circumstances the ontogenetic myth came to deemphasize somewhat the differences between Afrikaans and Dutch and concentrate on their panchronic similarities.

This task had two basic requirements. Ideally, the first requirement was a demonstration that beyond some indisputably non-European lexis, the linguistic features of Afrikaans are properly included in that of continental Netherlandic. A handbook for teachers published in 1914 went so far as to say: "Voor het verstaan van elkaar is het verschil tussen Hollands en Afrikaans voor de Afrikaner maar een *STOOTJE*, waarover hij gemakkelik heenstapt en voor de Hollander is het niets, of alleen een *PLOEGVOOR* [emphasis in original]" and "het verschil tussen Afrikaans en Hollands lijkt groter als het is" (van Rijn 1914:8, 31).[11] The second requirement was more overtly racist insofar as there had to be a dissociation of the Cape Dutch Vernacular from its black speakers. D. F. Malan's speech "Het is ons ernst" (1908) is famous for the ubiquitously cited exhortation to his countrymen to elevate Afrikaans to a written language. It has perhaps been all to easy to overlook the fact that his attempt to substitute *volk*-consciousness for group consciousness contains a more explicit expropriation of the Cape Dutch Vernacular from its black speakers: "[Afrikaans] wordt nu gesproken door drievierden van de gehele blanke bevolking van Zuid-

---

[11]"As far as mutual comprehension is concerned, the difference between Dutch and Afrikaans is, for the Afrikaner, only a little hump which he easily steps over and, for the Dutchman, it is only a plow-furrow" "the difference between Afrikaans and Dutch seems larger than it is."

Afrika en door verreweg de meeste naturellen, DIE NIET MEER EEN EIGEN TAAL HEBBEN [my emphasis]."[12] In a radio talk entitled "Is Afrikaans 'n taal?" J. J. le Roux provided an effective synthesis. The *praatjie* takes the form of a dialog in which a certain Oom Frederik confronts a professor with the following observation: "In my jong dae het ons die skone Hollands geleer. Maar Afrikaans is mos nie 'n taal nie; dis somaar 'n verbastering" (1939:8).[13] Afrikaans, Professor X explains, is sufficiently differentiated from Dutch and elaborated to be considered a language in its own right; at the same time it is sufficiently proximate to be considered a daughter. By deft sleight of hand, le Roux reassures the listener that there is nothing odious about linguistic "bastardization," for this is merely a lay understanding of "normal" linguistic evolution. (If Afrikaans is a "verbastering" of seventeenth-century Dutch, then it follows that Modern English is a "verbastering" of Old English.) It is natural for languages to give birth to daughters, and that is precisely the relationship between Afrikaans and Dutch (1939:8-10).

From a developmental perspective, the expectation is that extraterritorial languages will adapt themselves to novel conditions by hybridizing with other languages. By acknowledging this fact, the present generation of Afrikaner scholars have done somewhat better justice to the African and Asian determinants, even while continuing to oppose creolization models of the genesis of Afrikaans. At the same time, they have done little to dispel the perceived isomorphism between ethnic group (race) formation and language formation (see Roberge 1990). To evaluate changes and continuities in the ontogenetic myth, one looks not to linguistic scholarship, but to extrapolations intended for popular consumption. Consider W. A. de Klerk's remarks on the origins of Afrikaans (1975:15):

---

[12]The text of Malan's speech is reprinted in Nienaber and Heyl, eds., pp. 93-103. The quotation occurs on p. 97. "[Afrikaans] is now spoken by three-fourths of the entire white population of South Africa and by far and away the most natives who no longer have a language of their own."

[13]"In my young days we learned pure Dutch. But Afrikaans is not really a language: it is just a mish-mash, a mongrelization."

The two elements of the emergent Afrikaners, each moving away from the other, already shared a common speech. They were now using the language of Van den Vondel, Bredero, Grotius, and others, the elevated High Dutch of the Golden Age of the Netherlands, in a new way. Their daily conversation with slaves, many of whom had come from the Malay Archipelago, compelled them to re-structure syntax, accept certain words from the languages of their servants, find apophthegms to express their observations and sentiments and build a new vocabulary. It was the growth of a vernacular.

Linguists will immediately recognize a variant of the "imitation of error" model of hybridization, according to which superstrate speakers employ simplified registers with indigenes and slaves. De Klerk's account is significant for its failure to make allowance for concomitant "broken language" on the part of substrate interlocutors, much less independent linguistic development within the substrate itself.

The new set of political realities taking shape in South Africa is likely to foster the emergence of both conservative and radical countermyths. Coverage of an Afrikaans language festival in Mmabatho (Bophuthatswana) in the February 1988 issue of *Panorama* is suggestive of a concern on the part of the Bureau for Information not only to dissociate Afrikaans from narrow Afrikaner nationalism, but also to reconstitute its image as a language that transcends ethnic and racial divisions. The piece portrays Afrikaans as a "language of Africa over which [White Afrikaners] do not possess sole right. Those of all races with Afrikaans as mother tongue will have to make it their task to break down the negative image of Afrikaans which has developed over the years. Efforts will have to be made to make Afrikaans the binding language of South Africans of all colours" (p. 27). As for those seeking to discredit Afrikaner linguistic mythology and promote a radical literary commitment in Afrikaans, Hein Willemse, for example, has written that "Afrikaans, vulgarized Dutch, became the valued possession of the Afrikaner. Afrikaans has been USURPED [my emphasis] and used as a prominent ideological vehicle in the Afrikaner's ensuing battle for political hegemony" (1987:239). If, as Henry Tudor (1972:138) claims, the essence of a (political) myth lies not in its content but in its dramatic form and service as practical argument, the raw material for a "counterhegemonic" myth may well be in place.

In sum the ontogenetic myth is a typical myth. It is partially consonant with historical reality; it deviates from the facts, for example, in appropriating the "driver" of linguistic transformation primarily for one group (Europeans) and assigns the other a subordinate, if not marginal role; it has been codified and deployed for political purposes; it accommodates a measure of internal contradiction, factual error and scientific implausibility; and it adapts to changing circumstances. Elements disappear when they become peripheral to the ideology or when the dominant group perceives they have ceased to serve its interests. To conclude that Afrikaner politicians and intellectuals have simply falsified linguistic history, as Cornevin and others have done, requires a certain degree of hubris. Such a conclusion accepts the widely propagated view of history and linguistics as scientifically neutral and objective, devoid of underlying beliefs and motivations, and that the lack of objectivity in Afrikaner history and linguistics is egregiously deviant. It ignores the fact that the historical image of a language is believed to be true not because the evidence is intrinsically compelling (or made so through adroit manipulation) but because that image both explains how present experience came about and establishes a plausibility metric for what people think ought to have happened in the past.

References

Boshoff, S. P. E. 1921. *Volk en Taal van Suid-Afrika.* Pretoria: De Bussy.
Cornevin, Marianne. 1980. *Apartheid: Power and Historical Falsification.* Paris: UNESCO.
Crapanzano, Vincent. 1985. *Waiting: The Whites of South Africa.* New York: Random House.
de Klerk, W. A. 1975. *The Puritans in Africa.* London: Rex Collings.

Kok, B., et al., eds. 1974. *Afrikaans: Ons Pêrel van Groot Waarde.* Johannesburg: Federasie van Afrikaanse Kultuurvereniginge.
le Roux, J. J. 1939. *Praatjies oor Ons Taal.* Cape Town: Nasionale Pers.
Macnab, Roy. 1973. *The Youngest Literary Language.* Johannesburg: SABC.
Nienaber, P. J. 1959. *Die Wonder van Afrikaans.* Johannesburg: SABC.
Nienaber, P. J., ed. 1968. *Dr. Arnoldus Pannevis: Vader van die Afrikaanse Taal.* Cape Town: Nasionale Boekhandel.
Nienaber, P. J. and J. A. Heyl, eds. n.d. *Pleidooie in Belang van Afrikaans.* Vol. II. Cape Town: Nasionale Boekhandel.
Pienaar, E. C. 1946. *Die Triomf van Afrikaans.* Cape Town: Nasionale Pers.
Postma, Willem. 1912. "Die Afrikaanse taal. Die ontstaan daarvan." *Die Brandwag,* March 1, 1912:623-27.
Roberge, Paul T. 1990. "The ideological profile of Afrikaans historical linguistics." In *Ideologies of Language,* ed. by John E. Joseph and Talbot Taylor, 131-49. London: Routledge.
Thompson, Leonard. 1985. *The Political Mythology of Apartheid.* New Haven: Yale University Press.
Tudor, Henry. 1972. *Political Myth.* New York: Praeger.
van der Merwe, H. J. J. M. 1974. "Die oerwortels van Afrikaans." In Kok et al., eds., 21-33.
van Rijn, C. J. 1914. *Het Zeer Nauwe Verband tussen het Afrikaans en het Nederlands.* Cape Town: T. Maskew Miller.
Venter, Hertzog. 1959. "Die taalhelde as draers van die wonder van Afrikaans." In *Die Wonder van Afrikaans,* ed. by M. S. du Buisson, 11-24. Johannesburg. Voortrekkerpers.
Willemse, Hein. 1987. "The black Afrikaans writer: A continuing dichotomy." *TriQuarterly* 69. 236-46.

Border Literature in Afrikaans

Johan P. Smuts
University of Stellenbosch, South Africa

The term *grensliteratuur* 'border literature' in Afrikaans includes all literary texts dealing with the armed struggle in which the South African Defence Force has been engaged, beyond and later even inside the borders of the country to preserve the status quo and to maintain law and order.

This struggle should be seen against the backdrop of colonial developments in Southern Africa. As far back as 1966, Botswana became independent and got a black government. After the military coup in Portugal in 1974, independence was granted to the Portuguese colonies of Angola and Mozambique, and black governments came to power. In 1980 Rhodesia gained independence as Zimbabwe, and also got a black government. South Africa and Namibia to the northwest were therefore completely surrounded by countries with black governments. Their neighbouring countries were willing to host so-called terrorist groups like SWAPO and the ANC which wanted to subvert the white minority governments in South Africa and Namibia. As a result, South Africa began to defend her borders. In doing so the enemy were sometimes pursued beyond these borders.

South Africa had already had her first taste of the so-called bush war in the late sixties when some of her police and troops went to the aid of Rhodesia. The real border war, however, was chiefly fought on the border between Namibia and Angola.

Robert S. Kirsner (ed.), *The Low Countries and Beyond,* 247-254. Lanham, MD: University Press of America, 1993.

The Angolan border presented a complex problem. Not only did Angola allow SWAPO to establish bases in her territory, but, after independence, there was also an ongoing civil war between the communist-orientated MPLA government and the more western-orientated UNITA movement. From 1975, the MPLA forces were strengthened by large numbers of Cuban soldiers who came to aid them in this struggle. This meant that the South African army in its fight against SWAPO in Angola often found itself pitted against Angolan and Cuban forces.

1976 was the year of the Soweto uprisings, and from that time on internal unrest has been a constant factor. The intensification of internal unrest in 1985 led to the proclamation of a state of emergency, which did succeed in containing the violence to some extent, but not in defusing the situation.

1989 saw new political initiatives on the part of the South African government. This led to the negotiated settlement of the independence of Namibia and the total withdrawal of the South African armed forces from the territory. Since the beginning of 1990, the South African government has also been negotiating with the ANC on a new political dispensation for South Africa.

South Africa was not in a position to sustain its growing military involvement in the seventies with just a standing army. Therefore, a new system was introduced whereby male school leavers, of approximately eighteen years of age, were expected to do military service, including a period of service on the border, which forced the young serviceman to be actively involved in a guerilla war.

Many of the servicemen felt that they were in a kind of Vietnam situation. From among this generation of young soldiers, a number of authors emerged whose writing expressed the rebellion, doubt, aimlessness, reproachfulness, and defeatism with which the war had left them. These texts were mostly short stories, but there were also a few novels and plays.

The first border stories were published during the seventies, but the most significant border texts have appeared since 1982. These have been written by young authors who have done military service themselves and personally experienced the war.

For these writers, the border has become the realm in which the major crises of the youth of our time are acted out. It places him in mortal danger and forces him to kill others. He becomes estranged from his family and friends because of an area of experience not shared by them, and because of a sense of guilt that they are possibly not even aware of.

It is striking how many border stories do not even take place on the border, but instead deal with the problems the dislocated soldier faces on his return to society.

Rather than attempt to give an overview of this group of border writers, I shall focus on a story regarded as one of the best border texts, *My Kubaan* ('My Cuban') by Etienne van Heerden, the most important of the younger prose writers.

The narrator in this story is a military serviceman who is doing border duty. He begins his story by saying that he has a Cuban soldier tied to him with a rope. The entire story is concerned with the fact that he constantly feels a strong bond with the Cuban. Only at the end of the story does it come to light that he shot dead a Cuban soldier while parachuting into Angola and that he is still feeling the burden of emotional guilt.

The Cuban is tied to the speaker in much the way Lucky was tied to Pozzo in Beckett's *Waiting for Godot*. But the converse is that the speaker is also tied to the Cuban, and this means that there is a bond that neither can free himself of.

The Cuban is the obsession with an enemy which has taken on a symbolic form, but he also becomes a double, a figure to whom one reaches out and in whom one finds completion, even if it is a fatal completion which burdens one with guilt. Thus he is the person one hates, but also loves.

The narrator's use of language reveals that he is a sensitive and linguistically skilled intellectual. This explains why he does not choose to give a realistic account of the events, but instead uses pertinent literary techniques when recounting what befalls him. He allows, for one, the focus to fall strongly on his role of storyteller, so the text takes on a distinctly metafictional flavour.

As part of his narrative strategy the real author creates two addressees in the text: the Cuban, a silent conversational partner to whom the narrator unburdens himself and through whom he reveals part of his story, is the immediate listener; and the implied reader, who is more of an external addressee. The narrator often adopts a patronizing stance towards the Cuban, while he meets the implied reader on equal terms and builds a confidential relationship with him, addressing him directly, for instance. In these parts, the narrator distances himself from the Cuban in the style of the Epic Theatre and estranges the Cuban from the reader so that the latter is able to view him more critically and actually develop a more objective view of the war situation.

The reverse also occurs: the narrator consciously identifies with the Cuban and talks about the reader. The result is that the reader begins to distrust the narrator. He realises that he might be dealing with someone who is unbalanced. This feeling is strengthened by the growing signs of obsession in the narrator as the story unfolds.

The text is made more dense by the use of concentrated metaphorical language. Here are two examples. The incursion into Angola is compared with rape, and in this way strong criticism is made of the effect the invaders have on the land and its people. In addition, the parachutists are compared with seeds which are carried by the wind and eventually fall to earth where they will live or die. The recurrent phrase "disselsade, heldedade" ('thistle seeds, heroic deeds') swells into a haunting refrain.

Perhaps this necessarily short treatment of a work which most readers of this volume will not know will suffice to indicate that the border narrative in Afrikaans — at its best — has developed into a sophisticated literary text, giving a disturbing picture of the grim reality of war on the one hand, and, on the other, by using refined literary techniques, giving one an insight into the spiritual burden with which the young serviceman is left.

The same obsession with the past and with being burdened with an emotional inheritance is also found in many outstanding short stories by other writers. Again and again one finds the image of the dislocated man pictured within an aimless existence or during a fatal moment which has arrived for him through no fault of his own.

Initially the border narrative was set on the borders of the country or even beyond them, but as a result of internal unrest the battle zone has gradually been extended. This has meant that this type of story now also uses the sphere of uprising and terror, particularly that in urban areas. This is the start of what is beginning to be termed township literature.

The war story is one of the most common of thrillers. In choosing his narrative strategies, the writer who sets out to write more than a mere adventure story has to take account of the expectations which many readers will have, particularly in assuming that the accent will be on the external.

The border stories show that the writers build in correctives to ensure that their stories move beyond this kind of expectation. Tension is often built up on more than one level so that the story gains depth. In virtually all cases the accent falls on the emotional life of the characters so that the purely war adventure becomes of secondary importance.

The writers also make use of recognized literary techniques such as the letter and diary format, and a number of the texts have typical post modernist traits.

I want to explore one aspect in particular which has contributed towards making the border story into serious literature. This is the way in which the border concept is utilized in many of these texts and developed into metaphor.

The Afrikaans word for "border" is *grens,* and this word can be a noun or a verb. As a noun it refers either to a division between different things or the farthest point to which something can be taken. In both cases there is a literal meaning, as well as numerous figurative ways in which the word *grens* can be used. The verb *grens* has a totally different meaning: it means "to cry."

Many nuances of meaning of the word *grens* are pressed into use in the stories, thus developing it into one of the most important codes in these works so that a great number of interpretations becomes possible.

The first dictionary meaning given defines *grens* as a line which arbitrarily divides two adjoining pieces of land, as in the case of the border of a country. In the first instance, this is the border of the border story — there is general reference to the border service which servicemen must do. The problem, however, is that the border concerned is not the country's border — but the border between Namibia and Angola, and Namibia was never really a part of South Africa; merely administered by her. This is precisely what contributed to the emotional problems of the South Africans who had to fight on and across this border.

In the second place, the border concerns the division between white and black in this war. But it is not even as simple as that, because the South African Defence Force had a large percentage of black soldiers, and many of them fought against SWAPO. Added to this is the fact that many of the white servicemen were ideologically radically opposed to South African government policy, but were compelled to take part in the war.

This brings us to the next border that is used in border literature: the schism within Afrikaner ranks between those who cling to traditional values and those who adopt an opposing stance. This brought division between people who were formerly close to each other.

The border also becomes the narrow dividing line between normality and abnormality, and it is striking how obsessional many of the characters in the border stories are.

The border is also the division between war and peace, Europe and Africa, life and death, and sometimes the wall of incomprehension which divides people.

Another border situation affects sexuality. Partly because of the isolated nature of the soldier's existence but also because man in a crisis situation or in the face of death arrives at an honesty and self-knowledge, the borders of sexuality are also at issue, shifting the dividing line between heterosexuality and homosexuality.

The strongly documentary nature of this work means that the border between reality and fiction is traversed. And in the later post modernist stories, one finds that the borders surrounding the border story have also been breeched. The border story is already being satirised and shown up and finally deconstructed.

Finally, the word *grens* is also being used in its verbal form. The soldier sometimes cries — something which is inappropriate in the hypermanly world of the soldier — and the full intensity of his emotional stratum is thus revealed.

The political situation in South Africa at the moment is extremely fluid, but there are very encouraging signs that we are moving away from war as a means of resolving political differences. The Defence Force has been withdrawn from Namibia, at the end of 1989 military service was reduced from two years to one, armament projects have been curtailed, and the army is being reduced and its budget has been cut. The process of negotiation currently underway between the government and the ANC could mean that the sporadic outbreak of subversive incidents could end.

It could be that border literature is a largely completed episode in Afrikaans literature, as the deconstruction of the border story among the latest work suggests. Some of the best known border writers openly admit that they are beginning to think about other themes for the nineties — ecological problems, for one.

It is impossible to predict the course a literature will take. However, one can look back on Afrikaans border literature and realize that it has produced outstanding texts during the past fifteen years. This literature has captured the imagination of the reading public because they were confronted with the disturbing realities facing South Africans in one of the most difficult periods that the country has ever experienced.

References

Smuts, J. P. *Koker: Kortprosatekste sedert Sestig.* Kaapstad: Tafelberg 1989.
Van Heerden, Etienne. *My Kubaan.* Kaapstad: Tafelberg 1983.

Rethinking Afrikaans Language and Literature: Facets of a Current Debate[1]

Hein Willemse
University of the Western Cape, Bellville, South Africa

Those superficially acquainted with South Africa invariably associate Afrikaans with the Afrikaner; they identify the Afrikaner as the oppressor and Afrikaans as the language of the oppressor. This statement, for all its effectiveness as a slogan, does not reflect the complex nature of relationships, history, invented traditions and mythologies. In order to grasp the complexity of the proposition — *Afrikaans is the language of the oppressor* — one will have read it against the background of the ideological discourse prevalent in South African society.

The present paper is intended to introduce the reader to the topic of "alternative Afrikaans." It will not advance intricate internal polemics but will rather provide a descriptive introduction to the debate. It consists of three sections: "Afrikaans as the language of the oppressor," "Afrikaans as a site of struggle," and thirdly, "Rethinking Afrikaans." These are broad brush strokes, rather than in-depth analysis, and I offer them as a literary critic rather than a linguist.

---

[1] Unavoidably the present paper heavily relies on my earlier work: "The black Afrikaans writer: a continuing dichotomy." 1987. In *TriQuarterly* 69. Evanston: Northwestern University; "The liberation of Afrikaans." 1987. Johannesburg: Congress of South African Writers; "Die skrille sonbesies — emergent Black Afrikaans Poets in search of authority." 1990. In Martin Trump (ed.) *Rendering Things Visible: The South African Literary Tradition since 1976.* Johannesburg: Ravan.

Robert S Kirsner (ed.), *The Low Countries and Beyond,* 255-265. Lanham, MD: University Press of America, 1993.

Afrikaans as the language of the oppressor

In the past fifteen years Afrikaner Nationalism has been repulsed most powerfully by the majority of South Africans, to such an extent that we are now, at the beginning of the 1990s, entering a phase of changed strategies, a time in which old certitudes are ceaselessly interrogated.

In a direct sense the uprisings of 1973 and more particularly 1976 were the beginnings of an abiding season of the most intense strife and struggle in South African history. It was chiefly with the uprising of Soweto 1976 that Afrikaans became more intimately identified with the Afrikaner. Afrikaans, the creole language, usurped in the beginning of this century by the ideologues of Afrikaner Nationalism as the Afrikaner's exclusive language signified with the proclamation of the Bantu Education Act (No. 47 of 1953) oppressive Afrikaner and Nationalist Party rule.

In 1954 and 1955 new syllabi were introduced under the provisions of the 1953 Bantu Education Act. These *inter alia* stipulated that instruction be given through the medium of the mother tongue, i.e. an African language, with the two official languages Afrikaans and English, introduced as subjects during a child's first year at school. After seven years of schooling 50% of subjects were to be taught through the medium of English and the remaining 50% through Afrikaans. In practice the 50:50 policy, as it became known, meant the following:

Mother tongue instruction:	Religious instruction, Music, and Physical Education
English:	General Science and practical subjects like needlework and woodwork.
Afrikaans:	Mathematics, Social Studies, Geography, and History.

Especially at secondary schools the 50:50 language policy was the subject of deep resentment.[2] African educationists and parents demanded that only one language be used. The government responded in a rigid, undemocratic manner: "It's in the Bantu's own interest that he should learn Afrikaans, it is not their right to determine in which language they must be taught. In the white area of South Africa, where the Government pays, it is certainly our right to decide on the language division" (Andries Treurnicht quoted in *The Star*, June 17, 1976, Johannesburg).

Ideologically, Afrikaans equals Afrikaner rule. Afrikaans equals apartheid and repression. Steyn (1980:293) in a study on the survival of Afrikaans refers to the following example: "When [a black person] comes to a government office and says: 'Afternoon, sir, can I please...' The reaction is: 'Who is your sir?' Or: 'Can't you address me in a better way?' and while standing there another comes and says: '*Baas* [Boss], please the form...' he is immediately attended to." A telling literary example of this colonial and servile relationship is a poem by Motshile wa Ntodi. The nature of the worker's language is characterized by the practice of inequality.

>Morning Baas,
>Baas,
>Baas Kleinbaas says,
>I must come and tell
>Baas that,
>Baas Ben's Baas says,
>Baas Ben want to see
>Baas Kleinbaas it

---

[2] A doctrinaire ruling of the Nationalist Ministry responsible for Black education requiring Afrikaans to be used as the medium of instruction in the study of Mathematics and Social Science is generally considered the motorial cause for the period of the 1976 uprising. The ruling was unacceptable because few teachers spoke the language and English proficiency is a prerequisite for employment. Furthermore Afrikaans was unacceptable for ideological reasons. "The issue of the uprising of 1976 was not about the choice between English or Afrikaans. Rather it was about the unacceptable principle of the 50.50 system, its undemocratic manner of adoption, the obstacle it placed before secondary school students in the learning process and last but not least, the fall in academic achievement since its introduction" (ANC, 1990: 20).

> Baas don't use
> Baas Kleinbaas,
> Baas.

Jeremy Cronin (1986:55) in a analysis of the poem draws a valid correlation between the use of language and the social relationships represented through language.

> Afrikaans (unlike English) marks the distinction between the polite and the familiar second person pronominal form — *u/jy*. But in racist South Africa, in the contact between colonizer and colonized, boss and labourer, even the polite *u* is not sufficiently distanced. The flexibility and economy of the syntactical shifter are lost and nouns and proper names (all Afrikaans in this poem) are retained. The consequence is an enormous clogging up, an enormous redundancy of information. The poem enacts, ironically, at the level of dialogue, the inefficiency, the opaqueness of apartheid colonialism.

But Afrikaans is not exclusively the language of the Afrikaner. The language is also predominantly the language of the so-called "Coloured" working class. Against this background the premise "Afrikaans is the language of the oppressor" can be reconsidered. Eagleton (1979:63) in an insightful essay discerns between the "emotive and cognitive structure of ideological discourse," which partially explains this perception. This notion of ideological discourse may be demonstrated with the proposition "Afrikaans is the language of the oppressor," with the implication "Afrikaans is *exclusively* the language of the oppressor." Viewed simply this could be regarded as a referential proposition: the Afrikaner speaks Afrikaans; the Afrikaner is the political oppressor; thus: Afrikaans is the language of the oppressor.

Taking into account that in the 1980 census of the South African government 47% of all Afrikaans speakers were black mother tongue speakers — in 1990 the percentage would probably be higher than 50% — this is obviously not a completely referential proposition, and could, in Eagleton's terminology, be decoded into "emotive ideological discourse": we hate the Afrikaner for violently enforcing apartheid; we hate the Nationalist government for denying us unfettered economic, political and social participation; therefore we reject the Nationalist government, the Afrikaner, its institutions and symbols, including the Afrikaans language.

The following extract illustrates compellingly the perception of that causal relationship between language and repression:

> The Afrikaners spoke Afrikaans, which is a mongrel Dutch with some German. Afrikaans has a guttural and ugly sound. It would later be very effective to use when the authorities ordered native families from our homes or commanded soldiers to fire into unarmed crowds. It is the language of genocide, and, in fact, it sounds like the German the Nazis speak in Hollywood movies (Makeba, 1988:5).

However, disentangling the discourse does not imply deprecation of a harsh political experience: what is at stake in the last analysis is not whether the proposition is true or false, but whether it defines a person's experience in the real world. "What is important to recognize is that the cognitive structure of an ideological discourse is subordinated to its emotive structure" (Eagleton, 1979:64).

The rejection of Afrikaans in 1976 thus served as a symbolic rejection of Afrikaner Nationalism and the educational policies of the Nationalist government. Moreover, it also helped to obscure all other relationships between Afrikaans and other speakers of Afrikaans, among them black speakers. It is only in recent years that attempts have been made to redeem the contribution of black Afrikaans speakers to the history of Afrikaans (see Belcher, 1987; Davids, 1987 and du Plessis, 1986).

Afrikaans as site of struggle

The debate on the origins of Afrikaans has been extremely controversial. Scientific and less scientific pronouncements perpetually rage within Afrikaans linguistic and literary circles on this issue. The debate ranges from the arguments for white purism, claiming that

Afrikaans is a branch of European languages essentially uncontaminated by African or Asian languages, to those linguists who maintain that Afrikaans certainly has the bearing of a creolized language. It is suggested that, for the purposes of ethnic mobilization, Afrikaner linguists over the years postulated Afrikaans as an European language: white purism contradicting the evidence of history. Valkhoff (1971:463), in discussing Afrikaner linguists and the debate on the origins of Afrikaans against the background of the Afrikaners' language struggle, remarks that, "[i]t is not astonishing that in their language struggle these linguists tended to transfer their ideal of purity of the white race to their mother tongue and its history."

For some commentators the issue of Afrikaans' uncontaminated origins belongs to the realm of myth and the invention of traditions. David Brown (1988:38) in his recent contribution to the general language debate holds the view that:

> This shying away from pidgin and creole linguistics in discussing the genesis of Afrikaans has been an essential component of the invented continuity of Afrikaner culture and new-Social Darwinist explanations of the origin of Afrikaans, which have dominated Afrikaans historical linguistics in South Africa.... Such explanations of the social historical origins of creoles are not uncommon but they are an invention of linguistic tradition in the desire of creole people to boost their sense of origin in the face of metropolitian prejudice.

Leaving aside the complexity of this historico-linguistic debate, it should be clear that not only the origins of Afrikaans but also the "proprietorship" of the language is very much in contention. The noted South African novelist, André Brink (1988:28) commented that a salient feature of South African and Afrikaner history is that official historical statistics represent only the whites — even in the Great Trek and other celebrated adventures. The absence of non-white Afrikaans speakers, according to Brink, is a tacit accusation of the way in which history has been manipulated by those in power. Black Afrikaans speakers were not the "agterryers" that history has condemned them to be. They were co-creators of and participants in the language.

Since 1976 more Black Afrikaans poets were published than in the preceding four decades. The contradiction is obvious: Afrikaans, the language associated with repression and exclusivity, is promoted as a language of black resistance. Leonard Koza (1984), a poet, observes that "We are primarily Afrikaans speaking... We still love the language, in spite of what the system did to us. This is our mother tongue. Through our feeling for the language, we show that we promote the language. The language is a bridge between people." In the wake of the Soweto revolt some aspirant writers experienced a schism with and denial of Afrikaans. "Although I grew up in an Afrikaans house my friends and I at one stage spoke English only," says Patrick Petersen in an interview, but with the confidence of the freshly converted he asserts, "Those days are gone. Today we have a free association with the language, because it is also my language" (quoted in *Die Burger,* July 16, 1988, Cape Town).

These writers experience life in South Africa as second class citizens and as writers are excluded from the established Afrikaans literary life. This sense of alienation led to a situation in which Afrikaans and the Afrikaans literary canon are perceived as sites of struggle. The issues of neglected language dialects or literary artifacts rendered invisible by established Afrikaans literary standards are more than a purely intellectual motivation for recognition. Debating these issues and identifying the restrictions imposed by the dominant order are seen as contributions to the overall liberation of South Africans. Through these actions Afrikaans becomes a medium of revolt and resistance.

Rethinking Afrikaans

The late seventies and 1980s saw a marked difference in particularly the Western Cape with regard to Afrikaans and the implications for political work. Major shifts in the nature of political and cultural activism, the organisation of popular political expression, the prominence of trade unions, the political dominance of the African National Congress and the rise of educational and political campaigns resulted in the rethinking of set ways of political and trade union organisation. A sensitivity developed in political and trade union activist discourses to the material composition of particular groups and classes. This is pre-eminently reflected in terms of language.

The shift to greater grassroots activity sensitized political activists to the expediency of Afrikaans. The Charterist tendency of left politics with its greater tolerance for language differences consciously employed language. At one of the Afrikaner universities during the 1980s Patrick Lekota, then a member of the United Democratic Front, even addressed his white student audience in Afrikaans. The strategy could not be more clear: the language is very much part of the message. In many areas of the Cape Peninsula, the Karoo, North Western Cape and the Eastern Cape Afrikaans has been used in political and grassroots campaigns. Whereas previously Afrikaans was limited to pamphlets in especially rural communities the late eighties saw the emergence of several "alternative Afrikaans" language newspapers, among others *Saamstaan* and *Alternatief*. (Although not geared at the black Afrikaans community organisational level — like *Saamstaan* and *Alternatief* — newspapers and journals such as the *Vrye Weekblad* and *Die Suid-Afrikaan* are playing an increasing significant role in redefining the emphasis of traditional Afrikaner politics.)

During the 1988 May Day celebrations in the Western Cape some of the speeches were in Xhosa, translated into Afrikaans — "because these are the languages of the working class," a Cosatu organizer said, (quoted *South*, May 4-11, 1988, Cape Town. p. 11). In the Cape Peninsula working class pupils protest in Afrikaans as well as in Xhosa and English. During the recent uprising in the Western Cape, school children were singing these battle songs:

PW is 'n terroris   PW is a terrorist (X3)
Le Grange is 'n murderer (X3)   Le Grange is a murderer (X3)
Ma, ek wil 'n Casspir hê (X3)   Ma, I want a Casspir (X3)
Ma, ek wil 'n Buffel hê (X3)   Ma, I want a Buffel (X3)[3]

---

[3]Casspirs and Buffels refer to the armoured vehicles of the South African Police. These were used extensively to quell uprisings during the latter part of the 1980s.

Or:

Die mammas, die pappas,	The mommies, the daddies,
die boeties, die sussies,	the brothers, the sisters,
die uncles, die anties,	the uncles, the aunties,
die hondjies, die katjies,	the doggies, the kitties,
is almal tesame in die struggle.	are all together in the struggle.

Or the trade unionists sing:

Klim op die wa (X2)	Climb on board the wagon (X2)
Klim op die Cosatu se wa	Climb on board COSATU's wagon
Almal wat Cosatu lief het,	Everyone who loves COSATU
klim op Cosatu se wa.	Climb on board COSATU's wagon.[4]

In related developments, especially in the area of cultural production, the current calls for "people's culture" also influence the attitude towards Afrikaans. A Cape Town "cultural worker" describes people's culture as an emerging cultural activity which is firstly patriotic and national. He says, "our Kaaps way of speaking Afrikaans, the Goema-Goema beat, tamatiesous and kerrie kos... those things are as 'African' as the Xhosa language, the Mbaqanga beat and pap" (Williams, 1987:13). Another confesses: "[o]n leaving high school I decided never to speak Afrikaans unnecessarily. This was my protest against the Afrikaner government, the Volk and the system in this country. Later in my development I came to realize that workers on the farms speak Afrikaans. I became aware of the fact that if I wanted to identify with the struggle of the working class I had to speak, understand and write the language we all know" (Jansen, 1986:80-81).

The use of Afrikaans for these political activists and writers is justified in terms of the exigency of communication. These specific politico-cultural developments in no uncertain way impacted on the writing of black Afrikaans poets. The conscious manner of producing writing in Afrikaans and the confidence of inserting it within the broader democratic political and cultural movement could otherwise not

---

[4]COSATU is an acronym for Congress of South African Trade Unions.

have taken place. A niche for Afrikaans — which shortly after 1976 was certainly unthinkable — has been forged in the furnace of the contemporary national liberation and workers' struggle.

The growth in black Afrikaans writing which I alluded to earlier could be ascribed to a series of multifarious conditions, among others the influence and effect of Black Consciousness; the general political and cultural developments in the late 1970s and early 1980s; the development of a rudimentary working class consciousness; the insertion of black Afrikaans writers in the rural areas and in the case of black Afrikaans exiled writers the need to recreate — in exile — something genuinely South African.

Increasingly black editors have initiated, in line with their need for autonomy and fueled by a critical evaluation of their position and relationship to the Afrikaans literary canon, little magazines such as *Praat, Skryf,* and *Akuut*. A publishing house, concentrating exclusively on black Afrikaans writing, has recently been established. Its establishment came about "because most Afrikaans publishing houses are extensions of Nationalist party ideology, and our work never sees the light of day," according to Patrick Petersen (1988).

In this short paper I have hopefully provided a glimpse of how — apart from the ruling definition of the language — another invisible fringe expression has been in struggle and that the certitudes of established mythology have to be examined to arrive at an understanding of language which recognizes the indelible contribution of black people to Afrikaans. But then again: these developments — be it in the area of Afrikaans writing or the popular perception of the language — should not be seen as mere attempts to bolster Afrikaans, or secure the survival of Afrikaans as a language (and the Afrikaner) in a new democratic South Africa. These developments are taking place within context of left politics underscoring the belief that Afrikaans as a language is more than just the Afrikaner's language and as such it is very much part of the future.

References

ANC (African National Congress). 1990. "A survey of the language policies in education in South Africa: 1948-1989." In: *Towards a Language Policy for a Post-Apartheid South Africa.* Cape Town: NECC.
Brink, André. 1984. "The future of Afrikaans." *Leadership.* 3:2. Johannesburg.
_____. 1988. "Afrikaans en bevryding." In: Randall van den Heever. *Afrikaans en Bevryding.* Kasselsvlei: CTPA. pp. 23-35.
Brown, David. 1988 "Speaking in tongues: Apartheid and languages in South Africa." *Perspectives in Education.* 10:2.
Cronin, Jeremy. 1986. "'Laat ons ranks vassa" — African poets and the use of Afrikaans." In: Julian F Smith et al.
Davids, Achmat. 1987. "The role of Afrikaans in the history of the Cape Muslim community." In: Hans du Plessis & Theo du Plessis (eds). *Afrikaans en Taalpolitiek.* pp. 37-60.
Eagleton, Terry. 1976. *Criticism and Ideology.* London: NLB.
_____. 1979. "Ideology, Fiction, Narrative." *Social Text.* 2. pp. 62-80.
Jansen, Beverley. 1986. "Paneelbespreking." In: Smith, Julian F. pp. 76-78.
Makeba, Miriam with James Hall. 1988. *Makeba: My Story.* Johannesburg: Skotaville.
Smith, Julian, F, Alwyn van Gensen, Hein Willemse (eds). 1986. *Swart Afrikaanse Skrywers.* Bellville: UWC. pp. 50-61.
Steyn, J. C. 1980. *Tuiste in Eie Taal.* Cape Town: Tafelberg.
Valkhoff, M. F. 1971. "Descriptive bibliography of the linguistics of Afrikaans. a survey of major works and authors." *Current Trends in Linguistics.* 7. pp. 455-500.
Williams, Alex. 1987. "Toyi-toying to the goema-goema beat." *New Era.* 2:2. Cape Town.

Anglo-Dutch Relations

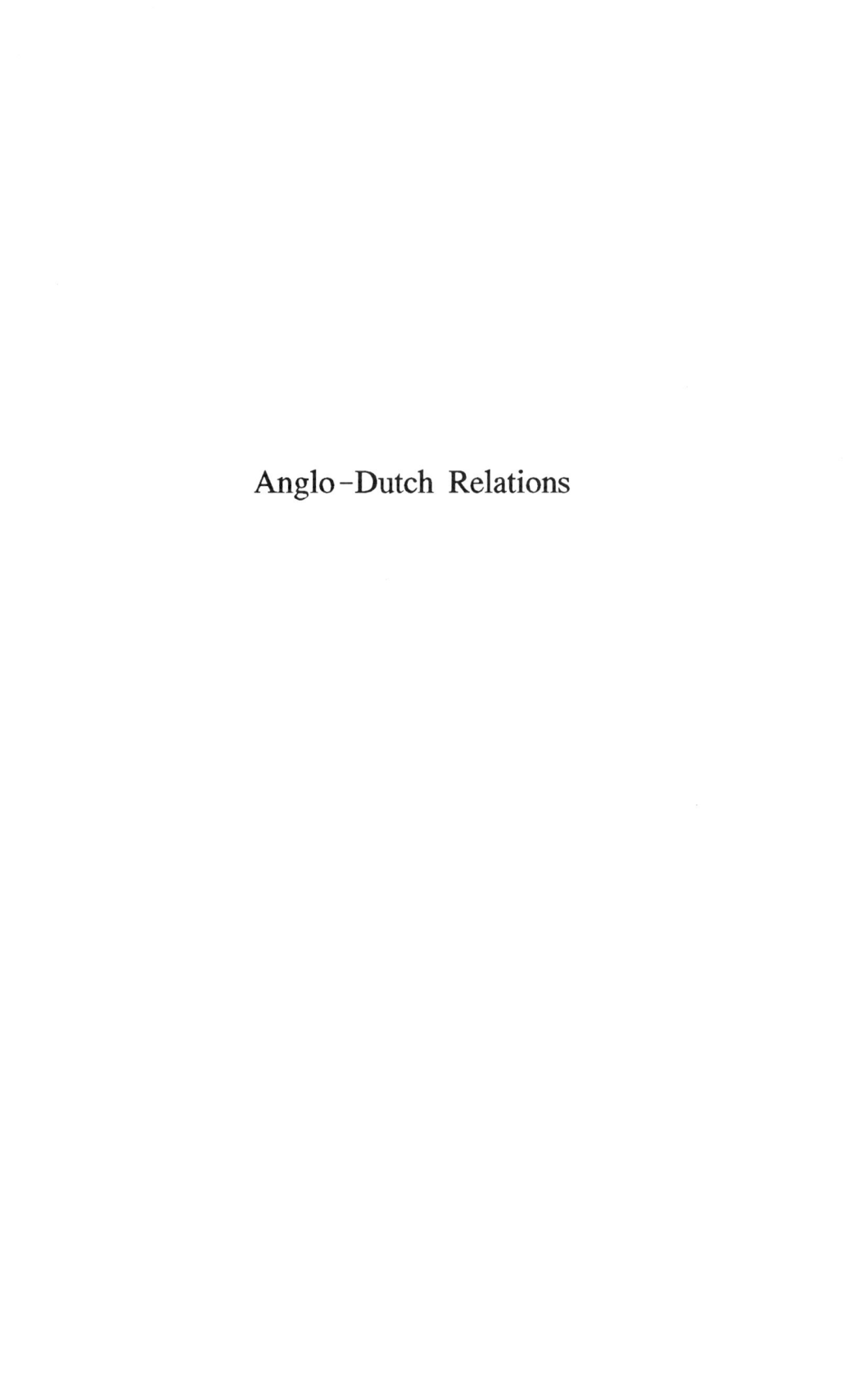

The Lazarus Motif in Donne and Rembrandt: Some Religious and Artistic Parallels

Mary Arshagouni Papazian
Oakland University, Rochester, Michigan

Recent scholarship has explored the very close ties between England and the Low Countries in the 16th and 17th centuries. It has also begun to explore the expression of Calvinist thought in the works of Donne and Rembrandt. This paper draws on both of these traditions in order to examine the presentation of the biblical Lazarus story in Donne's *Devotions upon Emergent Occasions* (1624) and Rembrandt's 1631 painting, "The Raising of Lazarus." Recounted only in the Gospel of St. John, the story of Christ's raising Lazarus from the dead has long been a favorite of artists and biblical commentators. According to the apostle John, Christ received word from Mary and Martha that their brother Lazarus was sick. He arrived in Bethany four days later — after Lazarus had died — ready to perform the miracle. Upon His arrival, Mary and Martha, who had been joined by many of their fellow Jews, greeted Him with expressions of doubt and incredulity. Christ responded by weeping with them, groaning in spirit, and reminding them that He is "the resurrection and the life" and that "he that believes in [Him], though he were dead, yet shall he live." At this point, John describes the actual raising of Lazarus, who emerged from the tomb at Christ's command, "bound hand and foot with graveclothes."[1]

---

[1]John 11:1-45, *The Bible,* King James Version (London: 1611).

Robert S. Kirsner (ed.), *The Low Countries and Beyond,* 269-279. Lanham, MD: University Press of America, 1993.

Commentators have generally interpreted this biblical event in two ways: first, as an example of the greatness of God's mercy; and second, as pre-figuring the raising of the faithful at the Last Judgment. In his sermon on "The Raising of Lazarus," Luther uses this story as an occasion to focus upon human sinfulness, faith, and God's love, and he interprets Christ's tears as signs of his compassion for the human frailty and weakness exhibited by Mary and Martha and their fellow Jews who have come to witness the scene. But although Luther believes with Augustine that Lazarus "signified those who are so entangled in sin that they go beyond all bound," he makes it clear that Christ loved him, just as he loves all of us who are also sinners.[2]

Like Luther, Calvin also reads this "specially remarkable miracle" as "a wonderful example of [God's] divine power... a lively image of our future resurrection." And he, too, focuses on man's need to turn to God because of his inevitable sinfulness. But Calvin begins to concentrate as well on the internal drama of the scene — the psychological action, if you will, that characterizes the portrayal of this event in Donne and Rembrandt. In particular, Calvin recognizes the paradoxical benefits of suffering for those loved of God, for, as he realizes, Christ will use the trials of the faithful as aids to salvation. As he explains, when "we groan in anxiety and sadness," "the Lord rejoices for our own good; and a twofold kindness shows in His not only pardoning our sins, but joyfully devising means to correct them." Moreover, Calvin adds, inverting the terms of life and death, "the fact that men live and breathe and are endowed with sense, understanding and will tends to their destruction." "Believers are said never to die," he continues, "because their souls, in that they are born again of incorruptible seed, have Christ dwelling in them." Rather, for the faithful, "death [ironically] is itself a sort of liberating from the bondage of death." These remarks reveal that the raising of Lazarus involves far more than simply demonstrating Christ's power and love, for they also call into question the very demand for life that Lazarus' sisters make. Thus, although Christ's tears confirm his compassion for both the suffering of Lazarus' sisters and for the sinfulness of mankind

---

[2]Martin Luther, "Sermon on the Raising of Lazarus, John 11:1-45. Preached on the Friday after Laetare, March 19, 1518," p. 45. Reprinted in *Luther's Works,* 51, ed. and trans. by John W. Doberstein (Philadelphia: Muhlenberg Press, 1968), pp. 44-49.

in general, they also suggest that Christ knows that raising Lazarus is not necessarily in Lazarus' best interest. As He recognizes, just as "we can see in Martha how many defects there are in the faith of even the best people," so too will the elect of God continue to suffer as long as they remain on earth.[3]

Calvin's emphasis on the very inevitability of sinning in God's faithful lies behind the paradox of perseverance that Donne recognizes in the Lazarus story. Although much debate still reigns regarding Donne's theological orientation — is he an Anglo-Catholic for whom the Jesuit influences of his early life remained forever present, for example, or is he instead a Puritan with sympathies to sister Reformed churches on the continent? — some church historians and literary scholars have convincingly demonstrated the Reformed coloration of his theology, particularly in regards to election and salvation.[4] It should come as no surprise, then, that his most important sermon on the Lazarus story takes on a Calvinist coloration. Although Donne's sermons contain dozens of references to the raising of Lazarus, the sermon on John 11:35, "Jesus Wept," "Preached at White-hall, the first Friday in Lent, 1622/3," offers his most detailed response to the miracle and provides a guide for reading his *Devotions*. In seeing the raising of Lazarus as "a pregnant proofe of the Resurrection," and in reading Christ's tears as symbols of His compassion for human suffering, Donne echoes many of the points on which Luther and Calvin had focused. But, in speaking specifically of Christ's tears, Donne takes the case even further, as he responds to the psychological dimension of the drama in Calvinian terms. Echoing Calvin, that is, Donne remarks that death is not undesireable in the faithful, despite the sadness that arises in those left behind. As Donne reminds us, "a good man is not the worse for dying, that is true and capable of a good sense, because he is established in a better world," and "to mourne passionately for the love of this world, which is decrepit, and upon the deathbed, or

---

[3]John Calvin, *Commentary on the Gospel of St. John*, vol. 2 (Grand Rapids: Eerdmans Publishing Co., 1961), pp. 1-14.

[4]See E. Randolph Daniel, "Reconciliation, Covenant, and Election: A Study in the Theology of John Donne," *Anglican Theological Review*, 48 (1966), 14-30; and Paul R. Sellin, *John Donne and 'Calvinist' Views of Grace* (Amsterdam: VU Boekhandel, 1983).

imoderately for the death of any that is passed out of this world is not the right use of teares." On the contrary, he explains,

> when Christ was told of *Lazarus* death, he said he was glad; when he came to raise him to life, then hee wept: for though his Disciples gained by it, (they were confirmed by a Miracle) though the family gained by it, (they had their *Lazarus* againe) yet *Lazarus* lost by it, by being re-imprisoned, re-committed, re-submitted to the manifold incommodities of this world.[5]

According to Donne, Christ's tears arose not only out of compassion for those mourning Lazarus' death, but more importantly, because Christ recognized that raising Lazarus to life meant committing him to continual sinfulness. William Perkins, the foremost theologian in England during Donne's formative years, similarly echoes Calvin's words as he explains that true believers should welcome — and not fear — death. "In this respect the day of death should be unto us most welcome," he explains, "because it doth unloose us from this miserable estate, in which wee doe almost nothing but displease God."[6] Like the passage from Donne's sermon quoted above, Perkins' words dramatically underscore the contrast for the elect of the liberating joy of death — a release from sin — and the inevitability of offending God through continued sinfulness on earth. Moreover, Donne's pious words highlight a grim irony in the well-know Protestant doctrine of the Perseverance of the Saints. According to the doctrine of Perseverance once an individual is Elect, he cannot fall from God's grace, though he will continue to fall into sin. But because of the corrupt nature of man's flesh, even the elect — those who, like Lazarus, as Luther explained, are loved of God and Christ — are not free from the temptations and sins of life on earth. In the words of the Articles promulgated at the famous Synod of Dort in 1618:

---

[5] George R. Potter and Evelyn M. Simpson, *The Sermons of John Donne* (Berkeley: The University of California Press, 1953), vol. 4, pp. 324-344.

[6] William Perkins, *An Exposition of the Symbole or Creede of the Apostles,* in Perkins, *Works* (London: 1605), p. 184.

whomsoever God, according to his purpose, calls unto the fellowship of his son our Lord Jesus Christ, and regenerates by the holy spirit, those certainly, even in this life, he frees from the dominion of sin, and slavery under sin, but *not altogether* from the flesh, and body of sin.[7]

According to Donne, then, Christ weeps as he turns to raise Lazarus from death because He recognizes that the miracle that He performs, though it will heighten the faith of the believers, will cause Lazarus further suffering. In short, Lazarus will be "re-imprisoned, re-committed, re-submitted to the manifold incommodities of this world."

Donne's *Devotions upon Emergent Occasions* (1624) and Rembrandt's "Raising of Lazarus" (1631) interpret artistically the psychological dimensions of this central paradox in the Lazarus story. In the *Devotions,* an account of spiritual self-suffering prepared for publication following a near-fatal illness in December 1623, for example, Donne makes explicit the parallel between his speaker and Lazarus in the Latin headnote to the twenty-first devotion, where he has Christ through the physicians address the speaker as Lazarus.[8] Our recognition of Donne's interpretation in his 1622 sermon of the Lazarus story as an expression of the paradox of Perseverance is helpful, for it enables us not only to perceive the importance of the explicit parallel Donne draws between his speaker and Lazarus but also to understand more clearly both the work's overall movement and its unusual conclusion. In the *Devotions,* that is, Donne presents the emotional and psychological responses of a speaker who falls suddenly into sickness. As he lies in his bed — thus parallelling Lazarus in his tomb — the speaker begins to imagine and hope that his death fast approaches. "I am dead," he plainly exclaims in his eighteenth prayer,

---

[7]*The Judgement of the Nationall Synode of the Reformed Belgique Churches, Assembled at Dort* (London: Printed for John Bill, 1619), V:i.

[8]The Latin headnote to the twenty-first devotion reads, "Atque annuit Ille, Qui, per eos, clamat, Linquas iam, Lazare, lectum" [And He <Christ>, who through them <the Physicians> calls out, "You may now leave thy bed, Lazarus," gives them the nod of assent.] John Donne, *Devotions Upon Emergent Occasions,* ed. Anthony Raspa (Montreal: McGill-Queen's University Press, 1975), p. 110. All subsequent references to the *Devotions* will be from this edition.

"I was born dead, and from the first laying of these mud walls in my conception, they have mouldered away, and the whole course of life is but an active death" (P18, p. 96). Echoing Calvin's inversion of life and death — he redefines death as the earthly, sinful life and life as the purity and peace that the elect achieve in eternity — Donne's speaker shows himself to be ready, eager, and even thankful for his final dissolution, for he knows that although elect, his physical recovery, as the doctrine of Perseverance teaches him, brings with it renewed sinfulness.

Thus, in the *Devotions,* Donne presents a healed sick man, not gladdened by physical renewal, but filled with increasing anxiety as the implications of his renewal become more and more clear to him. Just as Christ weeps as he restores Lazarus to life, so Donne's speaker weeps when he is restored to health, for he realizes that as a kind of Lazarus, he too will continue to suffer from sin. The speaker's final prayer, therefore, is anything but an expression of thanksgiving for physical recovery. Rather, it is a touching lament. The speaker cries, "since therefore thy correction hath brought me to such a participation of thyself... to such an entire possession of thee, as that I durst deliver myself over to thee this minute, if this minute thou wouldst accept my dissolution, preserve me, O my God, the God of constancy and perseverance, in this state," not from death or physical suffering, but "from all relapses into those sins which have induced thy former judgments upon me" (P23, p. 126). Recognizing that the experience through which he has just passed and from which he has just recovered will recur again and again, the speaker knows that, as he cannot prevent himself from sinning while still a man derived of dust and ashes, so neither can he reach true spiritual peace until God allows him to sever the bonds of earth and flesh. In short, he recognizes that he is in the same predicament as Lazarus after Christ's miracle, an act that caused Christ to weep for the suffering which he knows must inevitably befall Lazarus as his earthly life continues. As Calvin had remarked in his response to this biblical story, the faithful must learn not to weep for death, because only through death will they transcend sin. Whereas Mary and Martha could not see beyond their own suffering at the loss of their brother, Donne's speaker recognizes for himself that Lazarus' rising — and his own — incorporate the very irony of the perseverance assured the elect of God, for he knows that despite his best intentions, he (like Lazarus) can do little more than repay God's great mercy with continued sinning.

Comparison of the depiction of the Lazarus story in Donne's *Devotions* and Rembrandt's, "The Raising of Lazarus," is tantalizing, for like Donne, Rembrandt also represents the scene as one of anxiety and sadness rather than joy, an emphasis that suggests a Calvinian dimension to these works. Recent scholarship on Rembrandt has paid particular attention to Reformed elements in his work, and like Donne, recognition of his Calvinist orientation enables us to bring a new perspective to works such as these.[9] In his study of Rembrandt's portrayal of "six themes of Reformation art," William Halewood provides the most extensive discussion of Rembrandt's use of the Lazarus motif. According to Halewood, although "the story of Lazarus had special kinds of appeal to Reformation sensibilities and was appropriated in special ways by Reformation artists," Rembrandt's 1631 painting of the "Raising of Lazarus" is somewhat unclear as a statement of Reformation doctrine. Halewood reaches this conclusion, in part, because he finds that the painting portrays Christ as "heroic and statuesque, a commanding figure who more effectively expresses divine power than divine love" and not the humble figure that Reformers saw in the biblical passage.[10]

In the context of the treatment of the Lazarus story in Calvin's *Commentary* and Donne's sermon and *Devotions*, however, it seems to me that the painting very movingly expresses the psychological anxiety that the paradox of perseverance entails. The portrayal of inward psychological drama and emotion, one that shows "a careful savoring

---

[9]For interpretations of Rembrandt's work in a Calvinian context, see William H. Halewood, *Six Subjects of Reformation Art: A Preface to Rembrandt* (Toronto: University of Toronto Press, 1982); David R. Smith, "Towards a Protestant Aesthetics: Rembrandt's 1655 'Sacrifice of Isaac'," *Art History*, vol. 8, no. 3 (Sept. 1985), 290-302; Henrietta Ten Harmsel, "Introduction" of her translation of Jeremias De Decker, *Good Friday* (Jordan Station, Ontario: Paideia Press, 1984); and Shelley K. Perlov, "Visual Exegesis: The Calvinist Context for Rembrandt's Etchings of the Life of Abraham" and Robert Baldwin, "Rembrandt's New Testament Prints: Artistic Genius, Social Anxiety, and the Marketed Calvinist Image" in *Impressions of Faith: Rembrandt's Biblical Etchings*, Exhibition Catalogue (Dearborn: University of Michigan-Dearborn, 1989).

[10]Halewood, pp. 36, 45.

of the subtlest nuances of the biblical text," as we have seen, constitutes an important feature of Reformation art and literature.[11] The interpretation of the Lazarus story that Donne provides in his sermon and *Devotions* draws on Calvin's attention to Christ's groaning of the spirit and tears and emphasizes the internal, psychological dimensions of the story. Rembrandt's painting, too, focuses on similar emotional and psychological elements — specifically, on the emotions of Christ, Lazarus, and the witnesses of the miracle. Other scholars who have examined Rembrandt's works in a Calvinian context likewise have noted the psychological dimensions to his interpretations. In seeking to derive a Protestant aesthetic from Rembrandt's "Sacrifice of Isaac," for example, David Smith has stressed the psychological dimensions to Rembrandt's interpretation of the story, while Shelley Perlove has demonstrated that "through the vehicles of line, composition, facial expression, and light, [Rembrandt] produced highly imaginative, psychologically penetrating images dramatizing the Calvinist view of Abraham and his problematic relationship with God."[12] So too does Rembrandt use these techniques to underscore the psychological anxiety and internal drama in this depiction of the raising of Lazarus.

If we now turn our attention to the painting itself (Fig. 1), we can begin to examine how the work portrays the central paradox in the Lazarus story so important in Calvin and Donne. In "The Raising of Lazarus," Rembrandt uses *contropposto,* the technique which in art "involves the establishment of dialectical oppositions, such as light and dark, high and low, strength and gentleness." Professor Smith has identified this technique as a central feature of a Protestant aesthetic because it reflects "the fundamentally paradoxical meanings of Christianity" so important to Augustinian theology.[13] In this painting, the contrast between light and dark, and between Christ's strength and Lazarus' weakness, strikes the viewer immediately. As we have seen, the doctrine of Perseverance, particularly as interpreted by Donne in his sermon on the raising of Lazarus, has at its core an essential

---

[11]Smith, p. 293.

[12]Perlove, p. 20.

[13]Smith, p. 281.

Figure 1

contradiction — an opposition between life and death, misery and happiness, and man's continued sinfulness and God's infinite mercy. Rembrandt's use of light not only highlights this essential paradox, but it also illuminates the expressions of the figures in the painting: Christ, Lazarus, and the onlookers. While the faces of the witnesses to this miracle, particularly that of the young girl with her hands raised up, express surprise at the miracle, Christ's eyes glisten from tears. Although Christ's stance seems to suggest triumph, nevertheless his face is not peaceful and smiling. Rather, it expresses anxiety and inner torment.[14] In the right foreground, on a vertical axis with the figure of Christ, Lazarus rises from the tomb, shrouded, pale and gaunt, and makes no eye contact with either Christ or the witnesses. Strikingly, Christ's face with its furrowed forehead and raised eyebrow, is as pale as Lazarus'. One can certainly argue that by using *contropposto* to illuminate the facial expression of the central characters in this drama, Rembrandt has chosen to highlight the psychological tension of the scene: Christ's anxiety over the miracle, in which he brings Lazarus, whom he loved, back to the world of sinfulness; the surprise and wonder in the faces of the onlookers, who peer out to see the miracle; and the reaction of Lazarus, who does not yet understand that this rising means that he will be "re-imprisoned, re-committed, re-submitted to the manifold incommodities of this world."

Although the Lazarus motif has long been a favorite of artists and biblical commentators, it does take on a specifically Reformed context with Calvin's focus on the psychological tensions in the scene.

---

[14]Comparison of Rembrandt's depiction of Christ with that of his early associate, Jan Lievens, is revealing. In reference to Lievens' 1630 etching, Halewood has remarked, "What is most interesting in the Lievens etching, apart from its connection with Rembrandt's drawing, is its evangelical concentration. It is above all an image of Christ and very nearly an image of Christ glorified, a figure absorbed into the divine light which obliterates all other background and operates as the active power in the scene" (p. 45). While the Christ in Rembrandt's painting looks directly at the viewer with troubled eyes, Lievens' Christ, enshrouded in light, looks up to the heavens as if contemplating the majesty of the miracle. The viewer is thereby confronted with a very different psychological experience. Cf. Gary Schwartz, *Rembrandt: His Life, His Paintings* (New York: Viking Press, 1985), pp. 83-85, who identifies the relationship between Lievens and Rembrandt from 1630 to 1632 and how this relationship was manifested in their collective production of five versions of the Lazarus story. Schwartz is interested in noting the rivalry between the two young painters rather than in interpreting the painings themselves.

Donne draws on many of Calvin's remarks as he reads the story as representative of the paradox of perseverance and the psychological anxiety that that paradox entails. Awareness of this essential contradiction in the Lazarus story, thus, leads us to renewed interpretations of Donne's *Devotions* and Rembrandt's "Raising of Lazarus." Our examination of the responses in each of these works, with their moving emphasis on contradiction, miracle, paradox, and anxiety, perhaps, will help us begin to define a Protestant aesthetics characteristic of 16th and 17th century Anglo/Dutch art and literature, one which highlights the most affecting qualities of Reformation art.

Early Printed Books and the Low Countries: Accessing the Past through the Computer

Henry L. Snyder
University of California, Riverside

The sheer quantity of printed literature contemporary to the early modern period of European history is enormous; but the retrieval of works relevant to our own particular studies can be a frustrating experience. For the early modern historian — working in the period from the beginning of printing to 1800 — that process of access and retrieval is in the midst of a remarkable revolution. It is fortunate for those of us interested in Netherlandic studies that the leaders in this revolution are The Netherlands, Great Britain, the United States and Spain. Their achievements in national bibliography are going to transform the study of the past.

The computer has introduced a whole new era in the management of libraries from acquisitions through cataloging to circulation and reference. The libraries in the United States are in varying stages of converting to computer-based records. In Europe they are less well-advanced, especially in Southern Europe. Readers are not necessarily aware of these developments until the card catalog is closed, when they are obliged to go to a terminal to find a book or journal. Few library patrons are aware of the vast bibliographic utilities in existence in the United States, housing records in the tens of millions. Of the two largest only one, the Research Libraries Information Network (RLIN), invites individual accounts. Its general database represents a marvelous bibliographic tool. And one of its special databases, the Eighteenth Century Short Title Catalogue (ESTC), has special software — indexing,

Robert S. Kirsner (ed.), *The Low Countries and Beyond,* 281-295. Lanham, MD: University Press of America, 1993.

keyword, and Boolean search capabilities — that makes it still more valuable to the scholar. The ESTC will be considered first in this paper, rather then the Netherlands Short-Title Catalogue (STCN), because it is the only one of those discussed herein which is currently available in the United States. Moreover, as the contents, search mechanisms, usage, and scope are comparable, the more detailed description of the ESTC has equal applicability to the STCN and other files.

The ESTC is a machine-readable catalog containing bibliographical descriptions of hundreds of thousands of items. Its scope includes all items containing letterpress printing published in Great Britain and its dependencies during the years 1701-1800, as well as all letterpress items printed in English anywhere else in the world during that period. Many items are included in the ESTC which have never before been included in any major catalog. Among these are advertisements, lists (among which can be found shipping lists, society membership lists, and lists of items for sale), and transport timetables. One of the most important groups of previously uncataloged items to which scholars can now gain access is the sessional papers of the House of Commons, which are valuable sources for students of political and economic history. Only a very few categories of material are excluded: periodicals published more often than once a year; job printing such as tickets, labels, and forms; engraved music; and separately published maps. In addition to the bibliographical description, each ESTC record contains a list of all contributing libraries which have reported a copy of the item described.[1]

Although still in progress, it already represents a formidable mass of data. The records are created by three editorial centers at the British Library, the American Antiquarian Society and the University of California, Riverside. On each side of the Atlantic approximately 500 libraries have reported, so that the total of contributing libraries now exceeds 1,000 world-wide. The ESTC now contains about 280,000 records and more than 1,000,000 additional locations. It is difficult to

---

[1]For full details of the file and its early history see R. C. Alston and M. J. Jannetta, *Bibliography, Machine-Readable Cataloguing and the ESTC* (London: The British Library, 1978).

guess the ultimate size of the file. We are now matching at close to 90% of the records processed. But we still have an estimated backlog of 300,000 reports from libraries at Riverside alone. I expect that the file will eventually total as many as 350,000 records and more than 2,000,000 additional locations by 1995, when we expect to finish the active phase.

The British Library published a microfiche edition of its recataloged holdings in 1983. We published a second, enriched edition of the ESTC in 1990 and expect to publish a CD-ROM edition in 1991. The current data in the file may occupy little more than half of a disc, so that one disc should easily accommodate the entire file when it is completed. Of course, the file has been available on-line on RLIN in this country since 1982 and via the British Library Automated Information Service or BLAISE in Britain since the same year.

Perhaps the most single important consequence of this enormous canvass is the identification of all surviving printed matter from eighteenth-century Britain in public repositories. That may be a somewhat overambitious claim. But it is approximately if not precisely correct. Until now one could only guess at the total extent of publication in the eighteenth century. Though countless items may have completely perished with no surviving copies, especially ephemera, the amount that has survived is formidable. And piece by piece, item by item, edition by edition, they are all being entered in the ESTC. We have found, for example, an extraordinary collection of broadsides in the Sutro Library in San Francisco that are otherwise unrecorded. Our canvass of the Public Record Office is, not unexpectedly, turning up thousands of unique or rare items. Already we have found copies of titles listed in the standard bibliography of American imprints on the basis of advertisements or notices in other publications but for which no surviving copies had been located. And I could add that in the University of Göttingen we made similar discoveries, including German-language publications by no less than Benjamin Franklin.

The extensive holdings information is of almost equal value. It is not enough to know that a particular title survives. Because of the vagaries of eighteenth-century printing the scholar may also want to be in a position to compare a number of copies. Literary scholars in particular have made the value of this comparison evident for decades if not centuries. But even we historians, who are less sophisticated in such matters, can find the comparative study of texts rewarding. I recall reading an article comparing two copies of a volume Abel Boyer's *History of the Reign of Queen Anne Digested into Annals*. The writer had found that one copy had a whole additional gathering of text that provided an important account of a critical debate in the House of Commons. I compared the description of those two copies with four others to which I had access. Of the six only two were identical. To the extent, then, that this title was an important original source for Anne's reign, its value was much enhanced by access to all the fragments of text that Boyer wrote and had printed in one form or another. We enter every copy of every relevant item that is reported to us. We have entered as many as fifty-six holdings at one time. In some cases the cumulative total runs to over a hundred for a single edition.

Another reason for listing all copies is accessibility. It will be of greater value for a scholar living in Kansas City to know of a copy of a text he or she wants to consult in the Spencer Research Library at the University of Kansas rather than one in the Australian National Library at Canberra. All too often, the kind of widespread reading that our studies demands is denied to us because of dispersal of the texts we wish to consult and the cost and time required to examine them. We are further frustrated when local photoduplication policies denies us that alternative. It is for this reason that we have cooperated with Research Publications in its monumental project of filming all unduplicated texts to which the ESTC provides access. A twenty-year plus endeavour, that is expected to encompass as many as 200,000 titles, it will put at least one copy of every ESTC title in the hands of any student who wishes to consult them.

How does one use the ESTC? Only by actually running a search can we understand and appreciate fully its capabilities. But some words on the subject will also help to illustrate its awesome potential and the value it can bring to bear upon one's studies. Almost every field in the machine-readable record of the individual entries is indexed. This means that searches can be conducted of those fields, individually or linked, through the whole of the file. These fields include author, title, place of publication, date, bookseller's name, library name, and call number.[2] With a few key strokes one can retrieve all the works attributed to a particular author. This can include those works whose authorship is unquestioned as well as other attributions that are one of several for a single work. The authority field and the notes field, a particularly valuable section of the record, can both be examined individually with one command or separately by a series of commands.

Perhaps the most valuable point of access is the subject access that the search of the title field permits. Eighteenth-century publications are notorious for the length of their titles and ours is a full-title rather than a short-title file, in spite of its name. There are certain omissions, especially in very long titles, but we try to preserve all the essential elements. One can search on one word, several words at once, or a title phrase. A theater historian queried us once about materials relating to costume. By searching on the words *hair, coiffure,* and other similar words likely to retrieve appropriate titles we were able to provide a listing of advertisements, tracts, spoofs and ballads that included many titles unknown to her. A scholar working on the Oxfordshire election of 1754 could retrieve all the entered publications that appeared in Oxford in that year as a preliminary to sorting out the items of interest. But the searches can be far more sophisticated. They are, in fact, only limited by one's inquisitiveness and knowledge of the genre one is exploring.

The title field serves as an index and access point that exceeds the imagination. For example, the published, public acts of Parliament for the eighteenth century number some 4,000. There is no comprehensive title access to them. All will be entered in the ESTC. A key word or title phrase search together with the uniform title will instantly access what has heretofore been an unwieldy and unmanageable corpus of material. Moreover, all the preliminary material, bills, reports, petitions, will be entered. They are generally very rare and many do not survive at all. But by entering surviving material from so many

---

[2]For information on the use of the ESTC see David Hunter, *Searching ESTC on RLIN,* published as Occasional Paper 5 of *Factotum,* the Newsletter of the XVIIIth century STC, and available from the ESTC editorial office at Riverside.

different repositories a kind of access and enumeration is provided that is without precedent.

Attribution is at once a particularly fascinating and frustrating topic of investigation, especially for political historians, as all polemical material was issued anonymously. But if we are trying to pinpoint a particular author's work in a given time frame, we can create a source pool by making a search of the publications of all his known printers or publishers within a specific year or span of years. We can pull out all the items with pseudonyms he was known to have used.

If we are working on a particular work and wish to know the publications related to it, or the works that emanated from a specific debate or controversy, a few key words will quickly identify a corpus of material for us. Some months ago I was trying to solve an attribution problem related to tracts dealing with the effort to augment Scottish tithes in the mid-eighteenth century. Two opposing tracts had been cited to the same author, obviously in error. But when I searched on the word *tithe,* the time frame, and other key words, I uncovered a whole body of material that the standard works which treated the topic had failed to identify. Moreover, I found that most of them existed, so far as they had been reported to us, in only one copy. And those copies were scattered throughout Scotland, England and North America. The point I wish to emphasize is that in the space of seconds I had been able to identify a whole range of pamphlets on this subject that would have eluded even the most knowledgeable and assiduous investigator prior to the development of the ESTC.

A member of the British ESTC staff made a fascinating exploration of false London imprints, books printed in French in the Netherlands or France, but giving Londres as a place of publication.[3] (False imprints are included because any imprint purporting to emanate from the British Isles and its dependencies is automatically included regardless of language.) He could determine when they peaked, and contrasted those of the two countries. A survey of the nature of the imprints provided further clues as to their origins and the reason for

---

[3] Jim Mitchell, "Investigating false imprints," in *Searching the Eighteenth Century* (London, 1983), pp. 43-58.

the subterfuge. The terms and printer's names, generally bogus, provide clues to identifying further titles. All this can be done with a few commands and a few seconds of machine time. These are only a few examples of the discoveries that can be made by mastering and exploiting the powerful search capabilities of the ESTC file and the immense body of data it contains. The ESTC when fully utilized can revolutionize many avenues of research and open up new ones that were formerly unmanageable.

A major enhancement of the ESTC is now in the planning stages that will greatly extend its value. I refer to our plans for a national bibliography of the English press to 1800, essentially the era of the hand-printed book.[4] The output of the press of England and its dependencies to 1800, which is the approximate date of the introduction of machine printing, is already largely recorded. The STC[5] with 36,000 titles to date, Wing[6] with 100,000 titles, and the ESTC with ultimately some 350,000 titles, collectively represent a national bibliography. At present, some of the records exist only in hard copy form. But we are now in the process of adding both the STC and Wing to the ESTC file. The result will be the English Short Title Catalogue, containing a record of all relevant imprints from the beginning of printing to the year 1800, almost the whole period of the hand-printed book. This will then become the first machine-readable national catalogue of the hand-printed book for any European nation.

Given the close relationship between The Netherlands and England and later Great Britain from the revolt of the Netherlands into the eighteenth century, the material made accessible by the EngSTC

---

[4]Henry L. Snyder, "The English Short Title Catalogue. A proposal," *The Papers of the Bibliographical Society of America*, lxxxii (1988), 333-6.

[5]A. W. Pollard and G. R. Redgrave, *A Short-Title Catalogue of Books Printed in England, Scotland, and Ireland and of English Books Printed Abroad, 1475-1540* (London, 1926); 2nd. rev, and enl. ed. begun by W. A. Jackson and F. S. Ferguson, compl. by K. F. Pantzer, 3 vols. (London, 1976-91).

[6]Donald F. Wing, *Short-Title Catalogue of Books Printed in England, Scotland, Ireland, Wales, and British America and of English Books Printed in Other Countries 1641-1700*, which appeared in three volumes between 1945 and 1951. A second edition was completed in 1988. A third edition of volume one is now in progress.

has great potential value for the scholar working in Netherlandic studies. Much of the material covers diplomacy, warfare and commerce dealing in part or wholly with the United Netherlands. Keyword searches quickly elicit places and topics of specific interest for Netherlandic scholarship. For example, searches in the imprint field for Dutch place names yields 332 items for Amsterdam, 220 for The Hague, and 18 for Leiden. A search in the title field yields another 142 entries for *Amsterdam,* as well as 673 for *Dutch,* 484 for *Holland,* and 107 for *Netherlands.* Many works of Dutch authors can be found in the ESTC. To mention only one name, the Huguenot émigré newswriter in The Netherlands, Jean Dumont, Baron de Carlscroon, has eighteen entries. These are only sample figures. More sophisticated searching will undoubtedly yield many more.

Although the ESTC is the most advanced, and the most complete file of its kind, it is not unique. There are projects comparable to the English STC in progress on the continent of Europe as well. For Netherlandic scholars it is especially rewarding to note that the national project most advanced is that of The Netherlands. The Short Title Catalog Netherlands (STCN) was conceived as early as the late 1960s and a working group was set up in 1974.[7] The next five years were spent in developing rules and testing them in two experimental stages. Responsibility for the project was then transferred from the now defunct State Advisory Board on Library Affairs to the Royal Dutch Academy of Arts and Sciences. An STCN Bureau was set up on August 1, 1982. Although the product was initially intended to be an STCN, the development of the STCN began to parallel that of the ESTC during the life of the working party. The ESTC was initiated in 1976 and its rapid development, because of the massive investment of the British Library, soon outpaced that of the STCN. So even though it was conceived earlier, in the form and scope that was finally adopted, the STCN closely resembles and to some extent is even patterned after

---

[7]For details see J. A. Gruys, P. C. A. Vriesema and C. de Wolf, "Dutch national bibliography 1540-1899: the STCN," in *Quaerendo* 13 (1983), pp. 149-60. A pilot project resulted in: J. A. Gruys and C. de Wolf, *A Short-Title Catalogue of Books Printed at Hoorn Before 1701. A Specimen of the STCN* (Nieuwkoop, 1979). *KB Short-Title Catalogue Netherlands* (Den Haag: Koninklijke Bibliotheek, 1990) provides a short description with an appended bibliography.

the ESTC, whose parameters were already well established by 1978.[8] Because of the existence of two respected printed bibliographies covering the period to 1540,[9] the STCN is designed to serve as a retrospective Dutch national bibliography for the period 1540 to 1800. It is intended to include all relevant works published within the present borders of The Netherlands in any language or published in Dutch elsewhere except for Belgium. The STCN has a somewhat narrower focus than the ESTC (and its extension into the English STC), because it omits broadsides as well as engraved material and periodicals. While one may regret these omissions, it is still expected that it will eventually comprise some 100,000 items for the seventeenth century and 200,000 for the eighteenth century.

The main drawback to the STCN project, as implemented, is the limited resources that have been allocated for its operation up to the present time. The staff is much smaller than that of the ESTC. Whereas the three editorial centers at one time had a total of more than thirty workers, the STCN has a staff of six, none of whom are full-time. Because of its limited workforce the project was designed in six five-year phases to last a total of thirty years. The first phase, completed in 1987, was to catalog the seventeenth-century holdings of the Royal Library. The second phase, on which the staff is now embarked, is to record the 1540-1700 holdings of other major libraries. Currently the staff is at work on the holdings of the University Library of Amsterdam and after completing that repository will probably go on to that of Leiden University.

It is not yet clear to what extent other libraries will be surveyed before the team returns to the collections of the Royal Library to catalog its eighteenth-century holdings. That stage will, in turn, be followed by a comparable survey again of other major libraries. The small size of the staff is revealed dramatically in the slow pace at which the file has been built. By the end of 1990, after more than a decade

---

[8]See Robin C. Alston and Mervyn J. Jannetta, *Bibliography, Machine-Readable Cataloguing and the ESTC* (London: British Library, 1978).

[9]M. F. A. G. Campbell, *Annales de la typographie néerlandaise au xve siècle* (La Haye: 1874–90), continued by W. Nijhoff and M. E. Kronenberg, *Nederlandsche bibliographie van 1500 tot 1540* ('s-Gravenhage: 1923-71).

of work, there were only 33,000 records in the file, only eleven per cent of the estimated total, which was to have been completed in thirty years. Foreign libraries and other specialized repositories are also to be surveyed. Exchange agreements have been established with the British Library and with the University of Göttingen as an initial step. In 1982 the Royal Library assumed sole responsibility for the project. But that has not yet resulted in any dramatic increase in funding. A commitment on the order of that made by the British Library Board to the ESTC must be made by the national government for a sustained period if the project is to have any prospect of being completed within the scheduled span of thirty years.

There may be reservations about the limited nature of the support provided by the government to this imposing national project. It does, after all, capture the record of the history and culture of The Netherlands in the period that saw it emerge as an independent state and become a European leader on a scale that belied its small size. There can be no such reservations, however, about the design of the project and the quality of its accomplishments to date. Like the ESTC the STCN is a full MARC[10] record. That is, it employs a format based upon an internationally accepted standard that makes its records compatible with those of most other European nations and with the ESTC. The titles are somewhat abbreviated but still extensive, retaining all substantive matter. There is full imprint information and a physical description, including pagination where present and signatures.

A special feature of the STCN is the fingerprint method employed to identify each unique printing. Although this scheme was developed at Oxford as part of an experimental project which was one of the forerunners of the ESTC, the fingerprint was not included in the ESTC because of the expense and time required to include it.[11] An

---

[10]An acronym for MAchine-Readable Cataloging. It identifies the most widely used format for computerized library cataloging. A MARC record is the computer equivalant of a catalog card and when displayed on the screen resembles one. Developed by the Library of Congress and standardized in this country as USMARC, variations of it are employed throughout much of the Western world (for example, UKMARC, UNIMARC).

[11]*Computers and early books. Report of the LOC Project investigating means of compiling a machine-readable union catalogue of pre-1801 books in Oxford, Cambridge, and the British Museum* (London, 1974).

essential feature of both the ESTC and the STCN is that the compilers go back to the book to create the record. The record is based upon a specific physical copy and the title-page information is taken directly from the book or a photocopy. Standard reference works or specialist bibliographies are, however, regularly cited. All the notes in the STCN are in English, which will facilitate its use in North America.

The STCN is created in the PICA cataloging system, a national bibliographic utility equivalent to OCLC or RLIN in the United States, although PICA is currently much smaller in scope. The total database contained less than one million records as of September, 1989. It does mean that the STCN is accessible from virtually any library in The Netherlands. The transition from a manual process with a printed catalog as a product to an automated system with machine readable records as a product was made by the early 1980s. At present it remains available only in The Netherlands. Negotiations are underway between the Center for Bibliographical Studies at the University of California, Riverside and RLG on one part and the Royal Library on the other to mount the file in RLIN. The Center and RLG also propose to issue periodic editions of the STCN along with several other national bibliographies of the handprint era in CD-ROM. That will make the file potentially available throughout the world.

The English STC and the STCN are not unique. There are similar sorts of plans if not projects afoot in most major Western European countries or language groups. There is one project in particular that merits more than passing attention from Netherlandic scholars. That is the *Patrimonio Bibliográfico* of Spain. The *Patrimonio* is the only other national bibliography currently in development that matches the EngSTC and the STCN in scope and depth. The *Patrimonio Bibliográfico* is a government-sponsored project administered by the National Library of Spain. Its charge is to create a complete record of Spanish imprints from the beginning of printing to the end of the nineteenth century. In addition to including publications that fall within its scope printed in any language in Spain itself, it will also include all imprints in Spanish regardless of country of origin.

The geographical scope of the *Patrimonio Bibliográfico* is even more ambitious than either the English or the Dutch projects. The

Spanish cultural heritage is an extraordinarily rich and influential one. Only England, through its colonial empire, has influenced the language and culture of the rest of the world on something like the same scale. The Spanish empire, however, was the oldest, and the one in which its language became the prevailing one and replaced indigenous languages as the means of communication for the entire population, a feat not paralleled in the English colonies. The Spanish printed heritage is therefore not only that of a major European nation, it is also a principal means of recovering the history of much of the rest of the world in the early modern period. This includes, of course, some of the earliest recorded history of what is now the United States and the whole history of its neighbors to the south. The significance of the *Patrimonio* for Dutch scholars is two-fold. It provides access to a rich body of printed literature regarding the revolt of The Netherlands and the subsequent war for independence fought with Spain, its former colonial master. The extraordinary growth of The Netherlands as the major European trading nation in the seventeenth century and the development of its own colonial empire in the same period brought it into regular contact and as regular conflict with Spain throughout the known world. That too is chronicled in the *Patrimonio*.

Until now there has been no major catalog or bibliography to which one can turn to retrieve the records of this rich heritage. The surviving copies of Spanish imprints, as with those of the other countries under discussion in this paper, are often few in number. Many titles may exist in only a single title. The material is scattered over dozens if not hundreds of libraries both in Spain itself and elsewhere in Europe and the rest of the world. Spain itself, of course, has the richest collections. The group of ten libraries managed by the National Library is the most important. But the existing catalog is manual only and not accessible outside the libraries themselves. The entries were made long ago when bibliographical standards were minimal. They are often so brief that it may not be possible to identify the item one seeks.

The National Library, charged and funded by the national government, is in the process of systematically reviewing its collections to retrieve all the relevant material. For titles published before 1800, the books themselves are being paged and full new bibliographic records, based upon the most modern standards and guidelines, are created with book in hand. For the nineteenth century, when the standardization introduced with machine printing makes the recording much less challenging, the new record is being based upon the existing manual catalog.

The *Patrimonio,* reminiscent of the STCN, at least in its earlier stages, is being published both in traditional book form and also in machine-readable records. The machine-readable records will eventually be made available to readers within the national library. It will also be made available through the national library's own bibliographic network, now in the process of creation, throughout the rest of the country. As is the case with the STCN, there is no current mechanism in existence, however, to distribute it throughout the rest of Europe or abroad. The Center for Bibliographical Studies and RLIN are also negotiating with the National Library of Spain to mount this file in North America and further to distribute it through a composite CD-ROM.

The task of creating the *Patrimonio* has been divided into four units based upon the centuries to be covered. The incunable or fifteenth-century unit has been completed and published. The existing sixteenth-century records have been reproduced but still await checking against the book in order to create new full bibliographical records. The seventeenth-century unit is well along and the published version has appeared through letter *E*. The eighteenth-century unit has recently been inaugurated. The nineteenth-century unit is also well along.

As the STCN, the *Patrimonio* and other national bibliographies are developed and become accessible to us, they can expand our bibliographic horizons by bringing in successive new clusters of records that will give us hitherto undreamed of control over the printed sources of early modern European history. Let me enumerate these briefly.[12] We expect to obtain a file of machine-readable records for Portuguese imprints for the period before 1801 as a result of the efforts of the

---

[12] For details on individual national projects, see Marcelle Beaudiquez and Philip Bryant, editors, "Special issue on retrospective conversion," *IFLA Journal,* xvi (1990), no. 1.

National Library of Portugal to convert its manual catalog to machine-readable format. The Italians are in the first stage of their union catalog and are currently working on the sixteenth century. The German effort is more fragmented; the sixteenth-century segment is organized by region and available only in hard copy. We have hopes that the seventeenth and eighteenth-century extensions, when initiated, will be computer based, though the German adoption of an incompatible record format creates a new host of problems. The Royal Library of Sweden has created a machine-readable bibliography of Swedish monographic publications for the eighteenth-century based primarily upon its own collections, *Svensk Bibliografi 1700-1829*.[13] That database currently contains slightly more than 42,000 entries. The French are still in the discussion stages, though the Bibliothèque Nationale is recataloging its anonymous holdings from the book in a machine-readable format. For the period before 1801 they estimate as many as 150,000 titles. We hope to mount that file as well. Regrettably, there is at present no national Belgian project, owing to linguistic and political divisions. This is the more regrettable for Netherlandic scholars because the STCN deliberately excludes imprints from what is now Belgium, even though printed in Dutch.

I think that we will all recognize the desirability to work at least initially within national files to create projects manageable in scope which will elicit the necessary funding. But we also recognize that national boundaries are arbitrary and that our interests as scholars not only transcend national boundaries but require access to the broadest possible range of materials. Hence, the optimum goal would be a European STC that embraces at least all Western European materials. I do not think that is an idle dream. As noted above, the Center is negotiating now with the Swedish, Dutch, Spanish and Portuguese to mount their records. Our plan is that they will be searchable as one joint special database or as individual national databases like the ESTC, with the same versatility in terms of access we now enjoy. Can you imagine a single search command for title words *treaty* and *Utrecht* or the equivalent *verdrag, traite, Vertrag, trattato*, or *tratado*? In our careers

---

[13]A description of the file by Gunilla Jonsson, head of the reference service and the reference library in the Royal Library, Stockholm, has appeared, *Factotum* 32 (Sept., 1990), pp. 6-7.

and lives as scholars we will be able to study the hand-press era in Europe and its dependencies unrestricted by the artificial time barriers that have previously been imposed upon us by the limited nature of the records available until now. The extraordinary search capabilities of the English STC and STCN, paralleled and even exceeded by the fullness of the records of other European nations, will be accessible to any interested individual.

Politics *versus* Poetics:
The Granting of the *Privilege* of Marnix' Revised Vernacular Psalm Translation of 1591 to Vulcanius[1]

Richard Todd
Free University, Amsterdam

The vernacular, Dutch-language, psalter of Philips van Marnix, Lord of St Aldegonde (1540-98), was first published in Antwerp in 1580.[2] It was reprinted in revised form at Middelburg in 1591, this time with a "privilege" or patent granted to Bonaventura Vulcanius.[3] The printer of the 1591 edition was Richard Schilders (fl. 1579-1634), noted as an orthodox supplier of puritan material for an English-language readership.[4] It is likely that Schilders was chosen because of Vulcanius' assumption that the psalter would be introduced not only

---

[1]This paper further develops part of the argument of my article "Humanist Prosodic Theory, Dutch Synods, and the Poetics of the Sidney-Pembroke Psalter," *Huntington Library Quarterly* 52 (1989): 273-93. See especially pp. 282ff. and pp. 291nn. 29ff. I would like to thank Theo Bögels, Department of English, Vrije Universiteit, Amsterdam, for helpful comment and bibliographical suggestions, and Stephen Todd, Department of Classics, University of Keele, for solving many problems with texts in neo-Latin. The translations from Dutch and French are my own.

[2]*Het Boeck der Psalmen Davids. Wt de Hebreische spraeke in Nederduytschen dichte op de ghewoonlijcke Francoische wyse ouerghesett* ... 't Antwerpen, By Gillis vanden Rade (1580).

[3]*Het Boeck der Psalmen, wt der Hebraïsscher sprake in nederduytschen dichte op de ghewoonlicke oude wijsen van singen overgese* ... (Middelburg, 1591).

[4]For a recent account of Schilders see Keith Sprunger, *Dutch Puritanism: A History of English and Scottish Churches in the Netherlands in the Sixteenth and Seventeenth Centuries* (Leiden: E. J. Brill, 1982): 28.

Robert S. Kirsner (ed.), *The Low Countries and Beyond,* 297-306. Lanham, MD: University Press of America, 1993.

in the Low Countries but also in Dutch Churches such as that at Austin Friars, London, and elsewhere in England.[5] Each of Marnix' versions comprises a critique of the 1566 psalter of Petrus Dathenus. The Dathenus metaphrase was based on the French Huguenot psalter of Clément Marot and Théodore Beza that had appeared in 1562. For whereas Dathenus had simply adapted Marot and Beza for liturgical use in Dutch, Marnix' rewritings demonstrate a more scrupulous attitude to the philological and scholarly concerns of European literary humanism, and involved returning to Hebrew sources.[6]

In this paper I shall re-examine some of the circumstances that occasioned the reissue of Marnix' psalter in 1591 and explore their implications. The two points I shall elaborate on are related yet conflicting, and are as follows. I have already indicated, firstly, that Marnix' 1591 reissue, unlike the 1580 printing, was accompanied by a privilege: this was granted by the States General to Marnix' former secretary and later intimate scholarly correspondent Bonaventura Vulcanius (1538-1614).[7] Secondly, what was probably the major such event of the decade, the National Synod held at The Hague in 1586, had stipulated — indeed urged — that while the Marnix psalter should indeed replace the apparently discredited metaphrase of Petrus Dathenus in the Dutch Reformed liturgy, it could do so only under certain preconditions that included further revision on Marnix's part, and the desirability of freedom of publication, that is the condition that NO privilege would be granted. In the event, this particular recommendation of the 1586 Synod (its seventeenth and final one),

---

[5]See MS Vulc. 104, fasc. 52 (Rijksuniversiteitsbibliotheek Leiden), fol. [2ᵛ]; also quoted (when evidently more legible) in J. J. van Toorenenbergen, ed., *Philips van Marnix van St. Aldegonde: Godsdienstige en Kerkelijke Geschriften*, 4 vols. (The Hague: Nijhoff, 1871-1891), I: lv, n. 2; see also note 19 below.

[6]Marnix had a small manual of the Hebrew text *(Hebraici textus enchiridiolum)* with him when he wrote to Bonaventura Vulcanius on 21 November 1580. *Oeuvres de Ph. de Marnix de Sainte Aldegonde VIII*, ed. Albert Lacroix (Paris, &c.: 1860): 302.

[7]The text of the privilege is summarized in the 1591 edition. It is dated 9 July and indicates the acquiescence of the States General two months earlier, on 13 May 1591. Cf. N. Japikse, ed., *Resolutiën der Staten-Generaal van 1576-1609*, 14 vols. (The Hague: Nijhoff, 1915-70), 7 [1590-1592]: 507. Vulcanius' request to the States General, made in French, is preserved in MS Vulc. 104, fasc. 52, fol. [1ʳ].

presented along with the rest to Robert Dudley, Earl of Leicester, remained unimplemented throughout the lifetimes of all involved. What had happened to bring these two elements, Marnix' patronage of Vulcanius during the 1580s, and the Synodal recommendation of 1586, into direct confrontation with each other? I shall seek to throw light on the problem by means of a brief presentation of the relevant Synodal recommendation, and an equally brief review of salient issues arising from Marnix' correspondence with Vulcanius.

I must first place in historical context the relationship between Marnix and Vulcanius (whose name is a Latinization of De Smet or De Smed: sometimes he is also referred to as "Fortunatus Faber"). After scholarly and secretarial work carried out in Spain, Germany, and Switzerland from about 1560 onwards, Vulcanius arrived in Antwerp in 1577 as secretary to Marnix, who ensured that he soon after became rector of the Latin school there. The very next year, however, Vulcanius moved with Marnix to Leyden. Although he was almost immediately named Professor of Greek and Latin at the newly-founded university of the Protestant province of Holland in Leyden, he did not actually assume the post officially until 1581, possibly in part because of the university authorities' desire to check thoroughly rumours that Vulcanius had incurred serious debts while in Antwerp, although if this is the case the replies from Antwerp cannot have left any doubt as to Vulcanius' character and learning.[8] Throughout the 1580s he and Marnix corresponded intermittently but with respect and affection. Much of this correspondence is concerned with the philological issues facing Marnix as he wrestled with the revision of his vernacular psalter. The 1591 reissue of the Marnix psalter was accompanied by a preface in which Marnix defends his undertaking on a number of grounds, and there can be no doubt that the correspondence with Vulcanius had exercised its influence on Marnix' thinking.[9]

---

[8]See P. C. Molhuysen, ed., *Bronnen tot de Geschiedenis der Leidsche Universiteit* I [1574-1610] (The Hague: Nijhoff, 1913): 6, 86*-89*. For the earliest definitive biographical sketch of Vulcanius see J. Meursius, *Athenae Batavae* (Leiden, 1625): 103-105 (sigs. N4ʳ-Oʳ).

[9]Since this paper was written, Willem Heyting of the Rare Books Department of the Free University Library has kindly drawn my attention to A. Dewitte, "Bonaventura Vulcanius en Philips Marnix van Sint-Aldegonde 1577-1606," in *Album Albert Schoutet* (Bruges, 1973): 57-74. Dewitte's article supplements the information given in the paragraph above.

At the same time, we should remember the conditions for the introduction of a psalter to replace Dathenus that the various national and provincial Synods were maintaining throughout the 1580s. As early as 1581, the National Synod held at Middelburg had passed a motion prohibiting introduction of the Marnix psalter should it be printed against the advice of the *Classis*.[10] Vulcanius presented the provincial Synod at Haarlem with a request to replace Dathenus' with Marnix' psalter in the following year.[11] Then in 1586 we have the proposals of the National Synod held in The Hague. These, since they seem to have fixed the terms of the debate, are worth quoting in some detail:

> As to the introduction of the Marnix psalter, as decided above on 10 July, the following clauses should be noted. First, the aforesaid Lord of St Aldegonde is requested to complete the corrections and simplifications [*versoetinge*] he is making to his psalter. Next, the printed version of the psalter will refrain from carrying its author's name. Thirdly, a foreword on behalf of this Synod will accompany the revised version, recommending and exhorting the people to use it. Fourthly, once the revised version has been printed, the ministers, along with the elders and deacons, and other prominent persons, will issue private recommendations on its behalf. Fifthly, once these preparatory steps have been carried out, appropriate occasion will be found to recommend the aforementioned improvements to the people from the pulpit, indicating their soundness while not in any way rejecting in so many words the new psalter's predecessor, that of Dathenus, in use hitherto, but on the contrary ensuring that children learn and grow accustomed to these psalms while still at school. Finally, His Excellency [Leicester] will be advised that there will be total freedom to print these psalms, without a

---

[10] See F. L. Rutgers, ed., *Acta van de Nederlandse synoden der 16e eeuw* (Utrecht, 1889): 420.

[11] See L. Knappert, "Marnix en zijne psalmen," in *Marnix van Sinte Aldegonde: Officieel Gedenkboek* (Amsterdam, [1939]): 162-63. This paper corrects some inaccuracies in Knappert's account, and takes issue with his suggestion (over-explicitly derived from van Toorenenbergen) that the motives for such a request are solely attributable to speculation within the book trade rather than at least partly to the humanist poetics repeatedly discussed in their correspondence by Marnix and Vulcanius.

privilege being granted to anyone. The local church authorities are free to finance the printing in whatever way they think fit.[12]

The more concise form of this aspect of the Synod's proceedings, as presented in French to Leicester in early July, read as follows:

> Finally, it has been resolved to ensure that the metrical psalms of [Marnix] will be introduced [into liturgical use], once they can be made more accessible *[commodement]*; a motion has been approved by the Synod to request and make known to your Excellency that he give permission to every printer to print the aforesaid psalms without patent or any special privilege, so that the printers will have no grounds for complaint and the [morale of the] people will not be undermined *[rongé]*.[13]

There are two points that emerge from these nuanced accounts of the proceedings of the 1586 Synod, accounts drawn up as it were for internal and external consumption respectively. Firstly, they are reticent concerning the reasons for the need for revision. It seems that, as it stood, Marnix' 1580 metaphrase presented formal difficulties when it came to singing the psalms to the French tunes, and the need to be able to sing them to those tunes was the *sine qua non* of their acceptance. Strict accuracy of translation seems to have played an ancillary role. Secondly, the summary presented to Leicester, although more compact, omits any mention of the financing of a reprint of Marnix. It is these points that seem to have led to the suspension of the entire proposal to replace Dathenus with Marnix as far as the ecclesiastical authorities were concerned. Later local Synods were to return to the question sporadically: thus at Leeuwarden in 1592 it was

---

[12]Because of limitations of space, the reader is referred to the published sources of contemporaneous material quoted in Dutch, French, and neo-Latin. In this case see Rutgers, 611-12.

[13]Cf. Rutgers, 643. It is hard to judge the precise nuance of *commodement*, which I have rendered as "accessibl[y]," and the extent to which this reflects *versoetinge* (see previous quotation in my text above), which I have rendered as "simplifications."

decided somewhat vaguely to postpone the entire question,[14] and at Franeker in 1595 an even more anodyne motion was formulated.[15]

What had happened between 1586 and the mid-1590s was, of course, that the sought-after Marnix revision HAD appeared, but with a privilege granted to Vulcanius. In the last part of this paper I shall trace the steps in this process along the two fronts of (i) the NEED for revision, and (ii) the stipulation of freedom to print, as laid down in 1586, while detailing Marnix' and Vulcanius' response to the 1586 Synod's recommendations.

After the 1586 Synod's report had been published, Marnix wrote to his friend Adrianus van der Myle on 19 July. More of Marnix' letters to van der Myle have survived than to any other correspondent. On this occasion Marnix addresses van der Myle in his capacity as President of the States General of Holland to express his disquiet at the outcome of the Synod, while evidently resigning himself to its conditions:

> Concerning the resolution of the Synod, I have sent a reply to my [friend] Kymedontius, and you may infer my opinion from that. In the matter of the Psalms you will collectively decide what seems best to you: I shall submit to the Church whether by working slowly or speedily.[16]

Marnix indicates that van der Myle was aware of the discussion between himself and Vulcanius concerning his revision of the 1580 psalter. That discussion seems to have begun in earnest when in a letter dated 10 March 1580, Marnix refers to improvements suggested by Vulcanius, particularly as concerns Marnix' frequent use of elisions. He speaks of Vulcanius' exertions on his behalf *(tuum erga me studium)* and certainly values Vulcanius' judgement as to the literary and

---

[14]Reitsma, J., and S. D. van Veen, eds., *Acta der Provinciale en Particuliere Synoden gehouden in de noordelijke nederlanden gedurende de jaren 1572-1620*, 8 vols. (Groningen: 1892-99), 6: 67.

[15]Reitsma and van Veen, 6: 83.

[16]Lacroix, 8: 329 (letter 54).

philological worth of Marnix' work. At the same time he shares with Vulcanius his fear that individual animosity may be preventing Synodal acceptance *(puto nonnullorum malevolentiam obstare)*.[17]

Marnix is already discussing a shared interest in humanist philology with Vulcanius, apparently on the basis of assumptions derived from Horace's *Ars Poeticae*, to which he more than once alludes. Concerning the difficulties attending the rendering of the language of the psalms in the vernacular, Marnix addresses some of the criticism that has been brought to bear on his psalter, evidently regarding much of it as ill-informed. Among the issues that come up repeatedly are the following: when (if at all) are elisions *(synaloephae)* justified? when should a line end with a stressed ("catalectic") syllable that leaves the metric foot incomplete, as opposed to an unstressed ("acatalectic") one? how can one ensure that the vernacular doesn't introduce tautologies that are absent from the language out of which it is being translated? In a substantial discussion in a letter to Vulcanius dated 21 November 1580, Marnix addresses these points, indicating that their importance is considerable, and although I cannot go into detail in the text of this paper, attention to that letter reveals Marnix agonizing over the responsibility of the translator of Holy Scripture: he must not confuse or oversimplify, thereby leading less able minds astray. The discussion concludes with Marnix now expressing the hope that it will be possible to grant Vulcanius, whom he evidently regards as sharing the scruples revealed in the discussion Marnix has set out, the privilege to a reprinting of Marnix' psalter. There is some indication of a difference between the two men that has arisen through Marnix' having forgotten to bring the necessary books from Antwerp, and Vulcanius' having become involved with printing work despite a lack of expertise.[18]

Vulcanius seems to have placed his initial request for the privilege with the provincial Synod held at Haarlem in the spring of 1582. It runs as follows:

---

[17]Lacroix, 8: 267 (letter 33).

[18]Lacroix, 8: 300-302 (letter 44).

In the afternoon [of 24 March] Bonaventura Vulcanius, professor of Greek, submitted a petition in which he requests that either the [Marnix] psalter be adopted for liturgical use or that the remaining printed copies be at least paid for. After lengthy discussion the decision was approved to reply to him that this Synod can do nothing other at this time than was decided concerning this matter at the general Synod, for this assembly has no wish whatever to deviate from the practice of its parent church. Furthermore that the delegates cannot be charged with deviating from that practice, there being for certain no general perception that people are ready for a change. As far as the financing is concerned, individual churches may be consulted, but this Synod is not empowered to answer for them. This answer was given orally to [Vulcanius] the next day.[19]

What we seem to perceive in all this is a conflict between collective ecclesiastical interests and individual literary-humanistic ones, a conflict I suggest is a distillation of that between politics and poetics. Marnix' 1580 metaphrase was felt to be unsatisfactory, both to Synodal authority and to their compiler himself, BUT FOR DIFFERENT AND IRRECONCILABLE REASONS. To the 1586 Synod it appears that they could not be sung as easily as could the settings of Dathenus to the melodies devised for their French Huguenot original. Yet at the same time the sheer philological inadequacy of Dathenus's metaphrase was evidently recognized by many literate people. Marnix was dissatisfied with his work on philological grounds alone. Resolving THAT dissatisfaction could not guarantee that his metaphrases would automatically become more "singable," a concept I believe to be reflected in the strangely reticent terms *versoetinge* and *commodement* as reported by the 1586 Synod. It seems fair to conclude that it was (and always had been) primarily in order to protect the philological integrity of his work that Marnix had enlisted the commercial support of Vulcanius. Yet the

---

[19]Reitsma and van Veen 1: 112. The reference to paying for the remaining printed copies implies that Vulcanius had been involved in the 1580 publication. I follow van Toorenenbergen in assuming MS Vulc. 104, fasc. 52 fol. [2ᵛ]: "Concerning England, I cannot in any way permit 50 copies.... What needs to be calculated is the level of payment that would be due on the basis of 2400 copies" *(De Anglia non possum quicquam permittere Exemplaria 50... Subducenda ratio emolumenti quod est rediturum... de 2400 exempl.)* to refer to what was expected to be the first of several printings (see note 5 above).

only way in which he could concretize that support was to propose that Vulcanius perform a role that was in effect finessed once and for all by Synodal recommendation in 1586. If we (rightly) think of the United Provinces in the later sixteenth and first half of the seventeenth centuries as (in English eyes at least) a place where freedom to publish (like religious tolerance) was so great as to seem practically anarchic to contemporaries living as late as Andrew Marvell (1621-78),[20] it is worth reminding ourselves of a sobering safeguard apparently built into a conception of freedom to print without the need for patent or privilege. Indeed, there are wider implications, since the fact that the conflicting parties are the various Synods (which desire the printing to be free of any commitment) and the States General (which issue the privilege) points to a conflict of interest between Church and State themselves. In the case in question, the fact that the privilege was granted indicates that the State supported a liberal position over an orthodoxy maintained by the Church: the Church's response was to prefer the manifest inadequacy of Dathenus over the enlightened struggle represented in the efforts of Marnix and Vulcanius. These men's undertaking of vernacularizing, popularizing, and thus making collectively available a literary form associated with cultural elitism, with its scrupulous insistence on high standards of humanist scholarship, could not avoid running into conflict with one kind of institutional pressure. We may prefer not to think of this conflict in terms of a form of Renaissance "censorship," but its effects were not dissimilar.

There is one interesting twist to the tail of this enquiry. In his last letter to Vulcanius, written on Easter Saturday, 13 April 1591, Marnix seems by inference to refer to something pertaining to the psalms having been obtained from England from Sir Francis Walsingham, who had died the previous year.[21] Walsingham, traditionally regarded as a crafty and accomplished diplomat, had served Queen Elizabeth's interests (or lack of them) in the Low

---

[20]See the remarks in Marvell's, "The Character of Holland," ll. 67-76.

[21]Lacroix, 8: 338 (letter 57). The Walsingham reference is cited in J. A. van Dorsten, *Poets, Patrons and Professors: An Outline of Some Literary Connexions Between England and the University of Leiden 1575-1586* (Leiden: Leiden U P, 1962): 130, who (as puzzled about it as I am) draws no conclusions from it.

Countries. He was also a great lover of books and learning. Walsingham had become father-in-law to Sir Philip Sidney in 1583, through Frances, daughter to Walsingham by his second, and surviving, wife Ursula. Whatever the truth about the motives behind the marriage of Frances Walsingham to Sir Philip Sidney (for through it Walsingham managed to cement a political alliance with Sidney's uncle Leicester), Walsingham seems to have been genuinely affected by Sidney's early death, not only offering great consolation to the afflicted young widow but undertaking to settle Sidney's financial affairs, thereby consolidating Sidney's posthumous reputation.[22] Could it be that Walsingham was also promoting Sidney's reputation as a literary humanist of pan-European stature, and that what Marnix had received was at least information concerning, or perhaps even a draft of, the psalter that Sidney's sister the Countess of Pembroke seems to have been completing during the course of these years? It would be tempting to think so: we should probably rule out any reference to one of the 50 copies of Marnix's 1591 psalter apparently destined for use among Dutch congregations in England.[23] For the outcome of the sequence of events I have been briefly reviewing, a particular instance of politics VERSUS poetics, of Church VERSUS State, is that Marnix' psalter (even though it represented an attempt to make the psalms available to a larger public) was NOT adopted liturgically, primarily it would seem on account of the consequences of its learning. Indeed, like the Sidneys' psalter (which was to remain in manuscript into the nineteenth century), that of Marnix would continue throughout the seventeenth century to exercise its primary appeal privately rather than devotionally, in what John Donne was later to describe as in "chambers" rather than in "church."[24]

---

[22] See Conyers Read, *Mr. Secretary Walsingham and the Policy of Queen Elizabeth*, 3 vols. (Oxford: Clarendon: 1925), 3: 423-25.

[23] We have no evidence that those copies had reached their destination as early as the spring of the year of publication, and in view of the privilege to Schilders being dated 9 July, it would seem that they could not have done, unless the dating is retrospective, which is, of course possible. Certainly the privilege is likely to have been the last part of the book to have been published.

[24] John Donne, "Upon the translation of the Psalmes by Sir *Philip Sydney*, and the Countesse of Pembroke his Sister," l. 39.

Dutch-American Relations

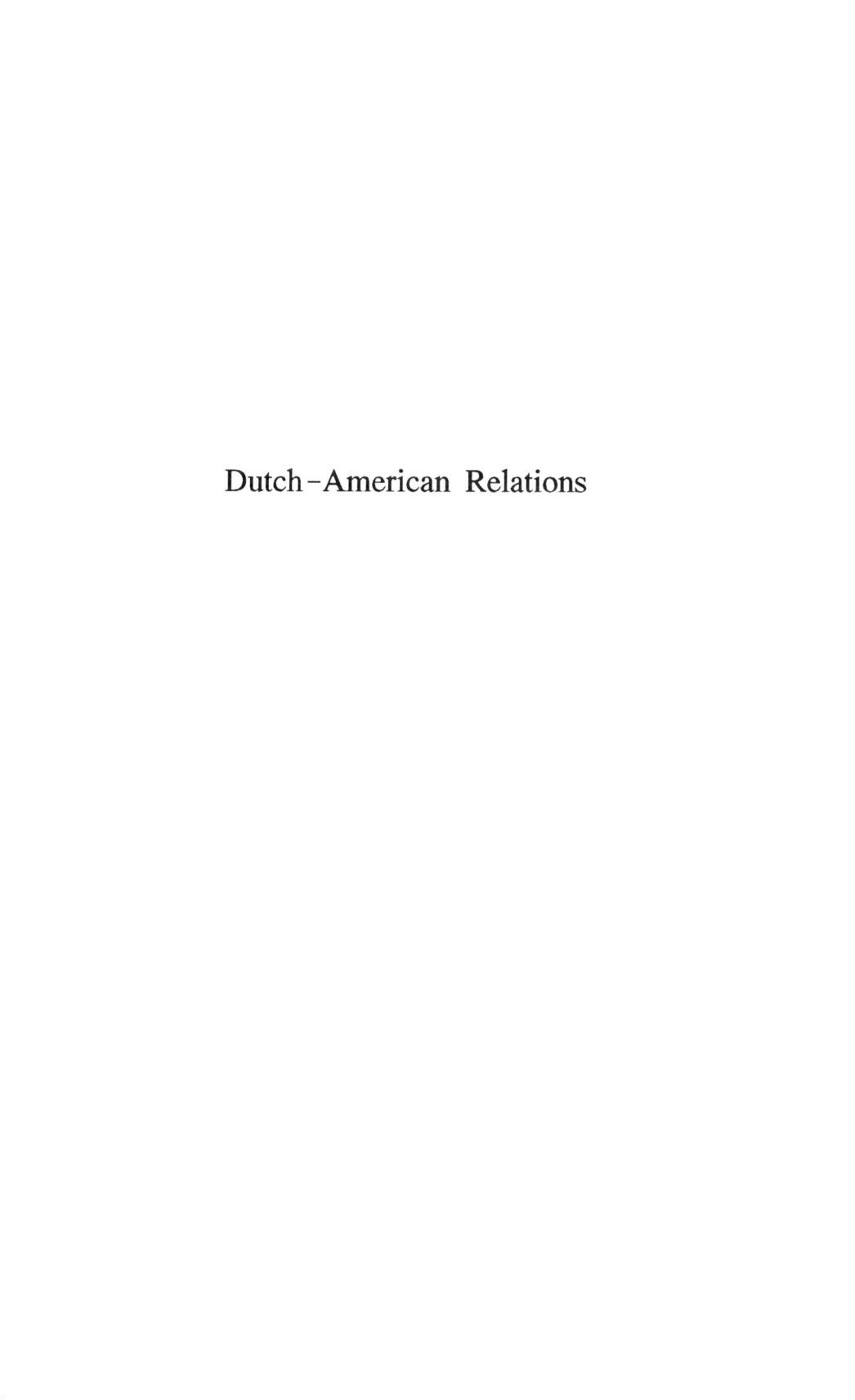

"Dutch" Towns in the United States of America

Augustus J. Veenendaal Jr.
Institute for Netherlands History, The Hague

When one hears the words "Dutch towns in America," people will first think of New York or, possibly, of other places in the Hudson River valley. Others may come up with the towns settled by Dutchmen in the nineteenth century, such as Holland, Michigan, and the surrounding towns, or the other Dutch Protestant settlements of Pella, Iowa, and its offshoots of Orange City and others of the same kind. Yet there is a different kind of Dutch town in the United States, one founded by Dutch capitalists as a business venture, sometimes connected with an emigration scheme, but not necessarily so, and then in most cases only as an afterthought. In this article I want to pay some attention to three towns that were founded or developed as part of financial schemes set up by Dutchmen and operated chiefly from the Netherlands.

Buffalo and the Holland Land Company

Turning to the first of the large-scale Dutch land companies, we find the Holland Land Company operating in the western part of New York State at the end of the 18th century.[1] It is well known that several Amsterdam banking houses had advanced large sums to the

---

[1] Paul D. Evans, *The Holland Land Company* (Buffalo, 1924), and A. M. Sakolski, *The Great American Land Bubble; The Amazing Story of Land Grabbing, Speculations and Booms from Colonial Days to the Present Time* (New York/London, 1932).

Robert S. Kirsner (ed.), *The Low Countries and Beyond*, 309-322. Lanham, MD: University Press of America, 1993.

young American Republic after independence, and six of these houses joined forces in 1792 to extend their operations in the USA and founded the Holland Land Company of Amsterdam. This new company started to buy land in Pennsylvania and in western New York, altogether some 3,300,000 acres. Governor Robert Morris, famous for his financial operations to keep the American revolution solvent, was one of the chief sellers of land to the Dutchmen. The six houses involved were Stadnitski & Son, Van Vollenhoven, Schimmelpenninck, Van Staphorst, P. & C. van Eeghen and W. & J. Willink, all famous houses in Amsterdam banking circles, and indeed in the world at large because of their large stakes in government debts all over Europe.[2] To manage their American interests — foremost among these the vast but uncharted possessions in New York State — they sent out Theophile Cazenove as their agent, and he took up headquarters in Philadelphia. Largely through his influence, the consortium continued to buy more of the western wilderness until the Holland Land Company owned over 5 million acres altogether.

Title to the new possessions was unclear, however. Both Massachusetts and New York claimed overlordship over the region; and after this legal mess had been untangled, the claims of the Seneca Indians to all lands west of the Genesee River had to be bought off. The Treaty of Big Tree of September 15, 1797, effectively ended Indian ownership except for a couple of small reservations on the shores of Lake Erie. Now one more hurdle had to be taken. New York State law forbade ownership of landed property in the state by foreigners. Largely through the persuasion of senator Aaron Burr, the law was changed in favor of alien ownership. Burr himself gained considerably from this deal, inasmuch the Holland Land Company paid him $5,500, officially as a loan, but never repaid by Burr.[3] The Company could now go ahead with its plans for selling its holdings in small parcels to individual settlers, a process that was to take several decades, and even then only partly successfull in the end. The later history of the Holland

---

[2]For the early Dutch involvement in American financial matters, see: J. C. Riley, *International Government Finance and the Amsterdam Capital Market 1749-1815* (Cambridge, 1980), and P. J. van Winter, *Het aandeel van den Amsterdamschen handel aan den opbouw van het Amerikaansche Gemeenebest* (2 volumes 's-Gravenhage, 1927-1933).

[3]Sakolski, *American Land Bubble*, 80.

Land Company has been described elsewhere and need not be recounted here, but some attention should now be paid to the city of Buffalo, as the first of the "Dutch" towns mentioned in the title of this article.

Buffalo Creek was already on the primitive maps of the eastern shores of Lake Erie in 1764; a very small community had sprung up there. The new Dutch owners of the land and the creek established a land office in Batavia and contracted Joseph Ellicott to make an accurate map of their possessions.[4] Ellicott came from a wellknown family of surveyors and his brother Andrew had laid out the new federal capital according to the plans of the French major l'Enfant in 1791 and 1792. Between 1797 and 1800 Joseph Ellicott surveyed the whole of western New York and he drew up plans for a new settlement on Buffalo Creek, to be named New Amsterdam in honor of the distant lords, now themselves temporarily under French rule. In 1802 or 1803 his plans were approved by the directors, and now New Amsterdam was started on its way to become the chief city of western New York. Several of the main thoroughfares of the new city were named after the Dutch directors and so Willink, Schimmelpenninck, and other avenues appeared on the map.[5] For the time being they were on the map only, as actual settlement was very slow. In 1805 the federal government made New Amsterdam an official port of entry, ignoring loud protests from neighboring Black Rock with its fine natural harbor, but just outside the Dutch land. Despite the optimistic beginnings, total population of the area was only some 1500 in 1810 and little more than 2000 ten years later. The war with Great Britain was disastrous for the new community: trade was disrupted and, in December 1813, British forces burned almost every house in the town in revenge for the burning by the Americans of Newark, the then capital of Ontario, a few weeks before.

---

[4]William Chazanof, *Joseph Ellicott and the Holland Land Company. The Opening of Western New York* (Syracuse, 1970).

[5]Henry Wayland Hill, *Municipality of Buffalo, New York. A History 1720-1923* (Vol. 1, New York/Chicago, 1923).

Fortunately this setback was only temporary and the development of the little town was actively resumed by Ellicott and the Holland Land Company. The selection of the place, by now better known as Buffalo, as the western end of the Erie Canal and the completion of a new harbor in 1821 further strengthened the growth of the town. In 1832 the city of Buffalo was incorporated and the name of New Amsterdam quietly dropped. By that time the Dutch character had almost vanished completely. Only a handful of town lots had been sold to Dutch settlers, although the Company had done its best to attract Dutchmen, farmers, artisans, and workers, but with very limited success. The Office of the Company at the corner of Clinton and Washington streets catered mostly to American customers. The now unpronouncable street names became a nuisance and so Willink and Van Staphorst Avenues became Main Street, Schimmelpenninck became Niagara, and Van Vollenhoven Erie and Stadnitski lived on as Church Street. Only Cazenove's name was retained in the name of a terrace below Erie Street.[6]

An abortive scheme for Washington D.C.

It is perhaps fitting to note, in connection with the Ellicott family, that Andrew Ellicott's plan for Washington D.C. also drew the attention of Dutch capitalists. The early development of the federal capital had been slow, chiefly because of lack of money in the treasury. Several schemes were started by speculators and other more serious businessmen to foster the growth of the young city, but nothing came of it. In 1793 James Greenleaf, recently appointed American consul in Amsterdam and with useful contacts in banking circles there, came forward with a new project. In combination with other financiers, among them Robert Morris already mentioned in the Holland Land Company story, he bought thousands of town lots in the capital, in the hope of selling them at a large profit later, after development. The money needed for his purchase was put up partly by Morris, and the rest was to come from Daniel Crommelin & Sons of Amsterdam. Apparently Crommelin had insufficient faith in Greenleaf's schemes and only cooperated when U.S. 3% and 6% bonds were offered as

---

[6]Wayland Hill, *Municipality of Buffalo*, 164.

collateral for the loan, but even with this incentive only a small sum was ever raised in Amsterdam for the purpose — certainly not enough to cover all of Greenleaf's purchases. Thus, Washington only narrowly escaped the fate of becoming a Dutch town.[7]

Spokane and the Inland Empire

The next really Dutch town in the series is Spokane, Washington. Lying at the falls of the Spokane River in the fertile Columbia Plain, bordered by the Cascades in the west and the Rockies in the east, the town of Spokane was ultimately to become the capital of the Inland Empire.[8] In the 1880s the Northern Pacific Railroad had completed its line through the town and connected the little settlement of some 1200 people with the outside world. The rich soil attracted the attention of prospective farmers and the Northern Pacific did its best to advertise the region in hopes of attracting more traffic. And with some success, as Dutch capitalists recognized the potential of the area for agriculture.

In the early years of Spokane Falls, as the place was then still called, its wealth had chiefly come from mining in the surrounding countryside, especially in Idaho and north towards the Canadian border. This industry was badly hit by the crisis of 1893 and consequently most of the real estate in the city was mortgaged to the several Dutch banks operating in the area. The first of these banks had been, in 1885, the short-lived Northwestern and Pacific Mortgage Bank of Olympia, despite its American name, financed from Amsterdam. After this first, but not very successfull venture, a whole series of Dutch mortgage banks was founded, mostly headquartered in Amsterdam, but all with offices in the U.S.[9] By 1918 nine of these Dutch banks had

---

[7]Sakolski, *American Land Bubble*, 156-160.

[8]Glenn C. Quiett, *They Built the West. An Epic of Rails and Cities* (1934, reprint New York, 1965), 496-541.

[9]Jacob van Hinte, *Netherlanders in America. A Study of Emigration and Settlement in the Nineteenth and Twentieth Centuries in the United States of America*. Edited by Robert P. Swieringa (Grand Rapids, 1985).

their chief sphere of interest in the Northwest, and of these nine, five had their offices in Spokane, three in Seattle, and one in Portland. Profits were large in some years, but losses were encountered as well. Years of bad harvests brought distress to the farmers and as a consequence many mortgages had to be executed, saddling the banks with much hard to sell real estate. Some of the banks formed separate companies to manage this land and town property, as the Nederlandsch-Amerikaansche Hypotheekbank of Groningen did in 1917 when it organized the Hollam Company expressly for this purpose. The Dutch banks never paid much attention to the mining industry; they concentrated instead on agriculture and related industries. After the collapse of silver mining in 1893, diversification was considered the key to prosperity anyway. From 1900 to about 1910 Spokane saw a phenomenal growth with the seemingly unlimited possibilities of agriculture and the Dutch banks gave a considerable impetus to this development. They also participated actively in industries such as the "Spokane Flour Mills," founded in Amsterdam in 1901, and operating mills in Seattle and Pendleton as well. The Phoenix Saw Mill was another Dutch business venture in the area, using the enormous stands of timber of the Pacific Northwest.

One of the driving forces behind the development of Spokane as a center of mining and agriculture was Daniel Chase Corbin, who had started as a railway entrepreneur in the area and who is now seen as the "father" of Spokane.[10] He introduced sugarbeet growing, helped in no small measure by the prohibitive tariff imposed upon sugar from the Dutch East Indies. He also recognized the advantages of irrigation, strongly stimulated by the Dutch banks in this respect. One of the outcomes of this innovation was the fruit growing in the Yakima Valley, where some Dutch farmers found a new home.

Yet, despite this strong influence from Holland, Spokane never became a town of Dutchmen. In 1910 only 168 Dutch-born were living there and only a handfull more ten years later. But Dutch capital had been very influential in the making of modern Spokane; and, when Corbin is seen as the father of the town, then R. Insinger, managing director of several Dutch banks in Spokane in the 1920s and for many

---

[10]John Fahey, *Inland Empire. D. C. Corbin and Spokane* (Seattle, 1965).

years president of the Chamber of Commerce, may be seen as the one who built on the foundation laid by Corbin.[11]

Cimarron N.M. and the Maxwell Land Grant

Turning now to the third "Dutch" town, we have to travel south to sunnier climes. In the territories of Arizona and New Mexico (ceded by Mexico to the United States in 1848), and in the adjoining state of Colorado, several large landgrants were to be found, granted originally by the Mexican government to Spanish-American landowners and later confirmed by the federal government in Washington. One of these was the Maxwell Land Grant given in 1841 to Carlos Beaubien and Guadelupe Miranda, and transferred a few years later to Lucien Maxwell, son-in-law of Beaubien. In 1860 the grant was confirmed by the U.S. government on Maxwell, who used his land the best he could, mostly for sheep and cattle grazing, with the small town of Cimarron as headquarters. His holdings, some 2,000,000 acres, comprised the northeastern part of New Mexico Territory with some land in Colorado as well.[12]

These enormous, but generally empty, tracts of land had already drawn the attention of British and Dutch capitalists, who had rosy views of developing the country for agriculture and peopling it with European farmers. The Costilla Estate in neighboring Colorado and northern New Mexico, comprising the ancient pueblo of Taos, had already been financed by English investors, together with the Amsterdam firm of Wertheim & Gompertz, who had put in about $1,000,000. Attempts to settle the Estate with Dutch and German farmers came to nought and Dutch interest in the Costilla soon waned.[13]

---

[11]About R. Insinger, who had been in Canada and California before coming to Spokane: Van Hinte, *Netherlanders in America*, 687.

[12]Jim B. Pearson, *The Maxwell Land Grant* (Norman, 1961), and Archives of the Amsterdam Stock Exchange (AASE), file nr. 21. I want to thank my friend Herbert W Günst, Archivist of the Exchange, for his generous help.

[13]Herbert O. Brayer, *William Blackmore: The Spanish-Mexican Land Grants of New Mexico and Colorado 1863-1878* (Vol. I, Denver, 1949), 95-123.

At the same time the potential of Colorado was actively boomed by such men as U.S. General William Jackson Palmer, and the Englishmen William Bell (publicist of some note on Colorado), and John Collinson and William Blackmore, both well-known London financiers. Palmer's new Denver & Rio Grande Railroad found most of its initial capital in Amsterdam through Wertheim & Gompertz, and the railroad promised to bring life to the undeveloped region.[14] Palmer envisaged his railroad as running from Denver, south by way of Raton Pass, to El Paso on the Mexican border, with branches to Santa Fe and other places, thus cutting through most of the Maxwell Estate. The Palmer interests now formed the Maxwell Land Grant & Railway Company and in 1870 bought out Lucien Maxwell for $1,350,000. Palmer became the first president of the new company. The necessary capital came from England and to a large measure from Holland, where the respected stockbrokers G. M. Boissevain of Amsterdam, and A. J. & M. Milders of Rotterdam raised several millions in 7% bonds from an enthusiastic Dutch public.

But all was not well on the Maxwell Estate. Palmer's Denver & Rio Grande lost the battle for Raton Pass to the competing Santa Fe Railroad, and Palmer withdrew from the Maxwell board. Problems were encountered with squatters on the Grant, who occupied the best land and who were not very eager to move of their own free will. Legal costs to remove them were staggering, although the courts generally upheld the Company's title to the land. A second bond issue had to be floated in 1872, again largely taken up by Boissevain and Milders who had trouble, however, placing the issue on the Dutch market. They were accused of making excessive profits out of the deal, and dissatisfied Dutch stock and bondholders, who had been promised large profits, were unwilling to see more of their money go down the drain. In a letter to the Amsterdam Exchange Committee, G. M. Boissevain defended himself honorably, stating that the Maxwell estate was to become a sure source of wealth, but only after the Santa Fe Railroad had built through the region to provide cheap transportation. Cimarron was bound to surpass Denver in wealth and population, and generally

---

[14]Herbert O. Brayer, *William Blackmore: Early Financing of the Denver & Rio Grande Railway and Ancillary Land Companies 1871-1878* (Vol. II, Denver, 1949), 37-69.

the business was sound, if only some more capital could be invested to develop the country to its full extent.[15]

To make sure this would happen, both stockbrokers sent out two engineers, Cornelis de Groot, who had many years of mining experience in the Dutch East Indies, and J. W. Leembruggen to investigate on the spot. In their report they were critical of the local management, or rather the lack of it, but hopeful about the potential of the Grant. Gold mining, the Aztec mine on the slopes of Mount Baldy foremost, could become profitable, but only after putting in more capital to develop the mine properly. Transportation was all-important and a branch from the Santa Fe mainline would be necessary. Coal in the N.E. corner of the Estate promised to be even more profitable than gold. Agriculture and cattle grazing were possible only on some parts of the Estate, but the engineers thought it best not to engage the Company in that business, and only let the land to others. One conclusion stood out: more capital was needed to make the Grant profitable in every respect.[16]

Despite this generally optimistic report, the Company went into receivership in 1874 as it could not pay the interest on the loans. As usual a Dutch protection committee was formed, consisting of several large stock- and bondholders. In 1877 this committee was able to buy back the Grant from new owners, who had bought the Estate at auction. They reorganized the Company according to the laws of the Netherlands, with directors both in Holland and America, a cumbersome and expensive arrangement. Troubles did not end with the formation of the new Company. Governing an area as large as Utrecht, Gelderland, and Overijssel combined, from a distant country across the ocean proved to be a problem, and the new American managing director, Frank Sherwin, turned out to be rather too independent and had to be bought out. Three directors set out in 1883 from Amsterdam

---

[15]G. M. Boissevain to Stock Exchange Committee Amsterdam, March 17, 1873. AASE, file 21. In that year only 75 white Americans and Europeans lived in Cimarron, plus 150 Spanish-Mexicans and halfbreeds'

[16]*Mededeelingen aan Belanghebbenden in de Maxwell Land Grant & Railway Company omtrent het onderzoek ingesteld door de heeren Corn.^{s} de Groot en J. W. Leembruggen* ('s-Gravenhage, 1874).

to accomplish this rather delicate task, and a young man, Albert Verwey, later famous as a poet, accompanied them as secretary. Verwey, then only 18 years old, was much impressed by the exotic circumstances in Cimarron, the vast prairies, and the beautiful nature of the Cimarron Gorge.[17] In his sonnet "The Far West" (1883), partly given here, he records his travel experiences:

> Vaal lag de prairie, door de zon gebrand,
> In middaghette; 't stoffig heidekruid
> Bewoog niet en geen vogelzang drong uit
> De doffe struiken van struweel en plant.
>
> En uit de spoortrein zag ik hoe langs 't land
> De rookpluim dreef en ginds met schor geluid
> Een gierenzwerm opwiekte om op zijn buit
> Weer neer te vallen in dat dodenland.

> Bare lay the prairie, scorched by the sun,
> in afternoon heat; the dusty heath motionless, and
> no birdsong escaped
> the dull bushes of brushwood and plant.
>
> And from the railroad train I saw the smoke-plume
> float along the land, and yonder with a rasping sound,
> a swarm of vultures took flight,
> to fall upon their prey in that land of death.

When the bondholders protested against a contract made with the Santa Fe Railroad for half-ownership of the Raton Coal and Coke Company, which was considered as too favorable for the railway, the directors stepped down. A new committee was formed in 1884 to investigate the books of the Estate.

---

[17]Marianne L. Mooijweer, "Albert Verwey in New Mexico, 1883," in Rob Kroes, ed. *The American West as seen by Europeans and Americans* (Amsterdam, 1989), pp.408-437. See also Francis Bulhof, "Albert Verwey, New Mexico en De Kristaltwijg," *Ons Erfdeel*, 16 (1973), no. 3, and Lucas Ligtenberg, "De reis van Albert Verwey," *NRC/Handelsblad* June 29, 1990.

In this committee some resounding names were to be found: chairman was A. C. Wertheim,[18] Jewish banker and stockbroker from Amsterdam and very active in social and economic affairs of his city; S. van Houten,[19] liberal politician and member of the Second Chamber of Parliament, and known for his social engagement; J. Voorhoeve Jr. of a well-known Rotterdam bankers and stockbrokers family; and a few other bankers, all good and honest men. Their report was severely critical: local management had been fraudulent; possessions of the Company had been squandered or put to private use; contracts made with others had been highly disadvantageous; Sherwin, the American director, had been more adept in furthering his own interests than those of the Company; and so on and so forth. They recommended the founding of a new company and the floating of a new issue of $2,500,000 prior lien bonds, to be able to buy off all claims against the Company and thus start with a clean slate. It took several years before an arrangement, acceptable to all parties, had been worked out, but the new Company was at last started in 1888, with Wertheim and Van Houten on the board in Amsterdam, and with the trustworthy Dutchman M. P. Pels as General Manager in Cimarron, with a place on the American Board of Trustees. A boost for the new owners was the decision in 1887 of the Supreme Court of the United States that the title of the Maxwell Company to all its possessions was valid. Problems with squatters diminished after this. From now on the aims of management were completely honest, but less spectacular than the far-reaching visions of the first years. No large-scale schemes for emigration any more, no goldmining by the Company itself, but only letting the mines to others in return for modest royalties; most of the grazing land was to be sold to large operators while retaining the mineral rights. Following this new policy, the Company managed to keep afloat and even repaid most of its outstanding loans. In 1908 only some 400,000 acres of the original 2,000,000 remained while land sales slowly continued. After Pels retired, Jan van Houten, son of the

---

[18] A. J. Rijnman, *A. C. Wertheim, 1832-1897. Een bijdrage tot zijn levensgeschiedenis* (Amsterdam, 1961), 152-154.

[19] G. M. Bos, *Mr. S. van Houten. Analyse van zijn denkbeelden, voorafgegaan door een schets van zijn leven* (Purmerend, 1952), 37-38, and *Biografisch Woordenboek van Nederland* (Volume I, 's-Gravenhage, 1979), 253-256, where no mention is made of Van Houten's Maxwell directorship.

director, became manager in Cimarron until his death in 1949. Income in this period came chiefly from lumbering, cattle grazing, and now and then from royalties paid by the Aztec gold mine. In 1949 the beautiful Cimarron Gorge, one of the scenic wonders of the Estate, was sold to the State of New Mexico, and numerous smaller lots were sold for use as vacation houses, especially in the Eagle Nest Lake area high in the Sangre de Christo Range on the other side of Taos Pass.[20] Cimarron itself, once meant to be a center of commerce and industry and the heart of the Dutch Maxwell operations, never numbered more than a thousand inhabitants at the most. Although at long last a branch from the Santa Fe mainline was constructed, the town remained outside the flow of traffic. Consequently it just fell asleep again and slowly disappeared in the dust.

All in all, the history of the Maxwell Land Grant Company was a failure. The original investors of the 1870s were looking for quick gains, and lost a great deal in the process by their unwillingness to put in more working capital to exploit the resources of the Grant to a greater extent. After the reorganization of 1888 the Company was just able to pay interest on its bonds, and only after land sales picked up the loans could be paid off, but no dividend was ever paid on its shares. The emigration schemes of the first years did not materialize; no Dutch farmer ever tilled the soil of the Cimarron Valley, and the cattle business did not attract any Dutch stock raiser.[21] The town of Cimarron itself never threatened the position of Denver and just withered away to the shadow it is today. Only the venerable St. James Hotel from the 1870s is still standing, almost the only remnant of the days of the Dutch Maxwell Company. Eagle Nest Lake and the Cimarron Gorge are attractive vacation destinations, but all traces of goldmining have disappeared from the slopes of Mount Baldy. Coalmining near Raton Pass is still continuing, but on a very limited scale.

---

[20]Details of the later history of the Maxwell Land Grant Company are taken from the Annual Reports of the Company in AASE, file 21, and from *Van Oss' Effectenboek* published annually since 1903.

[21]For the emigration projects, see: Van Hinte, *Netherlanders in America,* 666-667.

The town of Van Houten, southwest of Raton, once a thriving coal community, is now a ghost town. Its mines closed down in 1954.[22]

But the former "black sheep" of the Amsterdam Stock Exchange is still listed in the price lists there today and has even become a blue chip investment. In the 1930s and 1940s a wise and careful management invested part of the small annual profits in preferred shares of the Dordtsche Petroleum Maatschappij, one of the holding companies of Royal Dutch/Shell. Sale of land continued at the same time, until in 1963 the last part of Mount Baldy was disposed of. However, the mineral rights on some 200,000 acres have been retained to this day. In order to profile the new activities, the name of the company was changed in the same year to the Maxwell Petroleum Holding N. V. Dividends of the Maxwell now kept pace with the rising oil prices. From 25% in 1963 they soared to over 200% in 1988 and the value of the company was estimated at some 40,000,000 guilders. After a fashion the visions of Palmer, Wertheim, and Van Houten have come true, but in a way not foreseen by the original promotors.

Conclusion

These few examples of Dutch business ventures in the United States are only three from a long list of similar towns. Port Arthur, Texas, is another one of the more successfull kind, developed in the early years of the twentieth century in connection with the Dutch-owned Kansas City Southern Railway. The small town of Nederland, closeby on the same railway, was started as a community of Dutch rice-growers, and all along the railway through Louisiana and Arkansas Dutch names will be found testifying to Dutch interest. Another Nederland northwest of Denver high in the Colorado Rockies is living proof of the Dutch tungsten mine that was once located there. Kerkhoven, Minnesota, took its name from an Amsterdam stockbrokers firm that pumped millions into the ill-fated St. Paul & Pacific Railway and its associated Minnesota Land and Emigration Company. And

---

[22]James E. and Barbara H. Sherman, *Ghost Towns and Mining Camps of New Mexico* (Norman, 1975).

there are scores of similar names, most somehow connected with Dutch enterprise in the United States.

    The three examples given here illustrate nicely the development of Dutch investment in the United States. The oldest, the Holland Land Company, was started as a sound business venture, mixed to a certain extent with feelings of sympathy for the young sister republic across the ocean. Because of the revolutionary wars in Europe, nothing came of the optimistic emigration schemes, and eventually the land had to be sold to others than Dutch farmers. The Maxwell Land Grant & Railway Company was a child of the feverish speculation in American stocks of the 1870s. Shares and bonds of the most shady kind of railroads and land and mining companies were eagerly unloaded on a gullible investing public in Holland by respectable and less-respectable stockbrokers without much critical examination of the soundness of the schemes. The early investors in the Maxwell lost a great deal and only the later operations on a much smaller scale proved profitable. The mortgage banks operating in the Pacific Northwest are of a different kind altogether. Started cautiously by hardheaded Dutchmen in a region that promised to become a center of agriculture, they soon proved to be a good investment. Despite temporary setbacks, profits could be great, as long as the investors stuck to the policy of mortgaging only the more valuable land or town lots. Most banks specifically excluded from their operations churches, schools and other unprofitable public buildings! The Holland Land Company and the several Dutch mortgage banks in Spokane have had a great impact on the economy of the region they were operating in, but of the Maxwell this is much less true. One ghost town with a Dutch name is not enough to prove the importance of that unfortunate undertaking.

Contributors

Prof. **Gary Lee Baker**, Department of Modern Languages, Denison University, Granville, OH 43023, USA

Mw. drs. **Saskia Daalder**, Studierichting Nederlands, Vrije Universiteit, De Boelelaan 1105, 1081 HV AMSTERDAM, The Netherlands

Dr. **Bob de Graaff**, Instituut voor Nederlandse Geschiedenis, Prins Willem-Alexanderhof 7, Postbus 90755, 2509 LT DEN HAAG, The Netherlands

Prof. **John H. Grever**, Dept. of History, Loyola Marymount University, 7101 West 80th Street, Los Angeles, CA 90045, USA

Prof. dr. **Marcel Janssens**, Departement Literatuurwetenschap, Katholieke Universiteit Leuven, Blijde Inkomststraat 21, 3000 LEUVEN, Belgium

Ms. **Christa Johnson**, Department of German Studies, Stanford University, Stanford, CA 94305-2030, USA

Prof. **Robert S. Kirsner**, Department of Germanic Languages, 302 Royce Hall - UCLA, Los Angeles, CA 90024-1539, USA

Prof. **David Kunzle**, Department of Art History, 3209 Dickson Hall - UCLA, Los Angeles, CA 90024-1417, USA

Robert S. Kirsner (ed.), *The Low Countries and Beyond*, 323-325. Lanham, MD: University Press of America, 1993.

Mw. dr. **Ida Nijenhuis**, Levendaal 201, 2311 JK LEIDEN, The Netherlands

Prof. **Mary Arshagouni Papazian**, Department of English, Oakland University, Rochester, MI 48309-4401, USA

Mw. drs. **Justine A. Pardoen**, Studierichting Nederlands, Postbus 7161, Vrije Universiteit, De Boelelaan 1105, 1081 HV AMSTERDAM, The Netherlands

Prof. **Paul T. Roberge**, Department of Germanic Languages, University of North Carolina, Chapel Hill, NC 27599, USA

Dr. **Peter Romijn**, Rijksinstituut voor Oorlogsdocumentatie, Herengracht 474, 1017 CA AMSTERDAM, The Netherlands

Prof. **Thomas F. Shannon**, Department of German, 5317 Dwinelle Hall, University of California, Berkeley, CA 94720, USA

Prof. **J. P. Smuts**, Departement Afrikaans en Nederlands, Universiteit van Stellenbosch, Stellenbosch 7600, South Africa

Prof. **Johan P. Snapper**, Dutch Program, Department of German, 5317 Dwinelle Hall, University of California, Berkeley, CA 94720, USA

Prof. **Henry L. Snyder**, Director, Center for Bibliographical Studies and Research, Mail Code 016-Library, University of California, Riverside, CA 92521-0154, USA

Dr. **Richard A. Todd**, Faculteit der Letteren, Studierichting Engels, Vrije Universiteit, De Boelelaan 1105, 1081 HV AMSTERDAM, The Netherlands

Prof. J. van der Elst, Departement Afrikaans-Nederlands, Potchefstroomse Universiteit vir Christelike Hoër Onderwys, Privaatsak X6001, Potchefstroom 2520, South Africa

Drs. P. G. E. I. J. van der Velde, Instituut voor de Geschiedenis van de Europese Expansie (IGEER), Rijksuniversiteit Leiden, Postbus 9515, 2300 RA LEIDEN, The Netherlands

Dr. Augustus J. Veenendaal, Instituut voor Nederlandse Geschiedenis, Prins Willem-Alexanderhof 7, Postbus 90755, 2509 LT DEN HAAG, The Netherlands

Dr. Arie Verhagen, Vakgroep Nederlands, Rijksuniversiteit Utrecht, Trans 10, 3512 JK UTRECHT, The Netherlands

Prof. Patricia Vervoort, Department of Visual Arts, Lakehead University, Thunder Bay, Ontario P7B 5E1, Canada

Mr. Roel Vismans, Centre for Modern Dutch Studies, The University of Hull, Cottingham Road, Hull HU6 7RX, Great Britain

Prof. Hein Willemse, Department of Afrikaans, University of the Western Cape, Private Bag X17, Bellville 7535, South Africa

Prof. Manfred Wolf, Department of English, San Franciso State University, San Francisco, CA 94132, USA